Language and Learning

An Introduction for Teaching

THIRD EDITION

Marie Emmitt

John Pollock

Linda Komesaroff

OXFORD

UNIVERSITY PRESS

OXFORD

UNIVERSITY PRESS

253 Normanby Road, South Melbourne, Victoria 3205, Australia

Oxford University Press is a department of the University of Oxford. It
furthers the University's objective of excellence in research, scholarship,
and education by publishing worldwide in

Oxford New York

Auckland Bangkok Buenos Aires Cape Town Chennai
Dar es Salaam Delhi Hong Kong Istanbul Karachi Kolkata
Kuala Lumpur Madrid Melbourne Mexico City Mumbai Nairobi
São Paulo Shanghai Taipei Tokyo Toronto

OXFORD is a trade mark of Oxford University Press in the UK and in
certain other countries

National Library of Australia
Cataloguing-in-Publication data:

Emmitt, Marie.
 Language and learning: an introduction for teaching.

 3rd ed.
 Bibliography.
 Includes index.
 ISBN 0 19 551622 2.

 1. English language—Study and teaching. 2. Language arts.
 I. Pollock, John. II. Komesaroff, Linda R. III. Title.

428.007

Edited by Peter Cruttenden
Text designed by Heather Jones
Cover designed by Racheal Stines
Indexed by Lucy McLoughlin
Typeset by Promptset Pty Ltd
Printed through Bookpac Production Services, Singapore

CONTENTS

CONTENTS

CONTENTS

FOREWORD

Language is central to education. Language is an essential part of thinking which enhances the learning process. The teacher's use of language can either facilitate or hinder learning. Therefore understanding language is essential for making learning easier, particularly literacy learning.

This third edition builds on the sociocultural constructivist view of language and emphasises critical pedagogies and issues of language and power. Given that language is used within social and cultural contexts, it is bound up with issues of power and plays a central part in the struggles and politics of cultural groups. This book was written for teachers in preservice education and practising teachers in any context who want to re-evaluate their understanding of language. Our aim is to enhance your understanding of the nature and function of language and language learning in order to assist your decision-making in the classroom. This knowledge will also help you better understand and implement the national and state curriculum documents. It is also intended to encourage you to reflect on current policy in the light of your understanding of language theory. This is not a 'how to' book, although it is hoped that the perceptions derived through reading and reflecting on the ideas discussed will inform your decision-making and classroom practices. While implications for classroom practice are suggested throughout the text, detailed development of these should be followed up in the recommended reading and/or explored in classroom discussions with teacher educators.

One of the themes running through this book is that language reflects and helps shape culture—different cultures use language differently. We want to acknowledge our cultural biases early. We think that the task of education is to develop ways of thinking and acting that extend the opportunities and choices our students will be able to take, and we see language as playing a critical role in this process. This, however may not be the position of others, in particular those from other cultural groups.

There are many theories about language and language–learning, and research provides many helpful insights. For this book we have borrowed concepts and insights from a range of theories and focused on those aspects of language that we believe are most significant for learning about teaching, in particular for literacy education. In the process we have often simplified theories, but we hope that we have not distorted them.

It has been said that there is nothing more practical than a good theory—a theory that assists you in making sound decisions about a student's learning. However the most helpful theories for teaching are those that you construct for yourself. We hope that by working through this book you can construct a theory of language and language learning that assists your teaching, and can be used to explain your program to your colleagues, students, and their parents. Articulating your program is now seen as a critical part of a teacher's professional role.

References have been updated in this edition, though many of the original sources have been retained. It is important to appreciate that our current ideas are based on the work of many writers and thinkers over many years. We do not disenfranchise these thinkers/educators.

How to use this book

Learning is an active process that is most effective where there is some collaboration and negotiation of meanings. Hence we have tried to ensure that your reading of the text is an interactive experience, enabling you to participate and negotiate meanings.

Each chapter commences with a list of understandings that are the focus of the chapter, as well as pre-reading activities. Activities are interspersed throughout. Many of these require you to share and discuss your responses with others. Learning is often more effective and more enjoyable if we can collaborate with others and it is hoped that many of the activities can be carried out in class workshops. A list of references and further reading is provided at the end of each chapter. References that will be particularly helpful are indicated by asterisks. In case you find it difficult to remember the precise meaning and use of the linguistic terms, a glossary of some of the terms is included at the back.

The first chapter provides an overview of the concept of language and the contents of the book. It should be read first to give you a context for the other chapters, which can be read in any order that suits you.

Marie Emmitt, John Pollock, and Linda Komesaroff

ACKNOWLEDGMENTS

Our thanks to our many colleagues and students who, through their interactions with us, shaped our thinking.

We thank Andrew Perry for his insistence that we could write such a book and that we should, and also Diane Snowball for her help with particular aspects of the book.

The authors and publisher wish to thank copyright holders for granting permission to reproduce copyright material. Sources are as follows:

B. Bartlett & M. J. Usher, 'In-service Package for Secondary Teachers About Top-level Structures'.

B. Bartlett, B. Barton & A. Turner, *Knowing What and Knowing How, Book 1: Lower Primary*, Thomas Nelson.

G. Brown & G. Yule, *Discourse Analysis*, Cambridge University Press.

B. Cambourne, *The Whole Story*, Ashton Scholastic Ltd.

B. Carozzi, *Language: What Do We Use It For?*, Access Skills Project Team, Curriculum and Research Branch, Ministry of Education, Victoria.

C. H. Clark, 'Comprehension of normal and noncohesive text' in J. W. Irwin (ed.) *Understanding and Teaching*, International Reading Association.

J. Collerson, *Writing for Life*, Primary English Teaching Association.

P. Czerniewska, 'The experience of writing' in D. Graddol, J. Cheshire & J. Swann, *Describing Language*, Open University Press.

Education Department of South Australia, *Writing: R–7 Language Arts*.

V. Fromkin, R. Rodman, P. Collins & D. Blair, *An Introduction to Language*, Holt, Rinehart & Winston.

K. Goodman, *What's Whole in Whole Language?*, Scholastic–TAB Publications Ltd.

K. S. Goodman, E. Smith, R. Meredith & Y. Goodman, *Language and Thinking in School*, Richard C. Owen Publishers Inc.

Herodotus: *The Histories* (transl. Aubrey de Selincourt), Penguin Books Ltd.

R. Hudson, 'Higher-level Differences in Speech and Writing' in D. Graddol, J. Cheshire & J. Swann, *Describing Language*, Open University Press.

A. J. Moe & J. W. Irwin, 'Cohesion, coherence and comprehension' in J. W. Irwin (ed.) *Understanding and Teaching*, International Reading Association.

T. Parsons (ed.), *Max Weber: The Theory of Social and Economic Organization*, Oxford University Press.

K. Perera, *Children's Writing and Reading*, Basil Blackwell in association with André Deutsch.

C. R. Rogers, *Freedom to Learn*, Charles E. Merrill Publishing Co.

F. Smith, *Essays Into Literacy*, Heinemann Educational Books.

W. Sparke and C. McKowen, *Montage: Investigations in Language*, Macmillan Publishing Co.

Z. Strano, T. Mohan & H. McGregor, *Communicating!*, Harcourt Brace Jovanovich Publishers.

R. D. Walshe, 'How much grammar should be taught in the primary school?', in *Teaching in Australia*, 1980, No. 54.

Disclaimer

Every effort has been made to trace the original source material contained in this book. Where the attempt has been unsuccessful, the publisher would be pleased to hear from any copyright holders to rectify any omissions.

PART ONE

LANGUAGE AND CULTURE

CHAPTER 1

An Overview of Language and Learning

FOCUS

This chapter focuses on the understanding that:

- *explicit knowledge of language is important for fostering language learning*
- *language can be viewed from different dimensions or perspectives*
- *language is more than speech or writing*
- *language involves a number of verbal and non-verbal codes*
- *language and learning are about making and sharing meaning*
- *language is an integral part of culture and, as such, is tied up with politics and power*
- *literacy is part of language and understandings about language are relevant to literacy.*

PRE-READING ACTIVITIES

1 Write down why you think people want to study language. Why do you want to study language?

2 What do you use language for? Reflect on a day's activities and list the times when you used language, for what purpose, and what type(s) of language you used, for example, speech, writing, body language. What type of language did you use most frequently? Did you find that you used non-verbal language more frequently than any other type? What are the implications of your responses for a program to assist students' language development? What uses of language and what types of language should you focus on in developing students' language?

We suggest that you write your answers to these questions and file them for comparison with your views as they develop throughout the course of this book.

Why study language?

Valuing the language, culture, and lives of students, and empowering them to take control, is the foundation of language and literacy education. Language is integral to the process of conceiving meaning and a necessary pre-condition of the cultural process: 'It is not as though we have meaning and *then* have language—in order to express our meaning. Rather, language is integral to realizing meaning' (Lankshear 1997, p. 23).

In 1921, the philosopher Wittgenstein said: 'The limits of my language are the limits of my world.' If he meant by this that our understanding of the world is set by the limits of our language, then it is vital that we expand our students' language if we are interested in their learning and their growth as individuals. It is also true that, as teachers, we need a language to think and talk about language, and we need to extend the limits of our language and the assumptions built into it so we can best assist others in language learning.

Language is so much a part of us and our lives that it is very difficult for us to distance ourselves from it, and to reflect and examine it.

However, as we emphasise throughout this book, language is central to living and learning. As users of a language we all have intuitive knowledge of language but, as teachers, we must have explicit knowledge of what it is that we use all day in our teaching and what it is that we are trying to develop in our learners.

We can be truly professional only if we continually reflect upon and evaluate our practices. We need to know what we are doing and why; then and only then can we make informed decisions.

We aim for you to develop a more explicit understanding and appreciation of language, in particular an appreciation of the power of language and the importance of your students having access to that power. With your knowledge of language and language learning, you will have greater and more precise insights into your role in teaching–learning contexts.

Language use appears to be assuming a greater role in the lives of many people in the community as awareness of its importance grows. For example, nearly all jobs demand that workers engage in face-to-face and group interaction as speakers and listeners, and possess literacy skills. Almost all job descriptions now stress communication skills. It seems that the way language is being used in the workplace is changing along with the restructuring of work practices and is playing a different role in social control in the workplace. With changes in relations between groups there have been changes in the way language is used, for example between doctors and patients, between women and men, and between politicians and the public (Fairclough 1992). We need to help our students to understand the role of language in different contexts for them to be able to use it effectively.

Our understanding of the world is set by the limits of our language.

As teachers, we need a language to think about language, and we need to extend the limits of our language and the assumptions built into it so we can best assist others in language learning. Language is central to living and learning.

We can be truly professional only if we continually reflect upon and evaluate our practices.

All teachers need to understand the relationship between language and learning.

As teachers, no matter what our content or subject area, we need to understand:

- the relationship between language and learning, in particular how language can enhance learning
- how our use of language can impact on our students' learning
- how language structures and reflects meanings
- how language differs depending on the context
- how the texts of language can both inform and manipulate us.

As language teachers we need to understand:

Language teachers need explicit knowledge about language and language practices.

- the nature of language so we know what it is we want to develop, what it is we need to observe, and what we need to do to enable our students to become effective language users
- what knowledge of language or language awareness our students need to assist them in becoming effective users
- the factors involved in language learning so we can best support language and literacy learning
- that our use of language and literacy and what we validate as literacy practices in the classroom will impact on our learners' development of literacy.

In this chapter we want to highlight the key understandings underlying our concept of language and the way we plan to discuss language in this book. Due to the size and nature of this book our discussion can only be introductory. Hence we have been very selective in our discussions and focus on those aspects of language study that we think are most critical for language education. There will always be more to learn.

Who has studied language?

Language has been a focus of study for many years. Figure 1.1, a model of formal language study, indicates how language has been a part of philosophy, rhetoric, and psychology. Many of our language terms, such as gender, number, case, and person, come from medieval studies of language in philosophy. Only in this century has a special discipline been devoted to the formal study of language—linguistics. Many schools of linguistics have developed, and linguistics has been incorporated into interdisciplinary studies, such as sociolinguistics, psycholinguistics, and applied linguistics, which have enhanced our understanding of language in the classroom. While different models of language have been developed, any such model will only provide a partial view of language. Hence we will focus on key insights from different models or views of language.

Figure 1.1 Formal language study

Grammar, rhetoric, etymology
Greco-Roman times—writing-centred, prescriptive,
linked with composition, the study of literature,
logic, philosophy.

Philosophy
Late 18th century—historical studies of language,
descriptive, comparative.

Linguistics
Late 19th century—the scientific study of language,
descriptive, concerned with system and structure,
linked with sociology or psychology, focus on
language for conveying information.

- **Historical linguistics**
  Origin and
  development of a
  language; how
  a language has
  changed.

- **Descriptive/structural linguistics**
  Describing what is being
  used at a given time.
  Focuses on the
  sentence.

- **Generative/transformational linguistics**
  Describing the rules by
  which a language-user
  operates. Focuses on
  the sentence.

- **Systemic linguistics**
  Functional perspective—
  how language structure
  changes with different
  functions; studies of
  larger structures of
  language text.

- **Psycholiguistics**
  Investigation of
  processes involved
  in language.

- **Sociolinguistics**
  How the language
  is used in varying
  social contexts.

- **Applied linguistics**
  Language and education;
  second-language
  learning.

- **Critical linguistics**
  Combination of theories
  and methods of text
  analysis of systemic
  linguistics and theories
  of ideology and power.

5

What is language and why do we have it?

In one sense, we all know the answer to the question 'what is language?' because we are language users, but our knowing is very ill-defined. It is important, however, to attempt to answer this question more explicitly because in the process we can learn much about language and its use, which can inform our decision-making in the classroom.

The term 'language' is frequently used, but rarely defined. Many definitions and texts imply that language is speech alone or speech and writing; that is, codes based on words. Recognition of the legitimacy of native sign languages has extended this definition to include speech or signs. Language certainly involves producing and receiving information (speaking or signing and listening or watching), and decoding and coding text (reading and writing). The development of these processes is the basis of language programs. However, we believe that it is not very helpful to ignore non-verbal codes.

Language is a complex and abstract phenomenon that can be realised through a number of verbal and non-verbal codes.

Native sign languages are visual-spatial languages that are not derived from the language spoken by the surrounding hearing culture. Signs are visual symbols constructed with particular elements, including facial expression. It is not only in sign languages, however, that non-verbal cues are important. If you think of a situation where you use spoken language, such as in a conversation with a friend, you will realise that you frequently use more than one way of conveying and interpreting meaning. Speech is prominent, but so are a range of non-verbal cues, such as facial expressions and body gestures. Hence we see language as being more than speech and writing: it is a complex and abstract phenomenon that can be realised through a number of verbal and non-verbal codes. Today, language is seen as one of many social practices that operate interactively in a society to represent and make meaning (Halliday 1978; Hodge & Kress 1988; Fairclough 1989).

Language is a social practice; it is inextricably linked to social and cultural practices.

Language is centred on meaning: it is about constructing and sharing meaning.

Language is centred on meaning: it is the most powerful and pervasive means humans have for making and sharing meaning. Because language is centred on meaning, which is shared culturally, it follows that it is rooted in the culture of the group that uses it. It makes no sense to think of a language used by only one individual. This concept is basic to our understanding of language and the teacher's role in fostering language development.

In learning to make sense of our world we learn language and to do this we use verbal and/or non-verbal systems. For example, speech, gestures, scribbling, drawing, and writing are all used for making and sharing meaning. In the classroom it makes sense to appreciate that there are a variety of ways to make meaning and share meaning, for example, listening, reading, talking, writing, viewing films and videos, drawing, making diagrams, and producing plays. Separating the learning experience into little boxes of oral language, reading, writing, music, drama, etc., distorts the learning process.

We would still argue, however, that the verbal codes of speech and writing are very important. Words enable tremendous flexibility in thinking: try to think about such abstract concepts as democracy and education without words. It is virtually impossible! In addition, our society places great value on verbal skills. Success at school depends to a large extent on verbal competency, but success with words depends to some extent on non-verbal support, as do communicative competency and interpersonal relationships. Speech in particular is the major symbolic system available to humans.

> Separating the learning experience into little boxes of oral language, reading, writing, music, drama, etc., distorts the learning process.

Different dimensions of language

Language is so complex that it is difficult to study comprehensively—at any one time we tend to view language from a particular perspective using a particular model depending on our purposes. The story of the blind men trying to find out what an elephant looked like is an interesting analogy for different researchers trying to find out what language is. One blind man touched the elephant's side and thought the elephant was like a wall; another blind man touched its legs and thought the elephant was like a tree trunk; another touched its tail and thought the elephant was like a rope; another touched an ear and thought the elephant was like a fan; and another touched the elephant's trunk and thought the elephant was like a hose.

In this book we discuss language and learning from different perspectives such as sociocultural, linguistic and developmental, and use insights from different models of language such as traditional and functional. In addition we view language as a process—the social and cognitive processes involved in learning and using language; as a product—the demonstrations of our use of language including sounds, marks and gestures; and as having uses or purposes—communicating, thinking, and expressing feelings. We can view the deep structure of language (that is, the underlying meaning embodied in language) or the surface structure (that is, the form that language takes, the sounds or letters and words used). However, you need to keep in mind that language is more than any one dimension or perspective. All aspects are interrelated, although for study purposes we focus on one aspect at a time.

> Language and learning can be discussed from different perspectives—critical, sociocultural, linguistic, and developmental.
>
> Language is a process, a product, and it has purposes.

Function and form

We can examine language from either side of the one coin: function or form. We can study the functions of language—how we use language to fulfil all sorts of purposes. We can also study the structure or form of what we use as language. Previously these two aspects were studied quite separately, but we now appreciate how closely they interact—the function or purpose of language determines the type or form of language we use. Meaning cannot be divorced from the form of language. How we use language and how it varies in different contexts are discussed in chapters 2 and 3. The form or structure of language is discussed in chapters 6–8.

Meaning cannot be divorced from the form of language.

Language is both personal and sociocultural

Individuals learn language and use it for a whole range of purposes; different people use language for different purposes.

Individuals learn language and use it for a whole range of purposes; different people use language for different purposes. However, it is learned and used in a sociocultural context. What one learns has been developed by the group, but is redeveloped by the individual. The individual's use of language influences the group and vice versa. Also, as we are most interested in language in education, we need to remember that learning is a social process, and the environment in which school learning takes place is a social institution. 'Knowledge is transmitted in social contexts, through relationships, like those of parent and child, or teacher and pupil, or classmates, that are defined in the value systems and ideology of the culture' (Halliday & Hasan 1985). Hence it is important that we understand what is to be learned as language, how an individual learns it, and also how sociocultural factors influence an individual's language and how groups use language. Our thinking and language is shaped by our culture, hence the current focus on sexist and racist uses of language.

Knowledge is transmitted in social contexts.

Language is part of a culture; what the language is and how it is used depends on the culture. You cannot know a language unless you know the culture. This sociocultural view of language pervades this book, but is particularly emphasised in chapters 2 and 3, where language in use and language variation are discussed, and it underlies the approach to linguistics in chapters 6–8. The personal and social aspects are discussed in chapters 9–11, which consider language learning.

Language is part of a culture; what the language is and how it is used depends on the culture. You cannot know a language unless you know the culture.

Language, ideology, and power

Language and literacy educators since the late 1980s have been concerned with the way in which meanings constructed in text produce, reproduce, and maintain power (see, for example, Cambourne & Brown 1987; Gee 1990; McConnell 1992; Gilbert 1993). Because language is integral to the cultural process, it plays a central part in the struggles and politics of cultural groups. Dominant groups establish their language (as well as knowledge, pedagogical preferences and so on) as the legitimate form in education and society in general: '... for language, communication and meaning to be *socio-cultural* is for them to be *political*, for them to be inseparable from the production and operation of institutionally structured *power*. Language is deeply and inescapably bound up with producing, reproducing and maintaining arrangements of power which are unequal.' (Lankshear 1997, p. 46)

A critical view of language and literacy encourages scrutiny of attitudes, values and assumptions about social knowledge (such as gender relationships); the multiple reading of texts depending on how one is positioned in relation to that text, and the privileging of particular meanings in text: 'To explore the social context of language practices is inevitably to explore the networks of power that are sustained and brought into existence by such practices. It is to explore how language practices are used in powerful institutions like the state, the school, the law, the family, the church, and how these practices contribute to the maintenance of inequalities and injustices' (Gilbert 1993, pp. 324-5).

Gilbert (1993, p. 325) goes on to say: 'For teachers, it means engaging with issues that are often controversial, certainly contemporary, and perhaps quite volatile'.

In any complex society many different ideologies operate, often competing in different discourses and texts. Texts are defined here as the product of any language event, hence a text can be oral, written, or visual. Over time certain viewpoints become embedded in the language and come to be seen as natural. In this way, language users' choice of options in making and sharing meaning are influenced.

In any society, different ideologies operate and affect our language.

Through the ideologies in our language a particular reality is produced that seems like commonsense to the users, but may be in conflict with others' view of the world. As language is a means of communication and control, we can be both informed and manipulated by texts—often at the same time. One of the goals of critical linguistics and critical literacy therefore is to 'unpack' the ideologies underlying texts and assist us to become aware of how texts may be manipulating us.

Ideology influences an individual's making and sharing of meaning.

Halliday's functional linguistic theory (1985) provides us with a way of viewing power relationships in language, which are always present. He sees language as something that derives from a context of a situation. In any situation users take on roles and adopt certain styles of language appropriate to the role. Hence in any text two major functions are always present: it formulates some sort of information and it places the listener/reader/viewer in some sort of interpersonal stance. Halliday refers to these functions as ideational and interpersonal. Users of a language make choices as to what roles are appropriate. We make assessment of the power relations involved—for example, between parent and child, teacher and student, husband and wife, doctor and patient—and choose certain linguistic features appropriate to the roles assigned. A term used to describe this is 'positioning'. Speakers, writers, and film producers ascribe social positions to their listeners/readers/ viewers and take on social 'stances' when using language. The positions we ascribe and the stances we take depend on how we perceive our role and that of others in a group. Even in friendship groups some

Functional linguistics can be used to examine power relationships in language.

Texts position readers/listeners in particular ways.

individuals take on more 'power' than others; that is, they command more attention than others.

In any society some members may not be in the position to speak or be listened to. The positions we construct generally conform to appropriate institutionalised behaviours and values (culturally determined). Texts present information in particular ways (based on ideologies) and construct subjectivities (the ways people come to see themselves and the value positions they take up) in certain more or less predictable ways. For example, in popular romance novels authors tend to construct males as active and females as passive. Advertisements aim to position readers/viewers to construct certain images of modern life and persuade them to take on a product or service as socially desirable. People with differences are often constructed as disabled or deficient. We position ourselves and others through language.

Language users, speakers or sign-language users, writers and readers use language for some purpose in varying social contexts. As such, language users draw on their power and status in particular social groupings. The use of language involves positioning others in certain ways. It creates certain kinds of subjectivities that express or reflect particular cultural values and power orientations. For example, the reports on asylum seekers trying to reach Australia often used terms such as 'illegals' or 'queue jumpers'. An alternative construction is to talk about them as 'refugees' or 'dispossessed peoples'. It is important to note that from this perspective of language use, certain kinds of representations or subjectivities are oppressed, dominated, or subordinated, while others are oppressive and dominating. Subjectivity constructed along the lines of race, gender, and disability are other examples. Students need to become aware of the beliefs and values (ideologies) operating in texts (their own and others') and consider other ways of constructing texts that are less oppressive. This perspective will underlie our views on what knowledge of language our students need to have, which is explored in chapter 4.

Language positions and constructs people and issues in particular ways.

Some groups are oppressed through language policies and practices.

Students need to become aware of the ideologies operating in texts.

ACTIVITY

Read the editorials of different newspapers or the reports of a significant event in different papers. See if you can determine the different ideologies (belief systems) underpinning each article by identifying the different uses of linguistic forms, such as choice of vocabulary, use of passives, and nominalisations to delete the actors (where verbs are turned into nouns and sentences have no explicit agent—refer to chapter 8).

Language codes

In our concept of language as discussed above, language is perceived as being more than speech—it consists of a number of codes. What are these codes? If we investigate what we use for communication, we can begin to appreciate the potential range of language codes, both verbal and non-verbal, at our disposal.

ACTIVITY AND DISCUSSION

A number of language codes are listed below. Classify these codes into categories of your choice.

Codes
song, score (music), instrumental (played), Braille, native sign language, finger-spelling, semaphore, traffic code, graphics, writing, speech, sport (rules), cries, sculpture, painting, design, textiles (art), drama, dance, gesture, mime, flower arrangement, interior design, body language.

Q What categories did you make?

Q Why did you classify them that way?

Share your responses with others.

One way of classifying language codes is by the method of production, for example oral, graphic, or gestural. Another classification is by deciding whether or not words are the basis of the code, that is, whether it is verbal or non-verbal. Table 1.1 (Cameron & Saunders 1977) uses these categories to classify the different codes we use to make sense of our world. In addition you could add such mixed codes as drama, opera and interior design. Can you think of others?

Table 1.1   Matrix of language

	Modes		
	Oral	Graphic	Gestural
Verbal (predominantly)	speech song	writing braille	finger-spelling lip-reading semaphore
Non-verbal (predominantly)	cries	signs (directional)	signs (used by deaf)
	laughter	signs (mathematical)	signs (used in sport)
	music (sound)	music (score)	body position posture movement
		art (schools) object arrangement	facial expression

M. H. Cameron & M. T. Saunders, *An Overview of Language*, pp. 217–31.

Characteristics of language

If we look at these language codes and the ways in which they are classified, we can begin to appreciate the complexity of and variation in language use.

ACTIVITY AND DISCUSSION

List the characteristics that the codes shown in Table 1.1 have in common then list the functions of these codes. Share your responses with others.

Language is systematic, arbitrary, conventional, and symbolic.

From this activity you will realise that the codes possess a number of features and we can begin to describe the different characteristics of language and language codes. For instance, language is systematic—signs and symbols are selected and used according to rules. These rules have been developed by the users and determined by the culture, and have to be learned by new language users such as children and second-language learners. Language is arbitrary—there is no inherent reason why the word 'cat' refers to the small, furry animal; it has been agreed to by a group of language users. For meaning to be shared, the signs and symbols, and the way they are to be used in any language, have to be agreed upon by the language users. The agreement by groups of language users to use certain signs and symbols is not the kind of agreement that two or more people might come to in resolving a dispute. Rather it's the kind of agreement that occurs when groups of people come to share values, beliefs, and ways of doing things over time. In other words, the agreement is a convention. Language is symbolic. In the example above the word 'cat' is a symbol for a particular type of furry animal. There is no inherent relationship between the animal and the word or symbol 'cat'. What is wonderful about language is that it is generative; with a limited set of symbols and agreed rules for structuring (or stringing together) these symbols we can always create new meanings. Language is continually changing to meet the needs of language users. Words come and go and the meanings of words change over time. New words enter the language when there is a need to do so.

The nature and use of our language sets us apart from other animals. Through language we symbolise experiences; the mental representation is something that lasts in time and doesn't disappear when the phenomenon disappears. By putting our experiences into language we distance ourselves from them, transforming them into something that can be worked upon, creating new meanings. Others can respond to our representations and work with us on them. We can learn from these responses. This enables us to make great advances in our knowledge and understanding of our environment.

Given all these characteristics we can begin to define language as:

a system of arbitrary signs agreed to by a community of users, transmitted and received for a specific purpose, in relation to the shared world of the users.

Language, thinking, and learning

Language (which is culturally determined) influences what we think and how we think. Furthermore, language gives us a way of reflecting on our thinking, talking about our thinking, thereby enabling us to have greater control over our thinking. In this way language is like a pane of glass through which we can view our thinking. Language, meaning, thinking, and learning are all very closely interrelated. This concept is basic to understanding the role of language in learning.

But what do we mean by 'learning'? We have said that language is central to both learning and teaching. Learning occurs when we change or elaborate what is already known by us. Learning is a process of making connections, identifying patterns, organising previously unrelated bits of knowledge, behaviour, activities, into new (for the learner) patterned wholes (Cambourne 1990). We learn by attempting to relate new experiences to what we already know or believe. Learning is therefore about making new meanings for the learner—these meanings are generally developed and articulated through language. Learning and the role of language is discussed in greater detail in chapter 11.

Language and literacy

Written language is one code of language. Hence, whatever is discussed about language in general has implications for understanding reading and writing. Written language is different from speech, but there are many similarities between the codes because they are both verbal, that is, based on words. Development of one certainly enhances the development of the other. Learning oral and written language is discussed in chapters 9 and 10.

One important factor to keep in mind when thinking about language and literacy is the relationship between language and culture. Language, as discussed above, is a part of culture. It is used to pass on culture, but its use is also determined by the culture.

The concept of literacy is also culturally determined. Literacy is more than reading and writing: it is the use of reading and writing for a wide range of culturally determined purposes. Different cultures place different values on aspects of literacy and have different uses for reading and writing. McNaughton (1995) has described how literacy as practised by families socialises children into appropriate ways of using written language for a specific family within a specific sociocultural environment. Literature is one particular way literacy is used within a

Margin notes

Language can be defined as a system of arbitrary signs agreed to by a community of users, transmitted and received for a specific purpose, in relation to the shared world of the users.

Language, meaning, thinking, and learning are all very closely interrelated.

Learning is about making new meanings for the learner.

Literacy is more than reading and writing: it is the use of multiliteracies, including reading and writing for a wide range of culturally determined purposes.

Different cultures place different values on different types of literacies.

culture. The widespread use of technology in our society is leading to different uses of reading and writing—to the development of different literacies, for example, digital literacy.

It is important that, as adults, we consider the type of texts we give students to read, as this will greatly influence how they perceive literacy, their world, and their place in it. To learn to read is more than learning decoding skills; it is also about learning to use reading and writing for a wide range of socially constructed purposes, which allow us to make social sense of the vastly different forms of print we encounter. Hence it is important that we consider the content of texts for their social values, for example, in relation to gender, racism, ageism (Meek 1989). The approach taken in critical literacy is to urge the reader to interact with and question texts, to look behind a writer's words to the underlying sociocultural and political assumptions (Freebody & Luke 1990). 'Literacy is a social and cultural construction … its functions and uses are never neutral or innocent … the meanings constructed in text are ideological and involved in producing, reproducing and maintaining arrangements of power which are unequal' (Comber & Kamler 1997, pp. 30–1). In addition, we need to consider what literacies—or uses of reading and writing—are important for empowering our learners. Merely teaching reading and writing skills is not enough without enabling learners to become more aware of their world and be in creative control of it. This is the view of Paulo Freire (1972), a renowned liberatory educator who has written at great length on the importance of literacy for functioning as a human being. Central to his position is the argument that all humans must function equally if any are to function as humans. His view is overtly political and has come to be associated with the term 'Critical Literacy'.

> *It is not enough merely to recognize that language use is a social construction … understanding can be created most fully only if language users are wide awake both to the voices of others and to their own part in that construction. When we are aware of our own ability to choose how we constitute ourselves and how we constitute others, the nature of the conversations in which we participate becomes a kind of negotiation with others; in these circumstances, both our language and our understandings of one another change and grow.*
>
> (Fleischer, 1998, p. xix).

The more one engages in conscious action to understand and transform the world—one's reality—through the interplay between reflection and action, the more fully human we become, that is, we have greater control over our destinies. If we just accept the world as set by others we allow ourselves to become dehumanised—an object shaped and made by others rather than expressing our uniquely human potential to be involved actively in creating what we become. As human beings our shared vocation is to become active individual subjects

To learn to read is more than learning decoding skills.

Literacy should enable learners to become more critically aware of their world and aware of the construction of text—their own and others'.

engaged on an equal basis with others in the process of creating (or naming) the world. We should create history and culture rather than exist merely as passive objects accepting reality and the world as ready-made by other people. In creating history and culture we create our own beings in the process. This is a great challenge for literacy education.

To study literacy is to study contexts and relations.

QUESTIONS

Q Can you develop students' language and literacy without considering issues of power, control, relationships, and actions?

Q In what way is teaching people to read a political exercise?

Towards a definition of language

The different dimensions and complexity of language has been highlighted. Before you read on it is important for you to determine your own working definition of 'language'. In looking at different definitions it becomes obvious that views of language have changed over time and they differ depending on the discipline background of the writers. Definitions have generally moved away from language as speech and language for communication to a greater emphasis on the social nature of language.

ACTIVITY

To assist you in this process, examine the following definitions. Notice the way in which the definition of language has changed over time and consider the implications of adopting a particular definition.

Some definitions of language for discussion

1 Language is a purely human and non-instinctive method of communicating ideas, emotions and desires by means of a system of voluntarily produced symbols. These symbols are, in the first instance, auditory, and they are produced by the so-called 'organs of speech'—animal communication, if communication it may be called, as brought about by involuntary, instinctive cries, is not, in our sense, language at all.

Edward Sapir, *Language* (1921), p. 9.

2 Language is an organised system of linguistics symbols (words) used by human beings to communicate on an abstract level.

(a) Language is basic to all communication through words.

(b) Encompasses all forms of expression.

N. E. Wood, *Delayed Speech and Language Development* (1964), pp. 6–7.

3 Language is a system of arbitrary vocal symbols used for human communication.

General definition quoted by R. Wardhaugh, *Reading: A Linguistic Perspective* (1969), p. 34.

4 Language is a system of conventional symbols used for communication by a whole community.

A. C. Gimson, *An Introduction to the Pronunciation of English* (1970), p. 3.

5 Language ... [is] human vocal noise (or the graphic representation of this noise in writing) used systematically and conventionally by a community for purposes of communication. Occasionally language is used for purposes other than communication—for example, to let off steam ... or as a vehicle for our own thoughts when no one else is present. But such uses of language are secondary.

David Crystal, *Linguistics* (1971), p. 243.

6 Language: the sum total of explicit and implicit systems used by the individual to structure the environment.

M. H. Cameron & Marie T. Saunders, *Language and Speech* (1977), p. 217.

7 Language refers to the particular set of symbols that allows for intelligible communication in a culture. Language skills include the ability to speak, write and to comprehend the symbols of one's language.

P. Mussen, J. Conger & J. Kagan, *Child Development and Personality* (1979), p. 199.

8 Language is for negotiating meaning, building understanding and relationships and the activity of using language for any of these purposes always involves creating what is technically called a text—a stretch of language which is coherent and meaningful.

F. Christie, *Factual Writing in the First Years of School* (1987), p. 207.

9 Language, the possibility of making meaning, is the essence of being human. It is at the centre of individual empowerment. Through it, instead of simply being subject to the structures and activities that define the indifferent societal system, one interacts with and participates in the creation of the system. Through it one engages in the continual, active process of being.

B. Courts, *Literacy and Empowerment* (1991), p. 137.

10 Whenever language is used, it is used in events—events that capture and create relationships among people and between people and objects (material and otherwise) in the culture. What is learned when people learn language includes all those relationships that were parts of the events carried out through language use.

C. Edelsky, *With Literacy and Justice for All* (1991), pp. 80–1.

11 The fundamental task of every language is to link voice to meaning—
to provide words for the expression of thoughts and feeling. Language
is therefore like a coin whose two sides are expression and content ...
Content encompasses what we are attempting to say: expression
encompasses the way we articulate this content and language is the
mental code that links the two.

E. Finegan, N. Besnier, D. Blair & P. Collins, Language: Its Structure and Use (1992), pp. 3–4.

12 Languages are not purely linguistic entities. They serve social functions.
In order to define a language, it is important to look to its social and
political functions, as well as its linguistic features. So a language can be
thought of as a collection of dialects that are usually linguistically
similar, used by different social groups who choose to say that they are
speakers of one language, which functions to unite and represent them
to other groups.

J. Holmes, An Introduction to Sociolinguistics (1992), pp. 141–2.

13 All people put language to certain types of use and in so doing they all
learn a linguistic system which has evolved in the contexts of such
language use. But which parts of the language system they deploy and
emphasise ... are significantly determined by the culture—by the system
of social relations in which people are positioned and the roles they
learn to recognise and adopt.

L. Unsworth, Literacy Learning and Teaching (1993), p. 149.

14 Language is a symbolic system linking what goes on inside our heads
with what goes on outside. It mediates between self and society. It is a
form of representation, a way of representing the world to ourselves
and to others.

D. Barton, Literacy (1994), p. 46.

15 The view of language as social action differs considerably from the
view of language as a medium or vehicle of *communication*. The notion
that language is made for communication suggests that writers or
speakers simply convey or try to get across a message as 'pure
content' in some shape or form. This kind of view, which is very
pervasive in Western thought and history, tends to imply a view of
language users as transmitters and receivers of neutral information. ...
language is a tool for acting in an interested and engaged way, on and
in the material and social world.

J. Hodgens, in Deakin University Language Education 1 Study Guide (2000) pp. 19–20.

Q What is your definition?

Compare your response with your previous definition and file this
response with others for future comparisons.

Summary

This chapter briefly discussed the complexities of language and indicated the different aspects of language that we are focusing on. First and foremost we see language as a social practice and rooted in a culture. We emphasised that language is more than speech, and is also more than speech and writing. Rather, we use a number of systems, both verbal and non-verbal, to construct and convey meaning. Hence we see language as consisting of a number of codes. Different codes and combinations of codes are used, depending on the purpose and context. We need a range of language codes if we are to be effective language users.

We discussed the characteristics of language, that it is systematic, arbitrary, conventional, symbolic, and generative. Language is dynamic, it is agreed to by the users, and it changes with needs over time.

We emphasised that written language is a part of language and that the many factors that influence language use are also relevant for literacy. Language enables us to control our world. In today's world written language is particularly important.

Implications for teaching

1 In our classrooms we have the enormous responsibility of ensuring that we enable our students to have access to the language of power and that they know how to use it effectively and appropriately. We need to empower our students.
2 As teachers we need to have better knowledge of language in order to have greater power to assist our learners to be more powerful, to become more critically aware of their world, and be in creative control of it.
3 We need to have greater awareness of the language practices we validate in the classroom and their impact on our students.
4 We need to be aware of the types of texts we provide for our students to read because these influence not only how students perceive literacy but also their values.

References and further reading

Baker C. & Freebody P. *Children's First School Books*, Basil Blackwell, Oxford, 1989.

Barton D. *Literacy An Introduction to the Ecology of Written Language*, Blackwell, Oxford, 1994.

Cambourne B. 'Getting to the guts of whole language', in *Language as the Core: Teaching in the 90s*, Proceedings of a conference sponsored by ARA NSW and PETA, University of Wollongong, NSW, January 1990, pp. 15–41.

Cambourne & Brown 'A grounded theory of genre acquisition: learning to control different textual forms', *Australian Journal of Reading*, 1987, Vol. 10, No. 4 pp. 261–6.

Cameron M. H. & Saunders M. T. 'An overview of language', in *Language and Speech*, 1977, Vol. 20, No. 30, pp. 217–31.

Christie F. 'Factual writing in the first years of school', in *Australian Journal of Reading*, 1987, Vol. 10, No. 4, pp. 207–16.

Comber & Kamler, 'Critical literacies: politicising the language classroom', *Interpretations,* 1997, Vol. 30, No. 1, pp. 30–53.

Courts B. *Literacy and Empowerment*, Bergin & Garvey, New York, 1991.

Crystal D. *The Cambridge Encyclopedia of Language*, Cambridge University Press, Cambridge, 1987.

Crystal D. *Linguistics*, Penguin, Harmondsworth, 1971.

*Edelsky C. *With Literacy and Justice for All*, Falmer Press, London, 1991.

Fairclough N. *Language and Power*, Longman, London, 1989.

Fairclough N. *Discourse and Social Change*, Polity Press, Cambridge, 1992.

Finegan E., Besnier N., Blair D. & Collins P. *Language: Its Structure and Use*, Harcourt Brace Jovanovich, Sydney, 1992.

Fleischer C. & Schaafsma D. 'Introduction: further conversations: Jay Robinson, his students, and the study of literacy', in Fleischer C. & Schaafsma D. (eds) *Literacy and Democracy: Teacher Research and Composition Studies in Pursuit of Habitable Spaces*, National Council of Teachers of English, IL, 1998, pp. xiii-xxxii.

Freebody P. & Luke A. 'Literacies programs: debates and demands in cultural contexts', *Prospect: Australian Journal of ESL* 1990, Vol. 5, No. 3, pp. 7–16.

Freire P. *Pedagogy of the Oppressed*, Penguin, Harmondsworth, 1972.

Freire P. & Macedo D. *Literacy: Reading the Word and the World*, Bergin & Garvey, South Hadley, MA, 1987.

Gee J. *Social Linguistics and Literacies: Ideology in Discourses*, 2nd edn, Taylor & Francis, London, 1996.

Gilbert P. '(Sub)versions: using sexist language practices to explore critical literacy', *The Australian Journal of Language and Literacy,* 1993, Vol. 16, No. 4, pp. 323–31.

Gimson A. C. *An Introduction to the Pronunciation of English*, 2nd edn, Edward Arnold, London, 1970.

*Halliday M. A. K. & Hasan R. *Language, Context and Text: Aspects of Language in a Social-semiotic Perspective*, Deakin University, Geelong (Vic), 1985.

Hodge R. & Kress G. *Language as Ideology*, 2nd edn, Routledge, London, 1993.

Hodgens J. 'Language as social practice' in *Deakin University Language Education 1 Study Guide*, Deakin University, Geelong, Vic., 2000.

Holmes J. *An Introduction to Sociolinguistics*, Longman, 1992.

*Janks H. *Language, Identity & Power*, Hodder & Stoughton Educational with Witwatersrand University Press, Johannesburg, 1993.

Lankshear C. *Changing Literacies,* Open University Press, Buckingham, 1997.

Lankshear C. with Lawler M. *Literacy, Schooling and Revolution*, Falmer Press, London, 1987.

*Lo Bianco J. & Freebody P. *Australian Literacies*, 2nd edn, Language Australia, Melbourne, 2001.

Maybin J. *Language and Literacy in Social Practice*, Multilingual Matters & the Open University Press, Clevedon, UK, 1994.

McConnell S. 'Literacy and empowerment', *The Australian Journal of Language and Literacy*, 1992, Vol. 15, No. 2, pp. 123–38.

McNaughton S. *Patterns of Emergent Literacy*, Oxford University Press, Auckland, 1995.

*Meek M. *How Texts Teach What Readers Learn*, Thimble Press, Stroud Glos., 1988, in association with Primary English Teachers Association, Rozelle, NSW, 1989.

Muspratt S., Luke A. & Freebody P. *Constructing Critical Literacies*, Allen & Unwin, St Leonards, NSW, 1997.

Mussen P., Conger J. & Kagan J. *Child Development and Personality*, 5th edn, Harper & Row, New York, 1979.

Sapir E. *Language*, Harcourt Brace, New York, 1921.

*Unsworth L. *Literacy Learning and Teaching*, Macmillan, Melbourne, 1993.

Wardhaugh R. *Reading: A Linguistic Perspective*, Harcourt Brace Jovanovich, New York, 1969.

Wittgenstein L. *Tractus-Logico Philosphicus*, (transl. D. F. Pears & B. F. McGuiness), Routledge & Kegan Paul, London, 1961.

Wood N. E. *Delayed Speech and Language Development*, Prentice-Hall, Englewood Cliffs, NJ, 1964.

CHAPTER 2

Doing Things with Language

FOCUS

This chapter focuses on the understanding that:

- *language is more than communication*
- *language serves a number of functions in our society*
- *language is the means by which we make and share meaning with ourselves and with others*
- *we take up and allocate social roles through language*
- *we use language to establish group identity*
- *a major function of language is to structure reality, to make sense of our world*
- *we all possess different realities/worlds*
- *communication is a transactive process and effective communication is very important for teaching.*

PRE-READING ACTIVITY

1   Make a list of the social purposes for which you use language. Share and discuss your list with others who have made similar lists.

Functions of language

Language is more than communication. If you were to ask one hundred different people to explain what they used language for, it's likely that at least ninety-five would reply 'to communicate'. Of course they would be right, but their answers would tell only part of the story. Their responses wouldn't explain very much, particularly if you take the view that communication involves the deliberate passing of information from one person to another.

If you watch ants running along a path on a warm summer afternoon, you may notice individual ants stop to touch antennae. If a biologist were to explain this by saying that they were communicating with one another, would we have any clearer understanding of what they were doing? We might accept the fact that the ants were somehow checking on one another, or even passing information about the whereabouts of food or their nest, but we would have no clear idea about what they were 'saying'. In this sense, then, to be told that we use language to communicate doesn't tell us much about what sort of things we say, or can say, to each other.

There are further difficulties for us if we continue to describe language exclusively in terms of communication. What are we to make of the pre-school child who talks, seemingly to herself, as she paints at her kindergarten easel, or plays by herself in the sandtray? We cannot dismiss her behaviour because it seems to resemble the silent debates we may have with ourselves when we plan what we are going to do or say next time we are in a particular situation, or when we find ourselves involved in a complex problem.

A final, but not trivial, example that shows the inadequacy of communication as an all-embracing explanation for the use of language is the apparently meaningless greetings we exchange with friends and acquaintances as we see them from day to day. 'It's a lovely day, isn't it?' is hardly ever intended, or treated, as a meteorological comment. Imagine how we might respond to someone who proceeded to give such a detailed meteorological analysis. Clearly when we ask the question we intend to communicate, but what? Just as clearly, the response of 'Sure is' is also intended to be communicative, but what is communicated?

One approach to answering the question is to reflect on, or to observe, ourselves and others as we use language and construct a list of the different things that we see being done by people as they use language in their daily lives.

The use of language when we speak sign, or write involves action that can be seen.

At the most basic level, the use of oral, signed or written language involves action that can be seen. When we speak we move muscles that control our breathing and position our tongues, teeth, and lips so that we produce a symbolically significant pattern of sound. When people use sign language they use body movements and facial expression to produce symbolically significant signs. When we write we make symbolically significant marks on a page or computer screen. Some people may have difficulty doing what seems unconsciously natural for the majority of us, but for now let us focus on what we do with language.

Meaning and shared meaning lie at the heart of what we do with language.

Our actions are less obvious when we read or listen to someone else speaking. Nonetheless, reading and listening involve action because they seem to involve systematic and selective sampling of a printed text or stream of sound as we make sense of particular symbols. What seems to be common to these kinds of actions is that in each case we are involved in making meanings that we can share with others or use for ourselves. The notion that meaning and shared meaning lie at the heart of what we do with language is one that we will return to many times.

While these actions are not trivial, examining them won't give a clear indication of what purposes we use language for. In order to answer the question we need to look at the effects that our use of language produces. When we do this, a distinction can be drawn between language as action—language directed to others—and language as reflection, as thinking.

Making sense of our environment

There is no doubt that we do use language for communication, but language plays a much more significant role in our lives.

Carozzi (1976) in an article entitled 'Language: What do we use it for?' uses an extract from *Lord of the Flies* by William Golding to explain how language is used to make sense of our environment.

Consider the following extract from Lord of the Flies by William Golding. In the novel, a plane containing a group of boys crash-lands on an uninhabited island. Three of the boys—Ralph, Jack, and Simon—are exploring the island.

> *They scrambled down a rock slope, dropping among flowers and made their way under the trees. Here they paused and examined the bushes round them curiously. Simon spoke first. 'Like candles. Candle bushes. Candle buds.'*
>
> *The bushes were dark evergreen and aromatic and the many buds were waxen green and folded up against the light. Jack slashed at one with his knife and the scent spilled over them.*
>
> *'Candle buds'*
>
> *'You couldn't light them,' said Ralph. 'They just look like candles.'*
>
> *'Green candles,' said Jack contemptuously, 'we can't eat them. Come on.'*

How are the boys using language? For what functions is language being used? In the first place Simon is responding immediately to the bushes they have found, attempting to make sense of what he sees in terms of what he already knows. His words are tentative and provisional. He explores the possibilities, each attempt coming closer to representing 'in words' what he sees in the world: 'like candles. Candle bushes. Candle buds.' It is, in a sense, a poetic representation—one which Ralph must modify before he can accept it. 'You couldn't light them. They just look like candles.' Ralph's voice is very much the voice of common sense. For Jack, the bushes are assimilated into a still more practical frame of reference. They can't be eaten—therefore they are valueless.

B. Carozzi, *Language: What do we use it for?* p. 1.

Language is used for a range of purposes.

When we reflect upon our use of language it is clear that we use it for a range of purposes, many at the one time. For example, in a conversation we may communicate not only a particular message but we also convey things about ourselves—how we feel, our likes and dislikes, etc., and our feelings towards others. We use language to promote social interaction, control or direct behaviour, explain or instruct, question, praise and encourage, rebuke and threaten, etc. The activity you did before reading chapter 1 would have highlighted the range of purposes you have for language.

Language as social interaction

The rich variety of verbs in our language to account for ways of speaking (*talk, say, comment, question, argue, debate* and so on) is an indication of the variety of different actions we use language for as we deal with other people. While some of these actions may seem similar, the variety of terms suggests important, if subtle, semantic differences that rest on differences in social roles between participants in a conversation. For example, the difference in meaning between 'persuade' and 'beg' rests on a shared understanding of the roles of both participants; that is, the power of the person doing the asking and the person being asked.

Because we live in a society that holds to ideals of democratic equality, some people may be uncomfortable with the view that language is mediated according to social roles and is influenced by status and power differences between groups and individuals. However, the fact is that our culture does incorporate these differences and our language reflects this. This is discussed in more detail in the next chapter.

One way it does this is by making available the resources for doing particular things. For example, our language gives us ways of addressing one another depending on who we are and whom we are addressing.

Our culture compels us to recognise distinctions between people, and it does this by giving us a language that identifies and marks out those distinctions.

In your family you might call your parents by their first names, but if you do, you would also know that in some families calling parents by their first names would be regarded as outright impertinence. Our culture compels us to recognise distinctions between people, and it does this by giving us a language that identifies and marks out those distinctions. We have a range of titles to identify or address others whose rank or authority needs to be acknowledged. You may well have referred to your secondary high school principal as 'Old Creep' (or worse) when you spoke about her with your friends, but you would have been aware of the consequences of calling her that to her face. You may want to argue that it is simply common manners or politeness that determines how we will speak to someone. However, it is interesting that most native speakers are very aware of what is going on when someone in an interaction refuses to play the conversation game by the same rules as their partner.

One example reported by Farb (1974) concerned a dialogue between a police officer from a southern state of the United States and a black doctor:

> 'What's your name boy?' the policeman asked.
> 'Doctor Poussaint, I'm a physician.'
> 'What's your first name, boy?'
> ... As my heart palpitated: I muttered in profound humiliation: 'Alvin'.

In his discussion of the fifteen words of dialogue Farb makes the point that most readers would recognise the exchange as a deliberate insult of the black Dr Poussaint by the white police officer who refused to concede the respect that is implicit in the use of the term 'doctor'.

What seems to be clear is that our language not only gives us the resources to acknowledge power and status relationships in our communication with others, but in doing so requires that we recognise these different relations when we speak. Of course language changes from time to time reflecting changes in society or may be deliberately changed in order to produce or reflect changes that some may want to make.

Two examples may help make the point. For many years the language reflected, and helped to shape, differences in the social position of women by providing 'Mister' as the one respectful title for adult males regardless of their marital status, yet provided, and required, 'Miss' for unmarried women and 'Missus' for married women. In a deliberate attempt to challenge the ideological foundations of these distinctions, the written form 'Ms' was proposed as a general term of respectful address for all women regardless of their marital status. Since the written form was first proposed it has moved into the spoken language of those who accept the social assumptions behind its use. These speakers now quite freely use /məz/ as a form of address or as a spoken title when referring to women. It is interesting that this form can lead to misunderstanding or embarrassment when it is used to refer to women who either do not understand, or do not share, its ideological foundation. For example, some older women may be offended if letters are addressed to them as 'Ms' because they believe that the term should only be applied to unmarried women or active feminists.

A second example comes from contemporary French, which, like other Latin-based languages, uses two forms of the second person pronoun (in English 'you' and sometimes 'youse'). For example in French there are two ways of asking 'Where are you going?' These are:

(a) *Où est-ce que tu vas?*   (b) *Où est-ce que vous allez?*

The two words 'tu' and 'vous' indicate number; the former being the singular form, and the latter being the plural form.* However, differentiating between the two words serves another purpose by indicating the difference in status and intimacy between the speaker and the listener: 'vous' is respectful and formal, while 'tu' is intimate and is used between social equals. The distinction reflects, and makes possible, the expression of social differences in French culture. This point has not been lost on young French people who, to the expected outrage of their elders and betters, have taken increasingly to using the intimate 'tu' in situations where the respectful 'vous' might have been expected.

So, quite clearly more than a simple request for information is being communicated by a young person who asks an older person: 'Où est-ce que tu vas?' Such a deliberate breaking of the rules or conventions of language use has been taken to mean, as no doubt it is expected to mean, a challenge to the social rules that underpin the language and the culture that is intertwined with it.

The forms of address we use are not the only ways we use language to negotiate social interactions. The kind of language we use can quite deliberately include or exclude others from our social world. This is discussed in chapter 3. At the most obvious level there are the greetings that we exchange as we meet people we know or have to deal with each day:

How are you?
Hi
Good morning

These, and many others, are ways that we signal to others that we have seen them and acknowledged them as belonging to our social world. Our friends and acquaintances would be surprised, and even hurt, if we walked past them without some form of acknowledgement just as we would be surprised, and even hurt, if our greetings were ignored. If you consider what is actually said in these brief encounters you might come to the conclusion that we are strange creatures indeed. We can say 'Good morning' to someone regardless of whether it is in fact a good morning and our greeting 'How are you?' doesn't seem to be a question at all. We would be very puzzled if it produced a response that did answer the question. We certainly wouldn't expect a detailed description of our friend's present state of health. This may lead to momentary confusion in a doctor's surgery where it may not be clear whether we should reply conversationally or treat the utterance as a

---

*Although standard English now has only the one word that indicates both singular and plural, there was a time when, like French, it had different words. In Old and Middle English, the singular form was 'thou' (rhyming with 'do'), and the plural form was 'you'. The singular form is still used in some English dialects, and might be familiar with those who have some acquaintance with religious literature.

question that needs to be properly answered with a statement of our symptoms. Clearly, context is an important factor in clarifying meanings and framing our own responses. All of this suggests that exchanges serve the function of 'making contact' or 'recognition', an interpretation supported by the fact that we would begin to feel very isolated if each of our acquaintances ignored us as we met them casually in our daily life.

Many exchanges serve the function of 'making contact', for establishing social relations.

Language and social values

Apart from the examples already given that show how individuals and groups use language to negotiate social relationships, language also provides ways to negotiate social values. Of all the ways in which we use language, gossip is often regarded as the least consequential, or even as somehow unpleasant or antisocial.

Gossip may well result in the destruction of individual reputations and its consequences may be malicious, but gossip seems to be the means by which people keep in touch with the values of their associates and community. The stories we tell one another about the behaviour of those we know, or know of, and the moral judgments our stories invite, all contribute to a communally shared set of values about acceptable and unacceptable behaviour. Every time we participate in such a discussion we confirm or modify our own values and place them into the context of other people's values. Whenever we find ourselves discussing the awful predicament of an acquaintance or a public figure we are also checking our own reactions and interpretations of that predicament against those of other people. 'Isn't what happened to George dreadful?' we may ask, but if our conversational partner replies 'Yes, I suppose so, but he got just what he deserved', we may find that our sympathy for George has to be defended or perhaps qualified. In the ensuing exchange the views of both conversationalists come to be evaluated and perhaps modified.

Gossip is the means by which people keep in touch with the values of their associates and community.

Gossip may be about individuals known to the speakers or the public face of individuals presented to us through the mass media. Just as we grow to know and like (or dislike) people we have met, we also form opinions of politicians and other public figures whom we might never meet except through a thirty-second slice of the evening news. What seems to be crucial in how our response is formed is the way we gossip with others about the characteristics and behaviour of these public figures. Recent Australian history gives us examples of public figures who fell from grace because the community came to think of them as lacking compassion or sympathy, or as being ineffectual.

Gossip is inevitable, even if we don't always care for its consequences, because it is necessary to develop and maintain the kind of cohesion that groups of individuals need in order to co-operate in society. When we gossip, the subject of our conversation may be trivial and inconsequential, but the underlying agenda is the negotiation of

The underlying agenda of gossip is the negotiation of shared social values and attitudes.

shared social values and attitudes. We gossip to discover what others think and to find ways of positioning our own thinking on the same issues.

To some extent, *jokes* and *stories* do the same thing as gossip. What we laugh at is bound tightly to particular cultures so that there are not many jokes that travel well and, in fact, many jokes don't work outside the social world from which they arose. Many jokes depend for their effect on a shared sense of ridicule for particular individuals or groups and if the values underpinning the joke are not shared then it is more likely to be a source of offence than of humour. We have all heard jokes that were not funny because they touched our values in an offensive rather than amusing way. Racial, ethnic, sexist, and political jokes all depend on the joke teller and joke listener sharing stereotypes and values. It isn't such a long shot to argue that by telling jokes we invite others to share and perhaps reinforce those stereotypes and values. Telling and listening to jokes is not just an amusing way of passing time: it is an important way by which groups can maintain a shared set of values.

Telling and listening to jokes is not just an amusing way of passing time; it is an important way by which groups can maintain a shared set of values.

Stories are another way of establishing and maintaining the sets of values that come to make up a group culture.

Stories are another way of establishing and maintaining the sets of values that come to make up a group culture. They are obviously a little more complex than jokes, if only because their greater length allows for a more complex development of their components than is usually possible in the highly conventional joke form. The stories of a particular culture range from traditional folk tales, which may have originated from oral stories, to highly contrived literary forms of a literary culture. In either case there is the same exposure of the values and attitudes of the authors or tellers that invites some acceptance or response from readers or listeners. In the case of traditional tales we can sometimes trace the history of their development and match this against changing public values over time. Even a simple tale like 'Little Red Riding Hood' has a history that reveals changes in public morality or ideology over 400 years (Zipes 1983). In the original oral tale the main character is a robust and resourceful peasant girl who successfully negotiates her own sexual initiation. Later versions depicted her as a middle-class adolescent who pays for the wilful disobedience of her mother with her own life; in these versions the story became a piece of cautionary moral advice. In most modern versions Little Red Riding Hood is a simpering child who with her feeble grandmother has to be rescued from the wolf by a male woodsman or woodcutter. Through these changes from the original peasant tale we can see the changes in the perceptions of childhood, sexuality and the relationship between the sexes over the period that the story has survived. Changes in literary taste are not merely changes in fashion but are both reflections and shapers of the values and attitudes of the culture from which they grow. The book *Politically Correct Bedtime Stories* by James Finn Garner (1994) highlights how our language has changed to reflect society's changing values.

Changes in literary taste are not merely changes in fashion but are both reflections and shapers of the values and attitudes of the culture from which they grow.

Language to exchange information

As well as using language to establish and maintain social connections and shared values, we also use it to share information and sometimes misinformation. We tell each other things. We ask for information from each other. We assert or deny propositions, some of which can be true or false or a mixture of both.

We use language to share information, and sometimes misinformation.

Philosophers of language and linguists have written a great deal about the ways in which language encodes meanings that may be shared. In fact, for a long time, philosophers of language seemed to be concerned almost exclusively with the logical meanings of words and sentences. However, as we've already seen, what people say to one another can mean much more than the actual meaning of the words and sentences they use. Even so, few would want to agree with Humpty Dumpty who argued:

> 'When I use a word', Humpty Dumpty said, in rather a scornful tone. 'it means just what I choose it to mean—neither more nor less'.

We can 'share' information because those of us who belong to a 'speech community' seem to have come to an agreement to apply similar meanings to the language we use. We object, as did Alice in *Alice in Wonderland*, when others seem to apply personal meanings to words rather than adopt these shared meanings.

One philosopher of language, Grice (1975), tried to equate this social agreement with a set of rules that formed a kind of contract used by people when they speak. His rules, which are paraphrased below, were covered under four headings:

Quantity: provide as much information as the exchange requires
don't provide more information than the exchange requires
Relation: be relevant
Quality: try to say what is true
don't say what you believe to be false
don't say things you don't have supporting evidence for
Manner: be clear
avoid obscurity
avoid ambiguity
be brief
be orderly

At first glance these are pretty strange rules. They certainly don't look like rules of grammar that, if broken, produce nonsense. Grice's rules are more like advice that a teacher might give students who are writing an essay. And in a sense, the consequences of breaking them in speech may be similar to the consequences of breaking them in writing. Our listeners or readers may decide that we are saying something more, or less, than we intended.

What happens if we provide more information than is required in an exchange?

Hello Soula, I just saw your mother. You know the lady who lives at number 27.

Soula would be justified in thinking that her 'informant' was providing the already known, or unnecessary, 'information' for some purpose and would probably decide that this person was speaking sarcastically.

ACTIVITY AND DISCUSSION

Make up exchanges in which you try to break each of Grice's rules in turn.

Q What happens?

We know when our conversational partner or the author with whom we are having a dialogue is speaking or writing ironically, sarcastically, or metaphorically, because part of our knowledge of the language we are using consists of shared knowledge of the way the language should be used.

What is clear from all of this is that the 'communication' of ideas is not simply a case of passing ideas in the form of words from the head of a speaker or writer into the head of a listener or a reader. The listener, or reader, has an important co-operative role to play in the business of sharing information.

> The listener, or reader, has an important co-operative role to play in the business of sharing information.

Learning language functions

M. A. K. Halliday has written extensively about the functions of language and how children learn language and its functions. In his study (Halliday 1973) he classified the different purposes of language used by a young child into seven functions. He found that the representational/informative communicative function was developed after the other six functions, indicating perhaps the importance of children using language for their own purposes and to make sense of the immediate environment before using it for strictly communicative purposes. Smith (1983) used and extended Halliday's speech functions to ten and provided examples of non-verbal codes for each function. These are provided in Table 2.1. He also discusses one specialised use of language (that is, to talk about language itself): metalinguistics or metalanguage. These functions are neither discrete nor mutually exclusive—any one text or language event can serve a number of purposes. Others have described seventy different uses for language!

> The functions of speech are neither discrete nor mutually exclusive—any one text or language event can serve a number of purposes.

Table 2.1   The uses of language

Language Use	Nonlanguage Alternative*
1. **Instrumental:** 'I want.' (Language as a means of getting things, satisfying material needs.)	Pantomime, facial expressions, screaming, pointing, grabbing.
2. **Regulatory:** 'Do as I tell you.' (Controlling the behaviour, feelings or attitudes of others.)	Pushing and pulling people around; modelling behavior for others to copy.
3. **Interactional:** 'Me and you.' (Getting along with others, establishing relative status. Also 'Me against you'—establishing separateness.)	Waving, smiling, linking arms, holding hands, shaking fists, sport.
4. **Personal:** 'Here I come.' (Expressing individuality, awareness self, pride.)	Art, music, dress, cosmetics, ornamentation.
5. **Heuristic:** 'Tell me why?' (Seeking and testing knowledge.)	Exploration, investigation, experimentation.
6. **Imaginative:** 'Let's pretend.' (Creating new worlds, making up stories, poems.)	Play, art, mime.
7. **Representational:** 'I've got something to tell you.' (Communicating information, descriptions, expressing propositions.)	Pointing, rituals, diagrams, maps, mathematics.
8. **Diversionary:** 'Enjoy this.' (Puns, jokes, riddles.)	Games, puzzles, magic.
9. **Authoritative/contractual:** 'How it must be.' (Statutes, laws, regulations, agreements, contracts.)	Roles, rituals, regalia, uniforms, architecture.
10. **Perpetuating:** 'How it was.' (Records, histories, diaries, notes, scores.)	Photographs, sculpture, monuments, memorials.

*We refer to these as non-verbal counterparts.

F. Smith, *Essays into Literacy*, pp. 53–4.

Halliday collapsed his original seven functions to three major ones that became the basis for functional systemic linguistics: ideational, for the communication of ideas; interpersonal, for the expression of feelings; and textual, for the relationships within a text.

An alternative formulation for the function of language was developed by Britton (1970) to study children's writing. His three categories are:

- transactional, or language to get things done (related to a wide range of uses)
- expressive, revealing of the user, personal expression
- poetic, covering all creative and artistic constructions of language.

A number of different purposes for writing and possible forms of writing are shown on Table 2.2, which highlight how easy it can be for us to provide for a range of purposes in our programs.

Language for structuring reality

Sapir (1921) argued that the 'real world' for individuals is, to a large extent, unconsciously built up by the language habits of the group. Writers such as Britton (1970), Halliday (1973) and Smith (1983) emphasised the importance of language for structuring this reality, for making our meanings. Through language we learn to make meaning, to make sense of experiences. A baby is born into a world full of stimuli; gradually the infant labels objects, feelings and experiences, categorises and classifies events, and learns to make some sense of the environment. Initially, children are in the world without 'knowing' it; until they have some language they cannot separate themselves from their environment. Language makes it possible for them to objectify and conceptualise themselves and their world, and to share the responsibility for their destiny.

Britton (1970) states 'we use language as a means of organising a representation of the world—each for himself—and that the representation so created constitutes the world we operate in, the basis of all the predictions by which we set the course of our lives'. Language used in the process of labelling our experiences enables us to simplify and generalise our experiences to facilitate communication. Classification is the basis of language and thought. The story of Helen Keller, who was blind and deaf from the age of two, highlights the importance and power of language for making sense of the environment. Until she realised that she could label and categorise objects and events, her life and behaviour were bizarre. Once she could use a language code—sign language—she was able to make sense of her environment, begin to interact effectively with it, and gain power over it.

A critical stage in language development appears to be when the very young child realises that things have names and can be labelled. For example, a child of one of the writers called a number of things that were important to him (such as bottle, dummy, or rug) 'dum dum'.

Through language we learn to make meaning, to make sense of experiences.

Language used in the process of labelling our experiences enables us to simplify and generalise our experiences to facilitate communication.

Table 2.2   Purposes of writing and their forms

Purposes	Writing form
To record feelings, observations, etc.	Personal letters Science reports Poems Jottings of sensory impressions from observations, stories, drama, music, art Diaries, journals
To describe	Character portraits Reports of a sequence of events Labels and captions Advertisements, e.g. wanted to buy or sell, lost and found
To inform or advise	Posters advertising coming events Scripts for news broadcasts Minutes of meetings/Agendas Invitations Programmes
To persuade	Advertisements and commercials Letters to the editor Notes for a debate Cartoons
To clarify thinking	Note-taking for research topics Explanations of graphs, science diagrams, etc. Jottings
To explore and maintain relationships with others	Letters Making requests Greeting cards Questionnaires
To predict or hypothesise	Speculations about probable outcomes in health, science, social studies topics Endings for stories Questions for research or interviews
To make comparisons	Charts Note-making Diagrams, graphs Descriptions
To command or direct	Recipes Instructions, How to make a ... Stage directions Rules for games, safety, health, etc.
To amuse or entertain	Jokes, riddles, puzzles Scripts for drama, puppet plays Stories and poems Personal anecdotes

Education Department of South Australia, *Writing R-7 Language Arts*, pp. 17–18.

The role of language in structuring our 'world' underpins our concepts of the role of language in learning, in living, of the role of literacy in learning, and informs our perceptions of the teacher's role in fostering language development. As teachers we need constantly to be aware of how we can assist our students to use language to learn effectively—to make different types of meanings. We need to ensure that our students have the appropriate 'labels' for the different discipline areas.

Each knowledge discipline structures reality differently.

As teachers it is worth remembering that different knowledge disciplines structure reality differently; each discipline asks different questions about the world and develops different theories or constructs to explain phenomena. It could be said that philosophy asks questions such as 'What are the principles by which people should conduct their lives?'; anthropology asks 'How do cultures establish normal ways of living?'; geography asks 'How do people adjust to their environment?'; psychology asks 'What are the rules of individual human behaviour?; and education asks 'How do we systematically create and communicate knowledge?' Language is used differently in the different disciplines to achieve this.

These discipline perspectives are not concrete realities, but are realities constructed by a group.

It is important to remember and help our students become aware that these discipline perspectives of the world are not concrete realities, but realities constructed by a group. For example, we previously thought of history as consisting of a study of the unchangeable facts of the past. As such, the realities of any discipline can be challenged and changed. This has happened several times in science when established ways of thinking have been overthrown by new theories based on different perspectives. Often this awareness is reassuring for students who are experiencing difficulty understanding that reality. In addition, it allows students to feel freer to question and be more creative in constructing their own realities and less pressured to learn a whole lot of facts by rote.

Differing realities

Even if we come from similar backgrounds our worlds may be different, but if we possess different languages and cultures our worlds may be very different.

We are born with different genetic backgrounds, have different experiences in different sociocultural environments, and process our experiences differently; therefore we all represent the world differently. Even if we come from similar backgrounds our worlds may be different. This has very important implications for teachers when we appreciate that our society is multilingual and multicultural with students coming from a wide range of backgrounds. It must also be remembered that the world of the young child is very different from the world of the adult. As Donaldson (1978) reminds us, the teacher needs to become less egocentric and realise this difference, evaluating the child's behaviour from a child's perspective. We need to set tasks that make sense to the child and work on extending and developing the child's logic, not merely imposing an adult view on top. Goodman et al. (1978) succinctly explain the concept of reality and language:

We need to set tasks that make sense to the child and that work on extending and developing the child's logic.

A reality that exists within the limits of language may not be reality in some absolute sense, but it is as much as a reality as the individual and the language community will ever know. Eskimos [Inuit] reflect their own environment and their interest by their many classifications of snow unknown to inhabitants of the temperate zone. Arabs may distinguish endlessly among camels, and some Brazilian Indians have hundreds of words for different birds without a generic term for bird. Inner city children have many colorful words for police officers. The fact that people from other language communities can learn Inuit or Brazilian distinctions does not destroy the validity of these as examples of language culture delimitation. It is possible to learn other languages, including nuances and refinements, but one still only knows about them. Without the psychological depth and sensuous involvement that grow out of extended transactions of individuals with their environment through the medium of language, something will always be lacking to some degree when one learns another language. One's particular grasp of reality is determined by the structure of the language as well as by its references.

Everyone and every language community starts with the same physical world, but each sees it from a slightly shifted perspective. Our common humanity predetermines what we shall find in reality, but our common humanity also allows ample room for community and individual differences. Although we have begun to find ways of radically shifting our perspectives to those of other persons or cultures, ultimately all will be qualified by the final individual perspective. All world views, no matter how wide the horizons, turn on the axial 'I'; that is, they are egocentric.

K. Goodman et al., *Language and Thinking in School*, pp. 20–1.

Language is integral to the process of conceiving meaning and a necessary pre-condition of the cultural process (Lankshear 1997). Culture reflects relationships and social process, the structuring of lives according to shared meanings, beliefs, and understandings: 'It is not as though we have meaning and *then* have language—in order to express our meaning. Rather, language is integral to realizing meaning' (Lankshear 1997, p. 23). Because language is integral to the cultural process, it plays a central part in the struggles and politics of cultural groups. Dominant groups establish their language, knowledge and pedagogical preferences as the legitimate form in education and society in general (Lankshear 1997). In her discussion of Deaf culture, Carol Padden (1996, p. 89) provides an interesting example of the way in which language reflects and constructs power relations within and between communities:

Language plays a central part in the struggles and politics of cultural groups.

> *To invoke the labels of DEAF and HEARING is to call up a web of relationships between what is central and what is peripheral, what is known and what is not known, and what is familiar and what is foreign. To talk of these terms is to offer a counterbalance between two large and imposing presences in Deaf people's lives—their own community and the community within which they must live, among hearing people.*

The different use and meaning of language depends on what is central and what is peripheral in your community.

Padden goes on to explain the different use and meaning of language depending on what is central in your life. For the Deaf, the terms 'deaf' or 'hearing-impaired' are used to refer to different groups of people within their community. In the Deaf community, being hearing-impaired (rather than deaf) indicates similarity with the dominant hearing community—an ability to speak and hear to some degree. Therefore, to be 'very' hearing-impaired is to be very much like the dominant community, that is, a small degree of hearing loss. This term 'very hearing-impaired' is interpreted by those in the hearing community as meaning someone who is very deaf. Therefore, the one term has opposite meaning within two different communities.

ACTIVITIES AND DISCUSSION

In Indonesia rice is very important and in Bahasa Indonesian a number of different words are used to describe rice, such as *padi* for rice in the field, *beras* for husked rice, and *nasi* for cooked rice.

Q Can you think of other examples of the way in which language reflects cultural perspectives or positions of power in society?

Q What is your reality? With a friend think of a concept for example, love, family, femininity. Compare your views. How do your views differ? Why?

Q Could any of the differences be explained by differences in the following: race, ethnicity, class, gender, religion, age?

Q How could the differences interfere with communication?

Q How could differences between the teacher's reality and the realities of the students interfere with teaching–learning?

The different types of functions of language can be seen as hierarchical.

In summary, the different types of functions of language can be seen as hierarchical. The primary function of language is seen as structuring the environment. This function can be classified in terms of communicative and non-communicative functions. Non-communicative functions could be further divided into expressive, where overt use of language is serving a non-communicative purpose such as for self-expression, and meditational/thinking or cognitive functions, where covert and overt systems are used for thinking and learning. A whole range of more specific functions can be described; some of these have been listed in Table 2.1 above. In any one instance of language use, however, language may be serving a number of purposes, but generally an overriding purpose can be determined.

ACTIVITY AND DISCUSSION

Use a diagram to illustrate how you perceive the relationship between the different types of functions of language. Share and discuss your diagram with others.

Language and communication

ACTIVITIES AND DISCUSSION

Think about good teachers who helped you to learn something of value.

Q What were the characteristics of their teaching? They may have used different styles of instruction, but all would have expressed their ideas clearly and coherently. Much of what they said was comprehensible, useful, and relevant. They were good communicators.

Think about poor teachers you may have known.

Q What were the characteristics of their teaching? Poor teachers probably could not demonstrate or explain key ideas in ways you could understand. The style of presentation was dull and unstimulating; they could not control classes and failed to convince students that what they had to say was important or interesting. They were poor communicators.

We stated earlier that communication is a major function of language. Communication, or at least effective communication, is central to our lives. Numerous seminars are held about communication. As teachers it is particularly important that we communicate effectively—we have to communicate to our students, their parents, and our colleagues. If we are poor communicators our teaching will be ineffective. We need to be competent in the so-called communication skills and we also need to know how these skills work for communication. An understanding of the process, determinants, and effects of communication will help you, the communicator, to communicate effectively. Strano et al. (1989) believe:

> In communication we are constantly trying to translate our
> personal experience into a form of message—either through
> language or other forms of social behaviour—to which others can
> respond. It follows that the better we understand human
> behaviour, both our own and that of others, the more effectively

Communication is a major function of language.

we will be able to communicate. It follows also that our command of symbols will be a measure of our communication strength. So whether your symbols are words or pictures, command over their choice is vital to you.

Z. Strano et al., *Communicating!*, p. 7.

Because of its importance to teaching, we plan to discuss the nature of communication in some depth.

QUESTIONS

Q What is your definition of communication?

Q What factors inhibit effective communication in the classroom?

Q What processes are involved in communication?

Q How can you communicate more effectively?

What is communication?

Generally, communication refers to the conveying and the receiving of a message/meaning between two or more people (*inter*personal communication). Some people refer to *intra*personal communication—communication with oneself. In the past, definitions of communication focused on the transfer of meaning, but more recent definitions of communication discuss the importance of shared understandings, of the transaction of meaning (Strano et al. 1989), and the construction of meaning. (Current definitions of reading also emphasise the construction of meaning; the reader bringing more meaning *to* the text than provided on the page—Morris & Stewart-Dore 1984.) The two parties have to work together to arrive at shared meanings: it is not just the transfer of a particular meaning to another party. Unfortunately, in many communication situations there are differences in interests, needs, and beliefs, which interfere with the process of achieving shared meanings. In addition, some people's beliefs about the nature of communication work against effective communication. These people seem to believe that communication is merely transferring information and therefore do not work at sharing and making meaning together. Similarly, a teacher who perceives teaching as transferring information, rather than helping learners make their own meanings, will teach ineffectively.

Communication can be defined as the use of language where more than one person is involved in constructing meaning. This definition of communication is very similar to how we described the main purpose of language—to construct meaning. It is obvious that language and communication are therefore central to the process of teaching.

Communication can be defined as the use of language where more than one person is involved in constructing meaning.

Another way of thinking about communication and language is as a system of signs. A discipline called semiotics is the study of the construction of signs that are used to convey meaning. Signs are defined as 'artefacts' or acts which refer to something other than themselves; codes are systems into which signs are organised and which determine how signs are used in relation to one another. Semiotics classifies signs into three categories:

Icon: a sign that resembles the object it signifies; for example, photographs, some drawings, road signs such as for restaurants, toilet signs, accommodation signs, no smoking signs

Index: a sign that is causally connected to the object it signifies; for example, smoke to represent fire

Symbol: a sign that is arbitrarily and conventionally related to its referent or object; for example, words are symbols—we have to learn what meanings are assigned to them as the meaning is not instinctively obvious. In literary writing many symbols are used to suggest different layers of meanings. For example, snow can be an index of cold and used to suggest loneliness.

ACTIVITIES AND DISCUSSION

Many business logos are symbols.

Q Can you think of any?

Q What sign does the Australian Broadcasting Corporation use as a logo?

Q What logo or crest does your institution possess?

Q Can you think of other examples of literary symbols?

We need to emphasise again that our understanding and use of signs is basically cultural: 'We make sense of them and they help us shape our behaviour according to our cultural and social experiences, class, gender, age, and other aspects of our personal and social relations' (Strano et al. 1989). One of the difficulties of translating from one language to another is that literal translations ignore the literary symbols that are culture-based. A translator needs to be familiar with the symbols of both languages.

Factors influencing communication

The quality and quantity of meaning constructed in a communication event appears to be a direct function of a number of factors: the degree of similarity of the participants' experiential backgrounds; the degree of similarity by which participants structure their experience; and the context, purposes for communication, and relationships between the communicators.

Language and communication are central to the process of teaching.

Semiotics is the study of the construction of signs that are used to convey meaning.

Our understanding and use of signs is basically cultural.

A translator needs to be familiar with the symbols of both languages.

Individuals vary considerably in experiential backgrounds and the way they structure their realities.

This variation is explained by a nested hierarchy of determinants, beginning at the personal level, and extending through to familial, social, regional, and national levels.

Individuals vary quite considerably in experiential backgrounds and the way they structure their realities. Variation in experiential background and structuring of experiences can be explained by viewing the factors as being part of a hierarchy of determinants, beginning at the level of the individual's potential for language-learning and extending through to the level of national characteristics. Each level of the hierarchy is represented as a series of layers embedded within one another illustrating a progressively broadening scope of influence. Figure 2.1 illustrates this concept.

Figure 2.1   Nested hierarchy of language–communication determinants

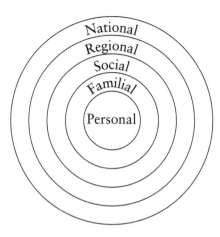

M. H. Cameron & M. T. Saunders, '*An Overview of Language*', p. 219.

Level 1: Personal

Genetic endowment establishes the potential for future language development. This may be modified adversely by the influence of environmental factors operating on the foetus or newborn infant prior to the time it functions independently of the mother's physiological system, or at any time throughout the individual's life. The personal level is the most important as, at all times, a person's genetic endowment interacts with the environment, represented in Figure 2.1 by the outer levels of the hierarchy.

The personal level is the most important because of its interaction with the environment, represented by the remaining four levels.

The familial level involves the influence of the family— its dynamic interaction with the individual in terms of qualitative and quantitative physical and psychological factors.

Level 2: Familial

This level involves the influence of the family and its dynamic interaction with the individual in terms of qualitative and quantitative physical and psychological factors. The physical factors consist of the amount and appropriateness of stimuli provided by the family environment. Early in the individual's life, the family environment provides the majority of experiences from which the child learns different ways of communicating and using language. Such experiences can be inferred from a study of the Matrix of Language codes in Table 1.1.

Level 3: Socio-economic

Socio-economic variables that impinge upon the family environment include:

- physical factors, such as residential location, schooling, social contacts, possessions, experiences outside the home, which all appear to be directly related to the degree of wealth in the family
- psychological factors, such as attitudes and methods of child rearing, individual roles within the family, attitudes about life, value placed upon literacy, the type and quantity of language used within the family, which appear to be strongly influenced by social groups.

Socio-economic variables that influence the individual directly include variables such as peer group, club, religious, and school affiliations, and type and place of work. These all influence the development and use of different language codes.

Socio-economic variables that impinge upon the family environment are physical factors that appear to be directly related to the family's wealth, and psychological factors which appear to be strongly influenced by social groups.

Level 4: Regional

This level covers the influence of broader forces, which may be classified by reference to:

- environmental variables, such as urban or rural lifestyles, degree of remoteness, distinctive geographical features
- ethnic variables, such as colour, religion, customs
- political variables, such as different legislation from region to region, which has direct and indirect influence on the individual's development and use of language.

The regional level includes the broader factors of environmental, ethnic, and political variables.

Level 5: National

This level incorporates factors that unite regions having similar:

- political structures
- religious philosophies
- cultural heritage
- cultural characteristics.

All of these factors influence the lower levels of the hierarchy. One of the most obvious national differences is speech. It varies in all linguistic parameters, the most subtle and interesting of which is rhythm. Even when the more obvious differences of a second speech code have been mastered, the rhythm of the new speech community often eludes the learner. In addition, global factors are influencing the way language is used.

Condon (1974) and Condon and Sanders (1974) discovered that healthy newborn infants manifest motor behaviour that is highly

The national level incorporates factors that unite regions having similar political structures, religious philosophies, cultural heritage, and cultural characteristics.

synchronised with the speech pattern of their culture. It appears that infants from the beginning move in rhythm with the organisation of the speech structure of the culture so that, by the time a child speaks, the basic rhythm patterns of a language are well established and probably resistant to change.

Figure 2.2 from Andersch et al. (1969) demonstrates the complexity of the communication process. Each participant receives a stimulus from the environment, which may come from a number of codes, then structures, evaluates, and processes a message based on this stimulus. The message is then received, constructed, and evaluated by the receiver, who then becomes a source or sender of more information. All participants have the roles of receiver and sender, and have responsibility for sharing and negotiating meanings.

All participants have the roles of receiver and sender, and have responsibility for sharing and negotiating meanings.

Figure 2.2   A model of the communication process

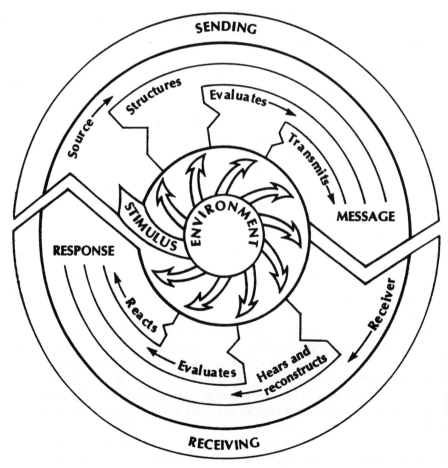

E. Andersch et al. in Z. Strano et al., *Communicating!*, p. 32.

Communication is more than words. In any communication event a number of sign systems may be involved. Words, pictures, diagrams, layout of print, and type of print all shape the message. In some communication events the different sign systems may convey contradictory messages. For example, the words may be carrying a positive message, but the facial expressions may indicate a negative message. What message do we take note of? What is the real meaning? It seems that the non-verbal message is the stronger system and that we are more likely to believe the non-verbal message, hence the reason why many people like to see other people's facial expressions. It also illustrates why it is inappropriate to separate verbal and non-verbal codes in our teaching.

It is important to remember that words and other symbols do not have meanings in themselves; rather they have meanings thrust upon them by the users. We all give slightly different meanings to words as we use them. In addition, many words in our language are used to represent different concepts, making the negotiation of meaning critical, if shared meanings are to be constructed. Furthermore, different groups assign different meanings to signs; for example, a shake of the head or looking at someone in the eyes. We need to be aware of these differences and help our students to become aware of them through discussions of language use and differences.

Words and other signs do not have meanings in themselves: meanings are thrust upon them by the users.

For effective communication negotiation of meaning is critical.

ACTIVITY

With your peers think of a word; for example, 'bank'.

Q What did you first think of—a riverbank, a money bank, an aeroplane banking, relying on someone?

Q If you thought of a money bank, what type of bank did you think of— a suburban branch, a bank as a financial institution participating in business?

The range of responses should have highlighted the different meanings we each hold about words, which can make communication difficult.

Improving our communication skills

How can we, as teachers, improve our communication with our students, their parents, and other community members? Communication is improved when the following indicators can be clearly observed among the communicators: warmth, empathy, respect, genuineness, and listening, and when the communication has concrete practicality. As teachers, we need to respect the views and values of others, and demonstrate the importance of this respect to others. Our students and their parents probably come from different backgrounds, sometimes vastly different, and are likely to possess different perspectives. The degree of success experienced by different students has

As teachers, we need to respect the views and values of others and demonstrate the importance of this respect to others.

much to do with how well their values mesh with those of mostly middle-class teachers. Success is more likely if the interests of the students and those of the school as an institution are shared. We hope that this and the next chapter will help you appreciate the validity of different views and attitudes about language and language use.

Summary

By now you should be clearer in your own mind as to what language means to you. This chapter stressed the importance of language for structuring our world and our reality, for making meaning, for creating an individual's and a group's reality. Language is about meaning, and these meanings are expressed through signs and symbols that are agreed upon by a group. The nature of language makes it a powerful tool for reflecting and learning. Language provides us with an important means for adopting and assigning roles when we interact with others. The kinds of social relationships we can enter with others through language are important shapers of our culture. Language enables us to establish and maintain group membership within larger cultural groups.

Language serves a great range of purposes—for communication, for thinking, for expressing ourselves. We use language to achieve myriad daily tasks.

Everyone's language is slightly different, and for that reason everyone's reality is different. This has many implications for teachers working with others to assist learning—to create new meanings. In particular, the teacher needs to accept the realities of other people and show respect for their different perspectives. In addition, we explored the nature of communication and argued that communication is about two or more people making and sharing meaning. For effective communication to occur the language must be similar.

We have argued that language is rooted in culture, that language is part of a culture. In chapter 3 we discuss the relationship between language and culture, showing that language reflects the culture and passes on the culture from one generation to the next. We emphasise how the culture influences the ways in which language is used, and how language influences the ways in which the individual perceives, thinks, and acts.

Implications for teaching

1 Communication is basic to the teaching–learning context and it is important that we, as teachers, are effective communicators both verbally and non-verbally.
2 This means that we, as teachers, really have to know and understand the cultural world of our students. It's not simply a

Success is more likely if the interests of the students and those of the school as an institution are shared.

Language is about meaning, and these meanings are expressed through signs and symbols that are agreed upon by a group.

Language provides us with an important means for adopting and assigning roles when we interact with others.

Language enables us to establish and maintain group membership within larger cultural groups.

matter of being friendly and nice to them. If we don't know their cultural rules and expectations, then our chances of being effective communicators with them are reduced.

3 Teachers need to realise that their view of the world and how they use language will be different from the students'—the greater the cultural differences, the greater will be the language differences. This will affect communication and the teaching–learning process. Our view, as teachers, is only one of many views in the classroom and the wider community, and is not necessarily the most valid view.

4 Our students need to become efficient in using language for a range of purposes, such as following directions, requesting information, entertainment, and self-expression.

5 Our programs should encourage students to use language for a wide range of purposes and assist them to use language more effectively to fulfil their purposes. The teacher should organise the classroom so that students can use language to satisfy the students' own authentic purposes. For example, when they first arrive at school each day children can learn to sign in, rather than the teacher taking valuable time marking the roll; older students could play a major role in organising excursions and other events; students could write their own notices to take home instead of the teacher or secretary doing them; students could be encouraged to keep diaries or be involved in advertising coming events; adult students could be encouraged to write their personal life stories for their children.

6 As teachers we need to be concerned particularly with the role of language in learning. Success at school depends to a great extent on how the student uses language for learning purposes. The strategies involved are not so likely to be learned outside the school context, therefore it is essential that they are demonstrated and practised at school.

7 We use a number of different ways to make and share meanings, often in interrelated ways. Different ways are more appropriate for different purposes and individuals. Hence we should allow our students to select the ways they consider most appropriate for their purposes, perhaps through painting, drama, or making a video. It therefore makes no sense to separate out the different ways of making meaning, such as listening, speaking, reading, writing, music, drawing, or drama. The curriculum needs to emphasise the importance of students answering questions and solving problems that have been negotiated with teachers. All ways of making and sharing meanings should be accepted and encouraged. Therefore, there needs to be much more integration in the curriculum. This does not mean that there isn't a place for focusing on particular aspects for teaching–learning purposes.

References and further reading

Andersch E., Staats L. & Bostrom R. *Communication in Everyday Use*, 3rd edn, Holt, Rinehart & Winston, New York, 1969.

Britton J. *Language and Learning*, Penguin, Harmondsworth, 1970.

Cameron M. H. & Saunders M. T. 'An overview of language', in *Language and Speech*, 1977, Vol. 20, No. 30, pp. 217–31.

Carozzi B. *Language: What Do We Use it For?*, Access Skills Project Team, Curriculum and Research Branch, Education Department of Victoria, Melbourne, 1976.

Condon W. 'Speech makes babies grow', in *New Scientist*, 1974, Vol. 6, No. 6, pp. 624–7.

Condon W. & Sanders L. 'Synchrony demonstrated between movements of the neonate and adult speech', in *Child Development*, 1974, Vol. 45, No. 2, p. 456.

*Donaldson M. *Children's Minds*, Fontana/Collins, Glasgow, 1978.

Farb P. *Word Play: What Happens When People Talk*, Jonathan Cape, London, 1974.

Garner J. *Politically Correct Bedtime Stories*, Macmillan, New York, 1994.

Goodman K., Smith E. B., Meredith R. & Goodman Y. *Language and Thinking in School: A Whole Language Curriculum*, 3rd edn, Richard C. Owen Pub., New York, 1987.

Grice H. P. 'Logic and conversation', in P. Cole & J. Morgan (eds) *Syntax and Semantics*, Vol. 3, *Speech Acts*, Academic Press, New York, 1975.

*Halliday M. A. K. *Explorations in the Functions of Language*, Edward Arnold, London, 1973.

*Janks H. *Language, Identity & Power*, Hodder & Stoughton Educational with Witwatersrand University Press, Johannesburg, 1993.

Lankshear C. *Changing Literacies*, Buckingham, Open University Press, 1997.

*Lindfors J. *Children's Language and Learning*, 2nd edn, Prentice-Hall, Englewood Cliffs, NJ, 1987, Chapters 11, 12.

Morris A. & Stewart-Dore N. *Learning to Learn from Text: Effective reading in content areas*, Addison-Wesley, North Ryde, NSW, 1984, pp. 13–24.

Padden C. A. *Early bilingual lives of deaf children*, in Parasnis I. (ed.) *Cultural and Language Diversity and the Deaf Experience*, New York, Cambridge, 1996, pp. 99–116.

Publications Branch, Education Department of South Australia *Writing: R-7 Language Arts*, Education Department of South Australia, Adelaide, 1979.

Sapir E. *Language: An Introduction to the Study of Speech*, Harcourt, Brace & World, New York, 1921.

*Smith F. *Essays into Literacy*, Heinemann Educational, Exeter, NH, 1983.

Strano Z., Mohan T. & McGregor H. *Communicating!*, 2nd edn, Harcourt Brace Jovanovich, Sydney, 1989.

Trevarthen C. 'Conversations with a two-month-old', in *New Scientist*, 1974, Vol. 2, No. 5, pp. 230–5.

Zipes J. *The Trials and Tribulations of Little Red Riding Hood: Versions of the tale in Sociocultural Perspective*, J. F. Bergin, South Hadley, MA, 1983.

CHAPTER 3

LANGUAGE VARIATION

FOCUS

This chapter focuses on the understanding that:

- *language and culture are interrelated*
- *language varies depending on context*
- *the concept of appropriateness is more useful than the concept of correctness when considering language in use*
- *there are different types of language variation*
- *we place values on different types of speech, which can influence our perceptions of our students*
- *our students come from language-difference backgrounds and not necessarily language-deficit backgrounds*
- *a range of language uses and varieties of language need to be fostered in the classroom*
- *students need access to the language of power.*

PRE-READING ACTIVITIES

1 Observe someone speaking in different situations. Note how their speech, posture, facial expressions, etc. vary.

2 Observe someone from a different cultural background speaking in various situations. Note how their speech, posture, facial expressions, etc. vary.

3 Do you feel confident about your use of spoken language? When are you most confident? When do you feel most insecure?

Q What are the implications of your response for your role in helping others become more confident and competent speakers?

4 Consider how you would communicate the one idea or message to:

- a peer
- a large mixed audience
- a minister of religion

- a child
- a celebrity

Q Does your speech vary in the different situations? If so, how does your speech change?

5 Give an account of a recent incident in which you were involved, for example a car accident. How would you relate the incident:

- to a friend in a conversation?
- to a friend in a letter?
- to an older relation?
- in a formal account?
- in a press report?

Note the differences.

Q How does your language vary with the different medium, audience, and purpose?

6 Consider an occasion when you met someone for the first time.

Q What were your original judgments about the person and on what basis did you make your judgments? Was the person's speech a factor?

Q After you got to know someone, did you have to change your original judgment?

Chapters 1 and 2 discussed briefly how a language is a part of a culture and how culture influences the type of language we possess and how we use it. In this chapter we want to explore this relationship further and examine in more detail how we use language.

Language and groups

The Gileadites seized the fords of the Jordan and held them against Ephraim. When any Ephraimite who had escaped begged leave to cross, the men of Gilead asked him, 'Are you an Ephraimite?', and if he said 'No', they would retort, 'Say Shibboleth'. He would say 'Sibboleth', and because he could not pronounce the word properly they seized him and killed him at the fords of the Jordan. At that time forty-two thousand men of Ephraim lost their lives.

New English Bible, Judges 12: 5–6.

All too often language serves as a barrier, rather than as a flexible and efficient means of communication. We do not all possess the same language. Even within a particular language community, individuals do not speak in the same way. It is by our language that we generally

It is by our language that we generally describe and define ourselves to others.

describe and define ourselves to others. Our language enables us to belong to a group and exclude others from the group.

There are numerous ways of using language to control who participates in interactions. Various 'in-groups' have particular ways of speaking and writing that keep the interactions within the control of the group and make it difficult for outsiders to participate. Every professional group develops its own jargon that serves as a code for specialised meanings that are important to the group. However, in the process, the jargon that is developed isolates the meanings from those who are not members of the group. Doctors and lawyers, and more recently computer experts, all use language to share meanings that are important to those in their professions. At the same time, this specialised language can be used to enhance the power and importance of the users as they deal with outsiders to their group.

Those of you who are being trained as teachers are already learning educational jargon and may already have had the experience of irritating your friends or family by 'talking like a teacher'.

Different professions are not the only groups who use language in ways that distinguish those who belong to the group from those who do not. Given that language exists within a social and cultural context, language develops and alters according to the needs and values of particular groups in our society. Skiers and sailors, for example, are notorious for using language in ways that demonstrate that they possess knowledge that is unknown to the rest of the community. Members of the drug culture use language as a test to help discriminate between those who belong to the culture and those who do not. The problem for drug users and other groups is that others can quickly learn their particular ways of talking so that the special language eventually loses its power to discriminate between those who share the group's values and those who don't; thus the special terms and expressions change more quickly than language normally changes in the wider community.

Young teenagers are another group who use language to establish the limits to group membership. You may remember using a secret language or secret words that you and your friends used as a private language. Your parents, teachers, and peers who were not members of the group may have been quite irritated by it all but, as users of a secret language, you would have drawn a sense of belonging and camaraderie through your inclusion in the group and the exclusion of others. Of course, just like members of the drug culture, or other groups who use language to distinguish those who belong from those who don't, teenagers' secret languages have to change frequently so they are not acquired by others, compromising their power to exclude others from their group. It is probably the power of language to identify those who belong from those who don't that drives the rapid changes to teenage slang. You will have noticed just how 'off' the use of last year's slang sounds, particularly when it's used by an older person who is trying to sound

Specialised language can be used to enhance the power and importance of the users as they deal with those who are not in the group.

'with it' or relevant to younger people. A principal of an exclusive girls' school used to advise her students never to use slang because 'it dates one so terribly'.

ACTIVITIES AND DISCUSSION

Q What groups do you belong to?

Q What aspects of language are specific to the group(s)?
Consider how your language may exclude others, for example, parents and children.

Q Do you speak a dialect (a recognisable variation of a language)?
If you do, how would you describe it?

Language and culture

What is culture? The term 'culture' is used frequently in daily conversation and the media, but rarely defined. For some people it means 'high culture', that is, opera, the kind of art shown in galleries, and the like. In the context of language, however, culture refers to 'a way of life', the context in which we exist, think, feel, and relate to others. Culture acts as the fabric of shared meanings between different people; it is the glue that binds people together and, as such, is the linchpin of national and personal identity. Culture determines what we place significance on and the way in which this is done. Thus culture provides the substance of meaning and the process of making meaning. Language, as you can no doubt appreciate, plays a central part in this. John Donne wrote: 'No man is an island entire of itself, every man is a piece of the continent, a part of the main' (*Devotions*, XVII). Culture is our continent, the collective identity of which each of us is a part. Culture mediates personal meaning and social structure. It draws people together and alienates those who don't belong.

Culture may be described as the ideas, customs, skills, arts, and tools that characterise a given group of people in a given period of time. Language is a part of all this. Culture provides guidelines for behaviour. It establishes for each of us a context of cognitive and affective behaviour—ways of thinking and feeling—a blueprint for personal existence. We tend, however, to perceive reality strictly within the context of our own culture, be critical of other cultures and others' realities, or unaware of, or disregard, the realities of others. This can result in great culture clashes; for example, the European settlement of Australia in which Europeans perceived land as a commodity to be owned, occupied, and traded, while the Aborigines saw the land as part of their 'Dreamtime', part of a continuum of the past, present and future.

Culture is a way of life, the context in which we exist, think, feel, and relate to others. It acts as the fabric of shared meanings that exist between different people.

Culture provides the substance of meaning and the process of making meaning.

Culture may be described as the ideas, customs, skills, arts, and tools that characterise a given group of people in a given period of time.

Differing cultures

QUESTIONS

Q Can you think of other examples of culture clashes?

Q Can you understand why there are such clashes?

We can't really learn a second language unless we learn about the culture.

Our culture influences our way of thinking and acting. To learn another language we need to learn to appreciate the culture in which the language exists. We can't really learn a second language—or, more precisely, learn the uses of that language—unless we learn about the culture, because many of the meanings constructed in the language are culture-specific.

If we want our students to relate to school and school learning, we need to accept what students from different backgrounds bring to school and we should not reject their language and customs as being inferior.

As teachers we need to appreciate that individuals who possess another language as their first language possess a different culture and a different way of creating meaning and reality. We need to accept what students from different backgrounds bring to the learning context and not reject their language and customs as being inferior. Furthermore, we need to understand the context within which they use language in order to make learning meaningful to them.

There are also non-verbal differences between different languages.

It also is important to remember that there are non-verbal differences between languages. For example, in most European languages nodding the head means 'yes' but in the Inuit culture it means 'no'. In a language in Japan 'yes' is conveyed by moving the arms to the chest and waving them. Other languages in Sri Lanka and India have other ways. Eye contact varies in different cultures. For example, in white Australian culture it is considered courteous to maintain eye contact when conversing with someone; if you do not, it would be thought that you were not interested and not paying attention. In contrast, in Aboriginal and many Asian cultures it would be considered rude to maintain eye contact, particularly if you were of lower status. In sign language, eye contact and facial expression are used in particular ways when asking questions indicating whether or not a response is required and who the question is addressed to. For example, in Auslan the eyebrows are drawn down in wh- questions such as where, when, who, what and why and raised (as well as leaning the body forward) in other questions. A sign language user can ask a rhetorical question by a roving eye gaze or indicate the person to whom the question is asked by direct eye gaze. There are also differences in

It is important to familiarise ourselves with the non-verbal culture differences of our students.

body contact and concepts of personal space. It is important to familiarise ourselves with the non-verbal culture differences of our students. Through our ignorance we could misinterpret or offend them and fail to make our meanings clear.

Language, culture, and thought

Anthropologists in the twentieth century widely acknowledged the importance of language in studying any ethnic group. Sapir (1921), an American linguist, was a key figure in discussing the relationship of language, culture, and thought. His name is associated with the theory of linguistic relativity, which argues that language determines thought and world view, and therefore culture and thought are dependent on language. Sapir believed that a study of a language was important for a study of a culture because the network of culture patterns is indexed in the language. Language, he said, was a guide to social reality. This belief is one reason why there has been so much debate about sexism in language and the trend to remove terms that seem to demean or diminish the importance of either sex. The civil rights movement in America raised awareness of the derogatory use of terms for black people and associated pride with the use of the word 'black'. In a similar way, many deaf people reject the term hearing-impaired, calling themselves 'deaf' or in some instances 'Deaf', using a capital letter to identify themselves as members of a cultural and linguistic minority; the term 'hard of hearing' being preferred by those with less significant hearing loss or who adopt the language and culture of the hearing community.

Some have argued that culture and thought are dependent on language.

Language is seen as a guide to social reality.

Whorfian hypothesis

The writings of another American, Benjamin Lee Whorf (1956), were particularly influential in the discussion of language in relation to culture, society, and the individual. His name is also linked with linguistic relativity, which is also referred to as the 'Whorfian Hypothesis'. Supporters of this view argue that the language habits of a community predispose certain choices of interpretation. They argue that we do not live alone in the objective world, or alone in the world of social activity as it is ordinarily understood; we are very much at the mercy of the particular language that has become the medium of expression for our society. The 'real world' is to a large extent unconsciously built up on the language habits of the group. What and how we see, hear, and otherwise experience is mainly due to the language habits of our community. Hence, Whorf would say that an English-speaking person would see snow differently from an Inuit because Inuit has four different expressions for the one English word 'snow': snow on the ground *(aput)*; falling snow *(quana)*; drifting snow *(piqsirpog)*; and a snow drift *(quiumqsua)*. In contrast, the Aztecs have only one word for cold, ice, and snow, and therefore would be expected to see the world differently.

The view that language determines thought is called the Whorfian hypothesis.

Comparisons of different languages are used to support these arguments. For example, the grammar of European languages analyses experience in one way: the subject acts on an object, with the emphasis being on the doer as the responsible agent. On the other hand, the American Indian language, Hopi, places the primary emphasis on the action and only secondary attention is paid to the objects involved. Some languages build into the verb system recognition of certainty or uncertainty of past, present, or future action. Other languages build into the verb system a recognition of the size, shape, and colour of the nouns referred to. Different languages divide the colour spectrum differently. For example, Russian has no equivalent to blue: the words *goluboj* and *sinij* usually translated as 'light blue' and 'dark blue', respectively, refer to what are, in Russian, distinct colours, not different shades of the same colour, as their translation into English might suggest. Consider the problem faced by a Russian translating an English language text, which includes the phrase 'a blue dress'. How should it be translated? Which word should be used? The English text gives no clues. Research has shown that colours for which we have single names—for example, pink, red, crimson, magenta, fuchsia, and carmine—are more easily recognised than others.

An Aboriginal language, Malak malak, uses three words for 'we' or 'our': *yanki* for 'I and you' (a single person is addressed), *yanot* for 'I and others' (not the person addressed), and *yeskil* for 'I, you and others'. Malak malak speakers are sensitive to whether 'we' includes the person spoken to or not. There is much greater precision on this point in Malak malak than in English. Often the differences are at a superficial level, but sometimes they are at the abstract concept level, and they indicate a more fundamental difference in thinking. For example, the single French word *conscience* means either 'consciousness' or 'conscience' in English, depending on the context. Bahasa Indonesia has no word for 'privacy'; privacy is not a relevant concept in traditional Indonesian life.

Consider the problems many translators and interpreters have in coping with language differences, and the difficulties experienced by some of our students when learning English as a second or foreign language.

Over the last three decades investigators have tested the Whorfian Hypothesis by studying different aspects of language in relation to extralinguistic factors in different cultures, such as terms of kinship, colour, number, disease, or modes of address. Although there have been conflicting results, there is consensus that:

- languages primarily reflect rather than create sociocultural regularities in values and orientations (language reflects the values of the culture, hence the concern about the use of sexist language)
- languages throughout the world share a far larger number of structural universals than was previously recognised
- if we can put aside the issue of 'what first causes what', we are left with the process of continuing interaction. In these processes, languages and societal behaviour are equal partners.

The Whorfian Hypothesis that languages embody particular world views has been extended by critical linguists to variations within languages; that is, particular texts embody particular world views or ideologies. The social meanings in texts of various kinds can be analysed and this is often now the basis of film and media studies, as well as literary criticism.

We need to accept that language is essentially rooted in the reality of the culture. Language cannot be explained without reference to this broader context. An utterance or text is intelligible only when placed within its context. Language is acquired in a cultural-social context and the meanings constructed are the result of interaction between the individual, the language, and the culture.

This awareness is of particular importance when we look at the teaching of reading and writing. In the past, learning to read and write have been treated as isolated skills in classroom activities that ignored the powerful importance of sociocultural factors in the learning process. Children were given books especially written for the teaching of reading (basal readers) and were taught to read and write in separate subjects as ends in themselves. Reading and writing were not related to how we use print for real purposes in our daily lives, such as reading TV guides, writing shopping lists, or responding to emails. Apart from making reading and writing culturally and socially relevant in the classroom, it needs to be remembered that the use of literacies and the value placed on them greatly determines how literacy is learned and what skills are involved.

> We need to accept that language is essentially rooted in the reality of the culture. An utterance or text is intelligible only when placed within its context.

> It needs to be remembered that the value and use of literacy in a society and its subgroups greatly determine how literacy is learned and what skills are involved.

Sexism and racism in language

The way language is used can shape the way both speakers and hearers view the people being described. Racist and sexist language greatly affects the self-conception of the people being discriminated against (Pearson 1985). Aspects of our language often discriminate against women, constructing them as being of lower status. Except for words referring to females by definition such as 'mother' and 'actress', English defines many non-sexual concepts as male. The underlying assumption is that people in general are males. For example when the term chairman is used we generally think of a male in the role. Pressure to redress sexist language has resulted in words previously used only for males to be extended to include women, such as the word 'actor' now used for a male or female. Words associated with males often have positive connotations, such as 'aggressive', 'confident', 'forceful', 'strong', and 'tough', whereas words relating to females are fewer and often have less positive connotations, for example, 'fickle', 'frivolous', and 'timid'; and when the more 'masculine' descriptions are being applied to women, for example 'aggressive', they often have negative connotations.

> Racist and sexist language greatly affects the self-conception of the people being discriminated against.

The driving force behind changing the language is to alter our ways of viewing males and females, particularly the latter, and the role relationships that exist between males and females.

While sexist language usually defines the world as made up of superior males and inferior females, in our culture, racist language usually defines the world as composed of superior whites and other inferior racial groups. Words and images associated with white are usually positive, whereas words and images associated with non-whites are often negative. The valuing or positioning of particular groups is also evident in the use of language to describe particular groups over others. For example, if you are part of the dominant hearing community, you would probably rarely think of or describe yourself as 'hearing'. Among the Deaf community, however, it is considered polite to introduce yourself as a hearing person, particularly if you are fluent in sign language and may otherwise be taken as a deaf person. Can you think of some other examples?

To the extent that our language is both sexist and racist, our view of the world is affected. For example, men are given greater opportunities than women to see themselves in a positive light, and similarly whites are given more opportunities than non-whites, non-disabled more than disabled, and so on. Language shapes the self-conceptions of those whom it labels in such a way that members of the linguistically slighted group come to see themselves as inferior. This is clearly an effect of the way in which language constructs others and does not only reflect social practices. For example, a deaf man who was born into a deaf family in which Auslan was the native language and deafness considered normal recalled his surprise, as a child, when he met hearing people who did not sign and did not seem capable of communicating other than moving their mouths in incomprehensible ways.

With some thought and care the sexual prejudices inherent in language can be avoided, particularly by eliminating the constant use of 'he' or suffix 'man' when gender is indeterminate. Words that use 'man' generically (non-specifically) to refer to humanity at large often pose problems. However, consider the following substitutions: 'mankind' could be replaced with 'humanity', 'human beings', 'human race', and 'people; 'man-made' could be replaced with 'artificial', 'manufactured', and 'synthetic'; 'manpower' could be replaced with 'labour', 'workers', and 'workforce'; 'manhood' could be replaced with 'adulthood'; 'firemen' could be replaced with 'fire-fighters'; 'policemen' with 'police officers'.

> Language shapes the self-conceptions of those whom it labels in such a way that members of the linguistically slighted group see themselves as inferior.

QUESTION

Q Can you think of other terms that do not discriminate in terms of either sex or race?

ACTIVITY

Collect samples of writing from your students. Highlight any examples of violence, sexist, racist, or other discriminatory content. What did you, or could you, do to counteract this? (A critical literacy perspective, for example, would emphasise the importance of making students aware of the way in which texts construct meanings, both in the texts students read and those they produce.)

Language and society

In the late 1950s, an early sociological investigation into the role of language in relation to social class and education in Britain created a new awareness of the language factor in society. There was concern about the number of intelligent, working-class students who were not successful at school. Basil Bernstein, a British sociologist, was a key figure in this debate. He believed that there is a systematic relationship between social class and language use. He believed that language in middle-class homes was used differently from language in working-class homes. Since language is first learned in the home, children from the different homes were predisposed to use language differently. The middle class tended to use language similar to the way it was used in schools, so he hypothesised that language-difference was a key factor in working-class students' lack of success at school. He described the language that was generally used by the middle class as a formal or 'elaborated' code. However, the working class, he suggested, was inclined towards the use of a public or 'restricted' code because of their different uses for language. Any speaker can use either code, but the speakers from different backgrounds are disposed to one more than the other. Schools generally favour the elaborated code so it was thought that children from working-class homes who were predisposed towards a restricted code were disadvantaged at school. Bernstein's thesis became a subject of controversy because it was considered an example of a 'linguistic deficit' theory.

Whatever the cause, children from particular backgrounds are not as successful at school as children from other backgrounds. This has to be of concern to teachers and school systems. The difference in values between the school and home is of importance, and creates an opportunity for students to learn the different types and uses of language. Some environments are more conducive to this than others. Teachers may have to structure the environment through their program planning to ensure that all their students have access to the different types of language (genres) that are important in a society (chapter 5 discusses different genres).

Bernstein believed that there is a systematic relationship between social class and language use. He believed that language in middle-class homes was used differently from language in working-class homes.

According to Bernstein, the middle class uses a formal or 'elaborated' code, whereas the working class uses a public or 'restricted' code. Since the language used by schools more closely resembles the language of the middle class, children from the working class were disadvantaged at school.

Teachers need to structure the environment through their program planning to ensure that their students have access to the different genres that are important in a society.

Language difference, language deviance, or language deficit?

In the latter half of the twentieth century there was much discussion and research about language variation. In particular, this debate concentrated on social class and language variation, and the implications for the school. Two views evolved: (i) the language-deficit hypothesis, and (ii) the language-difference hypothesis.

Language-deficit hypothesis

The *language-deficit* hypothesis depends on a view of language and learning that holds that some kinds of language are more logical and thus better for further education, and that an inferior language will cause a deficit in a child's further language development and education. Bernstein (1971) has been seen as a leading proponent of this view. He explained the difference in language in terms of 'restricted' and 'elaborated' codes, and that different social structures will generate different systems or linguistic codes.

In a restricted code, meaning to a large extent is implicit and the message is very dependent on context, whereas in an elaborated code, meaning is explicit and not so context-dependent. Bernstein believed that all people use a restricted code in familiar and personal situations with people whom they know well, such as peers, spouses and family; those who have access to an elaborated code use it in more formal contexts, such as business meetings. If two friends have coffee after seeing a film, they are likely to use a restricted code in discussing it. However, if others who have not seen the film join them and the film is discussed, the original couple would probably use more detailed language—an elaborated code. The first (restricted) conversation could go like this:

First friend: What did you think?
Second friend: Great. I didn't feel like going to sleep at all!
First friend: It was powerful acting, wasn't it?

Later with others; the second (elaborated) conversation:

First friend: We have just been to see *A Beautiful Mind*. It was incredible, more so because it was based on a true story ...

Bernstein described the restricted code as having the following features:
- sentences are shorter, grammatically simpler, and unfinished syntax (structure of a sentence) is loose; unacceptable forms are used; there are few subordinations (phrases, clauses etc.); short commands and questions are used
- active, simple verbs are used
- there is limited use of adjectives, adverbs, impersonal pronouns, and conjunctions

Two views on language variation have evolved: the language-deficit hypothesis and the language-difference hypothesis.

The language-deficit hypothesis depends on a behaviouristic view of learning.

Different social structures will generate different systems or language codes.

In a restricted code, meaning is generally implicit, whereas it is explicit in an elaborated code.

All people use a restricted code in familiar and personal situations; those who have access to an elaborated code use it in more formal contexts.

- idioms and clichés are used
- there is less formal coherence
- phrases such as 'you know' are used more frequently
- the meaning is implied by the context
- feelings and attitudes are communicated by intonation.

In contrast the elaborated code is described as having the following features:

- sentences are longer, grammatically more complex, and finished; syntax is controlled, acceptable forms are used; there are more subordinations (phrases and clauses); there is greater use of requests and explanations of various kinds
- active and complex verbs are used
- there is flexible and varied use of adjectives, adverbs, impersonal pronouns such as 'one would', 'it seems'; logical connectors such as 'if', 'unless', 'whether' are used
- there is more individual use of idioms
- there is greater formal coherence
- concepts are more abstract
- phrases such as 'I think', 'I suppose' are used
- the meaning is more explicit
- fact and logic are emphasised; attitudes and feelings are secondary.

Bernstein believed that the use of these codes was strongly determined by social class. He believed that working-class people have little use for the elaborated code with its verbally explicit meanings, whereas middle-class individuals use the two codes. He also suggested that an elaborated code is necessary for abstract thinking and 'school' learning. Therefore working-class children, who probably use only a restricted code, were labelled as being 'linguistically deficient and educationally disadvantaged'.

> Bernstein believed that the use of these codes was strongly determined by social class. So working-class children, who probably use only a restricted code, were labelled as 'linguistically deficient and educationally disadvantaged'.

Since the late 1950s, especially in the USA, there has been much research comparing the educational achievements of low social-class children with those of middle-class children. Educational categories, such as 'the culturally deprived', 'the linguistically deprived', and 'the socially disadvantaged', have been developed and, with this, the idea of 'compensatory education' and the introduction of programs such as 'Head Start' (an educational program in the United States). Despite the good intentions behind these programs, unfortunately they have not solved any of the problems: instead, the children's performances have tended to match the label of the category into which they have been placed.

Implicitly, children are told that their family and culture are not adequate, that they are not as good as those with middle-class values. The teacher will often have lower expectations of these children. The children are generally expected to drop their social and cultural identities at the school gate, and orient themselves towards different structures of meaning, whether it be reading John and Betty-type books, different types of speech usage, or patterns of social relationships.

Language-difference hypothesis

The above highlights the second view of speech variation, the *language-difference* hypothesis, which suggests that the deficiencies do not exist within the child, their family or community, but are to be found within the educational environment, the school itself, and its inability to cater for the differences between the children it is supposed to educate.

William Labov (1969), an American sociolinguist who carried out studies with black children, believes that all languages and dialects should be viewed as being equal in terms of their ability to communicate. They are not deviant or deficient but different. In other words, he believes that all non-standard dialects differ from standard English, not in lack of rules or in breaking the rules more often, but in having *different* rules. Speakers of Somerset or Glasgow or New York black dialects, or of Australian Aboriginal English, are not trying to speak standard English and getting it wrong: they are correctly speaking a different, non-standard English, not a sub-standard English. It is possible, of course, for someone to try to speak standard English and make mistakes. But equally, it is possible for an outsider to make grammatical mistakes when trying to speak a non-standard dialect.

Labov's research showed that sociolinguistic context determines the type of speech produced. He studied the speech produced by black children with white teachers in a test situation, and compared this speech with the speech produced in a less-threatening context with black research assistants. The test situation proved to be a poor indicator of language competency: the language in the test situation was very inhibited.

There is no evidence that any non-standard dialect is less suited for sophisticated, intellectual discussion than is standard English. As Labov (1969) demonstrated, a sequence of apparently incoherent and almost random remarks (to those who do not speak the dialect) can show impressive logical rigour and imaginative power when examined with understanding. Labov argued that, on the other hand, some middle-class use of language is very verbose and lacks any real logic or thought. It is important to remember that there is nothing inherent in one dialect that makes it superior to another. Rather, a dialect acquires prestige status because its users have the dominant power in the group.

There is a difference between Bernstein's codes and Labov's dialects. Bernstein's codes are involved with function and context, although social class factors play a part in the use of codes. Dialects are directly related to social factors. Certain features of codes could be features of dialects, such as verbal form stressing the active mood or infrequent use of impersonal pronouns as subjects. Other features, such as poor syntactic construction, are not common features, although to an outsider it may appear so. As discussed previously, Bernstein regards the 'codes' of language as being involved with context; for example, the restricted code is used within the family and the elaborated code is used

The language-difference hypothesis suggests that deficiencies do not exist within the child, their family or their community, but are found within the educational environment, the school, and its inability to cater for the differences between the children it is supposed to educate.

Labov believes that all languages and dialects should be viewed as equal in terms of their ability to communicate. They are not deviant or deficient, but different. They differ from standard English, not in lack of rules or in breaking the rules more often, but in having different rules.

Sociolinguistic context determines the type of speech produced.

There is nothing inherent in one dialect that makes it superior to another.

in formal situations. However, working-class people are restricted to using one code only. Labov, on the other hand, believes that we all possess different 'registers' or language varieties for varying contexts, and that the language used by a working-class person is not merely a register of a standard code, but could be a different dialect. The term 'dialect' refers to the different language, which has more broad-based differences, that different groups use. There are different registers for the different dialects. The differences between dialect and register are discussed later in this chapter.

The term 'dialect' refers to the different language, which has more broad-based differences, that different groups use.

A longitudinal study of 128 children in Bristol (Wells 1985) found that language differences could not simply be accounted for by differences in class or family background. The study did find that the most advanced children tended to come from higher socio-economic backgrounds and the least advanced children came from the lower end of the scale. Overall, however, in the vast majority of children there was no association between rate of development and family social class. However, when a sample of the children were studied at school, a strong relationship between family background and educational achievement was apparent. The way in which teachers interact with the different children may have some impact on their achievements. Wells (1985) suggests:

> *Familiarity with more abstract and less context-dependent uses of language, such as those associated with written text, seem to be of even greater importance [than oral language ability], and this tends to be associated with the place and value of literacy in the everyday life of the parents, which, in turn, is associated with their own educational and occupational experience. Where this familiarity is absent, children are at a disadvantage both because they lack the skills which are important for learning in school and also because this lack of skills affects the ways in which their teachers interact with them.*

G. Wells, *Language Learning and Education*, p. 98.

The above discussion does not preclude the fact that some children come to school with a language deficiency. Children who have had insufficient opportunity to hear and use language in a supportive environment may be deficient in their development. This condition, however, is not restricted to any one social class. A child from a wealthy, middle-class home can as easily suffer from neglect in language stimulation experiences as can a child from a working-class background.

In our schools many students come from language-difference backgrounds and not from language-deficit backgrounds. It is important that, as a teacher, you respond appropriately. It is important that you consider the values you place on different dialects of English. You also need to know something about the language your students bring to school.

In our schools, many students come from language-difference backgrounds and not from language-deficit backgrounds. As a teacher, you should respond appropriately.

Language variation and gender

Another important aspect of language variation is how males and females use language differently in our society. Consider this story. A husband and wife are in the car on a long distance trip. The wife asks the husband 'Would you like a cup of coffee?' The reply was 'No thanks, dear'. The husband could not understand why his wife was upset. If you are female you probably quickly realised that the wife wanted to stop for a coffee and her question was really a request to stop. Deborah Tannen (1990) has provided many examples of differences in how males and females use language in different contexts. It seems that women are likely to place more emphasis on creating involvement and rapport as opposed to simply exchanging information, and more likely to expect a high degree of conversational inference as opposed to explicit statements of meaning. Women appear to be concerned with building and supporting relationships whilst men seem to be more focused on controlling information and displaying knowledge. These differences are exhibited through different uses of specific features in ongoing conversations; for example, different patterns of interruptions (men interrupt more often to change the topic or to oppose a point, while women make more interjections designed not to take the floor but to provide supportive overlap), different patterns of intonation (women more often end clauses on a rising tone, opening their statements as questions), and the use of particular elements such as tag questions like 'isn't it?' (used more often by women and by speakers in a position of lesser authority). These differences can contribute to miscommunication. However, it needs to be remembered that the above characteristics can be used as stereotypes. It is preferable to think of these language stylistics as operating on a continuum with different men and women at different points along it. All men and women will not be at the same point. Certainly men and women from different cultures may use language quite differently from what is described by Tannen. You may wish to read the work of Anne Pauwels and others (1987) who have explored women's use of language in Australia and New Zealand.

This tendency to male dominance is increased by the differing ways in which boys and girls resist classroom authority. Boys react to authority by challenging it and by being disruptive and 'naughty'. Girls, on the other hand, react by opting out and going on with their own concerns. They are not interested in challenging authority; they just stop playing the classroom game altogether. A teacher can therefore ignore a disaffected group of girls, but teachers who ignore a group of disaffected boys do so at their own peril, and often their teaching style is driven by a need to placate such a group of boys.

The difficulties caused by male and female discourse styles are exacerbated when the teacher is female. Many researchers (Walkerdine 1981; Davies 1988; Clark 1990) note that teaching, particularly

Males and females use language differently. These differences can contribute to miscommunication.

primary teaching, is a predominantly female profession, and that boys may react against what they see as an environment dominated by female ways of talking and knowing. Boys may feel alienated from classrooms that are led by female teachers who maintain what are felt to be female norms, rewarding good behaviour, politeness, consensus, and neat work, and discouraging horseplay and other forms of display. Boys may resist help from their female teachers because they are female. Walkerdine (1981) and Clark (1990) describe boys who resist the authority of the teacher by undermining her at every opportunity. For example, Walkerdine (1981) documents cases of sexual harassment of female teachers by small boys trying to assert a male style in the only way they know.

Male teachers usually find it much easier to deal with boys. They are more tolerant of the means by which boys compete in their peer group, and they may even join in the jokes, verbal games, and horseplay so that their status as a teacher is reinforced by their ability to play the male hierarchy game. But such teachers, and of course not all male teachers are like this, are often not very good at talking to girls. Girls tend to remain unnoticed at the margin of the classroom, while boys compete to take the floor.

The final question is what teachers can do about differences in male and female talk. It is futile to pretend that these differences do not exist. One kind of response, then, is to assume that teachers should be helping males and females to be aware of the differences in the way they talk, and to make allowance for these differences. This is in line with suggestions made above about the importance of language awareness in learning to talk.

But this sort of approach runs the risk of perpetuating uncritically the existing differences between male and female conversation. There is a danger of seeing differences as somehow a 'natural' category, set in stone forever as a result of biological difference. But of course differences in ways of talking, although pervasive, are socially constructed and constantly changing. Thus another possible role for teachers is helping children to modify their conversational styles to make communication between the sexes easier. This does not mean that male and female differences should be obliterated; it means that both males and females should have experience of a broader range of ways of talking. Girls should have experience of trying to capture and hold the floor, for example, and boys should learn to support others and make constructive suggestions in a way that promotes the solidarity of a group. What we are suggesting is that there should be an extra dimension to all teaching of spoken language, which consists of an awareness of the gendered nature of classroom talk.

Teachers should help students become aware of the differences in the way they use language and the gendered nature of talk.

Many have explored how language and literacy practices are gendered—that is, 'literacy activities pattern differently according to gender' (Barton 1994, p. 79). Males and females from an early age read and write different types of texts, they have different conversational styles, and they use language for different purposes. Cameron (1992) reviewed the work in this area and explored many issues related to language and gender. Kamler, Maclean, Reid and Simpson's (1994) research with five years olds demonstrates how early these differences develop. The differences become greater as boys and girls move into adolescence and adulthood. Maltz and Borker (1982) give a cultural explanation for many of the differences. They believe that men and women grow up in different sub-cultures where language is used differently. During their early childhood and early teenage years, most boys and girls interact socially primarily with their own sex, even if they are in co-ed classes. Thus they have learned different ways of carrying out conversations. During these years boys tend to play in larger groups, in more competitive games, and focus their talk on the things they are doing. Girls on the other hand, are more likely to play indoors, in pairs or small groups, in non-competitive activities, with intense concern for establishing friendships and resolving inevitable conflict. Girls therefore learn to use words to create and maintain relationships of closeness and equality, using inclusive forms like 'we', and sharing confidences. They also learn how to criticise others in acceptable ways, often presenting criticism in terms of group norms or indirectly as the concern of someone else; and how to interpret accurately the speech of other girls, perceiving shifting alliances, and reading the attentions of others. Boys learn to use speech that asserts their own positions of dominance, including threats and name calling; that attracts and maintains an audience, despite ongoing challenges; and that allows them to assert themselves when others have the floor, and to offer challenges to a speaker, and thus assert their own identity even when others have the floor. By the time men and women become conversational partners in mid-to-late teens the differences are well established. These differences are not just differences in surface features, but also in ways of seeing, believing, and valuing. Hence there is great potential for miscommunication.

Boys and girls grow up in different sub-cultures.

The dual culture explanation given by Malzt and Borker above does not address the complexity of gendered language differences and the understanding that both sexes have of the differences and how this understanding can be used strategically. Eckert and McConnel-Ginet (1994, p. 437) give a common example of this operating in the home: 'The child's "Not really, mom" in response to her "Would you like to set the table?" tries to read mom's directive literally, thus forcing her to display openly her actual coercive authority'. Similar examples can be found in the classroom and in male and female interactions. Eckert and McConnel-Ginet (1994, p. 433) also remind us that:

Difference and dominance are involved in gender language differences.

> Not only are difference and dominance both involved in gender, but they are also jointly constructed and prove ultimately to be inseparable. These constructions are different at different times and places, and the constructors are people, not faceless

abstractions like "society". It is the mutual engagement of human agents in a wide range of activities that creates, sustains, challenges, and sometimes changes society and its institutions, including gender and language.

The explanations of language and gender differences by many tend to give the impression that ways of using language are fixed and that participants are passive in negotiating meanings and ways of using language. However, we are all active participants and we can resist existing patterns. It is important to note that gender cannot be isolated from other aspects of social identity and relations such as class, age, and ethnicity. As discussed in an earlier section, individuals typically belong to several groups, and gender and language interactions may be different in the different groups; for example, the home, the church, the workplace. It is interesting to note that the same linguistic features used by both females and males may be interpreted differently due to the values we place on the linguistic features and the gender of the user. For example, linguistic features that are considered authoritative in a male are often considered aggressive in a businesswoman. Gender and language relations are complex.

For educators it is important to appreciate that gender and language, like other social practices, are negotiated through interactions in social activities. Our students need to come to understand that meanings and practices are not fixed and that participants can be active in changing meanings and practices, ideally for the better.

Gender cannot be isolated from other aspects of social identity.

Students need to understand that participants can be active in changing meanings and practices.

How do we describe language variation?

The discipline of sociolinguistics considers how the use of speech is inextricably tied to the contexts (situations) in which speech is used, and how these contexts, in turn, are tied to the social structures and roles of speakers and listeners. Sociolinguistics is the branch of linguistics that studies properties that require a social explanation. The social explanations are of two main types:

- large-scale social settings, where language variation is correlated to categories such as class, sex, geography
- small-scale conversational text settings, where language variation depends on the actual situation of the speech and on the belief systems of the language users.

Sociolinguists have focused on speech, but the understandings derived from their work are transferable to understanding the use of written language.

Speech can vary in different ways, for example:

- at the phonological level, that is, the sounds used, the accent, the intonation used

- at the lexical level, that is, the words used
- at the level of syntax, that is, different syntax and word order used, such as 'We done it'
- at the text/discourse level, that is, different text structures or genres are used depending on context and purpose.

Differing syntax is the most significant in social stratification. Greater stigma is attached to certain syntactical variations than to sound or word variations. Language, in this instance, speech (although other codes of language should be considered), can be classified according to the following levels:

Greater stigma is attached to certain syntactical variations than to sound or word variations.

Language: such as English, French, and Japanese.

Dialect: a variety of language used by one group of people with differences in vocabulary, grammar, and pronunciation from other varieties of the language used by another group. A dialect may be:
— regional or geographical, for example, Australian or American
— social, frequently described as a 'sociolect', which is determined by socio-economic factors, for example, working-class English.

Idiolect: those idiosyncratic aspects of speech that identify one individual's speech from another's speech; for example a 'hello' on the phone is frequently enough to identify a speaker.

Register: the speech of an individual that varies according to the situation, in different contexts, and for different purposes; for example, a person will use an intimate form of speech at home and with close friends, whereas, when speaking to an employer or maybe the clergy, more formal speech is used. Registers can vary in sentence length, vocabulary, use of idiomatic expressions, and also in the precision of pronunciation. For example:
— formal, educated: I must say those cakes look lovely, may I have one?
— less formal: Will you pass the cakes please?
— informal: Can I have a cake please?
— slang: Shove over the buns, mate.
— vulgarity: Give us a bloody cake, will ya?

Note: Any important sociological distinction is likely to be reflected in language. Teenagers tend to speak differently from older members of the community. As a group, women do not speak identically to men in their community. Professional and other groups develop their own jargon. Families often acquire unique linguistic symbols. By our use of language we define certain people as being inside the group and exclude others. Language therefore becomes a 'map' of sociological divisions of a society.

For example, the speech of an Australian, educated to Year 12, talking to a friend could be characterised as 'intimate', 'individual', 'general Australian English', represented graphically in Figure 3.1.

Figure 3.1   Graphic depiction of an individual's speech

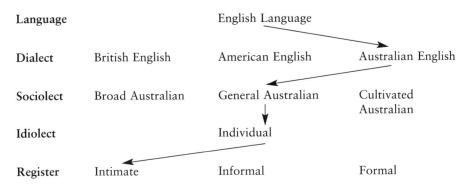

Language		English Language	
Dialect	British English	American English	Australian English
Sociolect	Broad Australian	General Australian	Cultivated Australian
Idiolect		Individual	
Register	Intimate	Informal	Formal

It is commonly accepted by sociolinguists that the speech of an individual varies in different social contexts, and that a speaker of a language can generally identify the social context of utterances and the background of another speaker.

Individuals normally possess a number of codes or registers, which are used in different situations. Generally we can switch from one register to another, and some can switch from one dialect or language to another. For effective communication it would appear important that an individual possesses a number of registers and be able to use them appropriately.

Initially, speech variation was studied in multilingual communities where speakers used different languages in different contexts for different purposes. For example, government functionaries in Brussels who are of Flemish origin do not always speak Dutch to each other; depending on the occasion they speak French, standard Dutch, or a regional variety of Dutch. In a study of Norwegian students, it was found that they subconsciously shifted from one language to another when discussing different topics. This phenomenon, which occurs very obviously in multilingual communities, exemplifies the speech variation that occurs in a less obvious way in monolingual communities.

In summary, when studying language variation and its social distribution, we need to keep four distinct factors in mind:
- different varieties of language exist side by side in the community
- these varieties are used by different sections of the community
- differing social values may be attached to them
- role relationships and social context influence language.

For effective communication it would appear important that an individual possesses a number of registers and be able to use them appropriately.

A discussion of these aspects raises the question of whether or not there is one correct way of speaking. Instead, it might be better to say that certain ways are more appropriate for particular situations. This concept is critical for language programming. Students need to become aware of and be competent in using the appropriate way for a particular context. They will need to see and hear different models and have experience in using different types of language in different contexts and for different purposes. Furthermore, in assessing the accuracy of a students' use of language or literacies, teachers will need to consider the context and purpose for which it is used.

Students need to be aware of and competent in using the appropriate way of speaking for a particular context.

ACTIVITIES AND DISCUSSION

Describe your speech using the categories of language, dialect, sociolect, idiolect, and register (register will vary according to context).

Think of some other examples of variation in expression with different registers.

Return to the beginning of this chapter and check your answer to the question 'Do you speak a dialect?' Many people answer 'no' to this question, believing that dialect means sub-standard speech and so they are convinced that they do not speak a dialect. We have stressed that some dialects may be non-standard but they are not sub-standard or inferior. We all speak at least one dialect.

Australian English

QUESTIONS FOR DISCUSSION

Q Are there differences in the way English is spoken in the various Australian states?

Q How would you describe the English spoken by ABC announcers? How has it changed over the years?

Q Is there a standard form of English in Australia?

Q What form of English should we model and encourage in the classroom?

Q How will you respond when students use a variation of standard English in the classroom?

Australian English can be described as a transported language, arriving in Australia with the First Fleet.

Australian English can be described as a transported language, arriving in Australia with the First Fleet. Initially the languages of England, Scotland, Wales, and Ireland, including the dialects, were the bases of Australian English; but over time many factors—such as different living conditions, different environment, the media, and the impact of other languages—have influenced its nature and use. Hence Australian

English is quite different from either British or American English. It now possesses a distinctive vocabulary and accent. Similarly Aboriginal English due to its history has a distinctive vocabulary, syntax and sound system (Malcolm 2002).

It needs to be remembered that although English is the dominant language, many other languages are also spoken in Australia. Aboriginal languages are still spoken in parts of Australia, the Deaf community uses Auslan and there has been a considerable increase in immigrant languages since World War II. Many of these languages have influenced Australian English. Aspects of different languages have become part of Australian English and speakers from non-English backgrounds often develop a different form of English. Therefore, as well as a large number of different languages, there are also a number of different types of English being used in Australia, such as migrant English.

Many people would claim there are differences in the way English is spoken in the various states in Australia. They give examples, such as 'togs' vs 'bathers' vs 'cossies'; 'sandshoes' vs 'runners' vs 'sneakers'; and 'ute' vs 'tilley'. Certain words are also pronounced differently. For example, 'castle' and 'pasty'. However, linguists generally agree that the differences between states are minimal and we cannot say that we have regional dialects. But there are obvious differences in the way English is spoken in Australia, and these are social dialects. Three categories of sociolects have been described:

- broad Australian English, associated with working-class Australian speech
- general Australian English, associated with middle-class Australian speech
- cultivated Australian English, associated with upper-class Australian speech.

English is the dominant language in Australia, but many other languages are also spoken here.

Australia does not have regional dialects, but there are three categories of sociolects: broad Australian English, general Australian English and cultivated Australian English.

QUESTION

Q Can you give examples of differences between the different sociolects?

In a classic study of seventeen year olds at school (Mitchell & Delbridge 1965), it was found that more girls spoke cultivated English than boys, and more boys spoke broad Australian English. This highlights that a number of complex factors such as sex, age, and social class influence the type of English learned and used. Why do you think more girls than boys spoke cultivated English in 1965? Would this still be the case?

It must be emphasised that all dialects are governed by rules. Speakers of broad Australian English are not making mistakes but are using different rules; for example, the negative constructions for 'they know something', 'I like somebody' and 'she will buy some' are 'they

All dialects are governed by rules.

don't know nothing', 'I don't like nobody' and 'she won't buy none'. The rule is that when the verb is negated, the indefinites 'something', 'somebody' and 'some' become the negative indefinites 'nothing', 'nobody' and 'none'. This was a rule that existed in earlier periods for all dialects of English.

The language of instruction

The language of instruction used by teachers in the classroom is an important aspect of language variation.

One aspect of language variation of importance to teachers is the language used for instruction by the teacher and in texts. Sometimes the characteristic language used in the classroom is called the 'curriculum genre'. For students to be successful at school they need, at the least, to have a *receptive* knowledge of this register. For a moment think about the terms used by a teacher relating to early literacy instruction: sound, letter, word, sentence, blend, write, read, etc. For many children these are new terms or at least terms that have new meanings. Research (Reid 1966; Downing 1970; Saunders 1979) has shown that many children are confused about these terms. Teachers need to check children's understanding of such terms and help them learn what they mean.

You need to remember that language serves different purposes in the classroom from the home: 'A predominant purpose of classroom discourse is to foster the expansion and reconceptualisation of referential/propositional knowledge—expanding frameworks of knowledge about the world and ways of reasoning within those frameworks' (Kutz 1997, p. 167). To achieve this, teachers need to create an environment or community that will support learning. Both implicit and explicit rules are developed. As in any community, language serves a range of purposes at any one time. Often, for example, teachers appear to be asking referential questions, but the purpose may really be to control behaviour. There is language of control and language of instruction. The discourse of many classrooms is dominated by the restricted discourse pattern in terms of 'Initiation/Response/Evaluation' (IRE): a rapid exchange where a teacher initiates a question, students respond with single word answers, and the teacher then offers a brief evaluation—'right' or 'no'. This pattern offers little opportunity for extended talk or development of thought. At home, talk is generally based on shared experiences and there is more of an equal partnership between adult and child, with the adult helping the child to express meaning. A teacher's procedure in giving commands may be quite foreign to a student; for example, the teacher may ask, 'Would you like to sit down please'—meaning 'Please sit down'. The teacher may be upset to find that the child takes no notice, but to the child it was not an order, rather it was a request where there was a choice. Outside of school, questions are generally asked when the speaker doesn't know something; the opposite is often the case in the classroom. The teacher, as speaker, generally knows the

A teacher's procedure in giving commands may be quite foreign to a child.

Students have to cope with different uses of questions in the classroom.

answer to the question, but asks it to assess the listener's knowledge or to maintain attention. The task of the listener becomes one of guessing what thoughts are in the teacher's head. Strategies the child has learned to use at home often don't work at school where language is more abstract and the child has to guess the teacher's meaning. It needs to be remembered, however, that a teacher is the authority figure who structures, controls, and mediates the discourse of the classroom. Hence it is the teacher's responsibility to find ways to bridge the gap between the discourse of home and school.

School discourse depends heavily on the language practices of the middle class, which are themselves influenced by the language associated with written texts (the recognised and acceptable ways of introducing and maintaining a topic, taking turns, and signalling stance and purpose). The sharing time event (morning talk) is one such context. Hence many children are at a disadvantage as they lack experience with these practices. For some, the way language is used at school is very strange and they may feel alienated and not participate. Teachers then make negative judgements about their language ability and intellectual potential. Catering for differences in language practices and experiences is one of the challenges teachers still face.

The terms used in textbooks, as well as the type of language and text structure used, may be quite unfamiliar to students and distract them in their attempts to obtain meaning from print. The teacher's instructions must cater for these difficulties. Different subjects use particular jargon as well as using language in different ways, which is something the student needs to master. Differences in text structure are discussed in the section on discourse analysis/text structure in chapter 5.

The terms, language, and text structure of textbooks may also be unfamiliar to students and distract them in their attempts to obtain meaning from print.

Language attitudes

What type(s) of speech should we use and encourage in the classroom? To answer this question we need to consider the values placed on different types of speech.

Norms about acceptable speech styles can be described along a continuum ranging from highly colloquial speech to prestigious speech. When speakers violate norms of acceptable speech in a particular context, they may be judged negatively, even when their speech begins to imitate the speech of the person to whom they are talking. For example, if an interviewee's speech pattern began to resemble the speech of the interviewer (which happened to be less prestigious), the interviewer would probably think worse of the interviewee, because more formal speech would be expected.

Norms about acceptable speech styles can be described along a continuum ranging from highly colloquial speech to prestigious speech.

Different forms of language are value-laden. As we learn language we acquire a set of notions about what is correct in certain contexts. We also judge people by the way they speak, not always by what they say. Research studies in Australia indicate that cultivated speech occupies a position of prestige relative to other varieties. University

Different forms of language are value-laden. We judge people by the way they speak, not always by what they say.

students judged 'cultivated Australian' speakers as having greater intelligence, competence, reliability, honesty, and status than 'broad Australian' speakers, although broad Australian speakers were evaluated higher on the scales of humorousness and talkativeness (Seggie et al. 1982, cited by Ball et al. 1989). Speakers with migrant-accented English are evaluated negatively in status in stressful situations such as employment interviews.

You may wonder why once a form is established as a prestige form that everyone does not learn to use it. It is because other forms of language develop positive values in certain contexts. For example, if a speaker used educated English in the home, in some cases it would be considered 'flash' and inappropriate. People identify with a particular language and maintain a sense of belonging through it. Hence in many contexts cultivated Australian English would be considered inappropriate.

Unfortunately, teachers seem to be no different from other people in judging others by their speech. Research indicates that teachers and student teachers rated cultivated Australian speakers more highly than speakers of broad Australian (Eltis 1989). This indicates that many teachers may be making false judgments about their students and their families. Teachers' evaluations of student learning may be negatively biased and, significantly in the learning environment, teachers' expectations of some learners may be depressed. It is well known that teacher expectation has significant impact on student learning.

> People identify with a particular language and maintain a sense of belonging through it.

> Many teachers may be making false judgements about their students and their families on the basis of the students' speech.

What should teachers do?

In the media there are often criticisms of young people's language, and teachers are exhorted to correct their students' speech, and teach grammar and spelling. But what is the teacher's role? From the discussion above it is obvious that we need to assist our students to become competent in using language for a wide range of purposes.

Many educators would also stress that we are responsible for ensuring that all our students have access to the language of power. In the community, the language used for government, education and in the media is 'general Australian English'. This dialect is the dominant dialect and could be called the standard dialect. It is the dialect that is taught to non-native speakers, and speakers of other dialects normally understand it. It is accepted as the literary dialect—the dialect to be used by all speakers for writing. Obviously, this dialect is the language of power and students need to have access to this language. However, we cannot reject the language the student brings to school, that is, the language of the home, of the family, and of the student. In rejecting the students' language we would be rejecting the students themselves and things that they hold dear.

We need to accept the language and be sensitive to the features of the students' dialects, particularly when responding to students'

> Teachers have the responsibility of ensuring that all students have access to the language of power. In the community, this is 'general Australian English', the language used for government, education, and the media.

> We cannot reject the language students bring to school. In rejecting the students' language, we would be rejecting the students themselves and things that they hold dear.

reading, writing, and speech. If a student is dictating a text to us, we should record it faithfully. If a student imposes a dialect on the reading of a text, do not treat the change as an error but, rather, realise that meaning has been constructed. Later you can go back to the change in the text and use it as the basis for a discussion of language differences. We can ensure, however, that students are exposed to a range of language models, oral and written, and have the opportunity to use language for different purposes, in different contexts, and with different audiences. Experiences with drama and literature are valuable for providing the opportunity to become familiar with different dialects and registers.

In addition, we need to be aware of the values we place on different types of speech. Too often we make judgments about others on the basis of their speech. As teachers we need to be careful that, just because a student speaks broad Australian, we do not assume that the student is not as intelligent as another, or that the student has come from a deprived background. Conversely, just because a student is a very articulate speaker of cultivated English, we should not assume that the student is highly intelligent.

As teachers we need to recognise the language differences of our students. These differences are not just in the structure of language but also in the way language is used. Because of the way language is used in their community, some students may find the language of the classroom quite alien, and as a result feel very hesitant about participating actively in discussions. Research (Cazden 1988) indicates that middle-class children and adolescents have often grown up in families who value the ability to hold the floor in conversation and construct monologues unsupported by listener responses. Working-class children and adolescents may not only have had less experience with these styles out of school but they may be accustomed to another style, one that values collaborative topic development and elaboration in the role of the listener. Classroom talk allows few opportunities to display competence of this second style, whereas opportunities are created for the first style. Working-class children may not only appear less competent to their teachers, they may also experience school as a place where oral language skills as they understand them are not valued. Students with different languages and cultures may also be accustomed to using language differently from ways that are expected in our classrooms.

We must appreciate that there are different ways of using language: the way that we think is appropriate (our way) is only *one* way. We need to ensure that we provide opportunities for different types of language use and show that we value them. We need to be aware of the values we place on different types of language and not make false judgments of our learners. Our students need to become aware of how language is used in the community to become competent and confident in using language appropriately in different contexts. This must be emphasised for learners of second languages.

We can ensure that students are exposed to a range of language models, oral and written, and have the opportunity to use language for different purposes, in different contexts, and with different audiences.

We need to be aware of the values we place on different types of speech. Because of the way language is used in their community, some students may find the language of the classroom alien, and therefore feel hesitant about participating actively in class discussions.

Students with different languages and cultures may be accustomed to using language differently from ways that are expected in our classrooms.

Students need to become aware of how language is used in the community, and they need to become competent and confident in using language appropriately in different contexts.

Slang

Slang and colloquial language are marks of informal language. New words are coined by groups of people, for example, 'gunk' or 'goof', or old words take on different meanings, such as 'wicked' and 'sick', and are used in a particular way by members of the group. Some slang words become so widely used that they become an accepted part of the language, such as 'dwindle', 'cockney', 'glib', and 'mob'. Different grammatical features such as using 'not' at the end of a sentence as in 'I am having a great time—not!' are also markers of variation in language based on age. Can you think of other slang words and variations in grammar?

Language change

What is considered acceptable language changes in different contexts.

The role of slang in the language highlights how language changes over time. What is acceptable in different contexts changes. It must be remembered that it is the community of language-users, not a textbook, that determines what is acceptable. Frequently aspects of language may be in a state of flux and a number of alternatives are acceptable. For example, at one time, 'different from' was the only acceptable expression, but now, 'different to' and 'different than' are acceptable to many speakers. Can you think of other expressions where there are different variants?

ACTIVITIES

Talk to older speakers to investigate an aspect of language that has changed or listen to the talkback callers to radio stations complaining about the way in which language has changed. Think about how you could have students investigate language change.

Informally survey some teachers for their attitudes to dialects and registers.

Q What type of language do they accept or reject?

Q Do they encourage students to vary their language for different situations?

Q What would you do if a student, when reading aloud, changes the syntax of a sentence or exchanges one word for another? Examples:

(a) Text. 'I asked Tom if he could come.'
Reader: 'I axed Tom could he come.'

(b) Text. 'Mother'
Reader. 'Mum'

Q What should you do?

USAGE TEST

Here are some expressions about which there has been much controversy.

What is your opinion of their acceptability in everyday speech? Do not be influenced by whether these usages do or do not violate traditional grammatical rules. Indicate by circling AC that you would be willing to use the expression listed or that you believe such an expression has become sufficiently current in educated Australian speech to be considered acceptable usage. Indicate by circling UNAC if the expression is unacceptable in educated circles.

1 His attitude makes me mad. AC UNAC
  (mad as a synonym for angry)

2 I will pay your bill if you accept my cheque. AC UNAC

3 The reason I'm worried is because I think she's ill. AC UNAC

4 His work is different than mine. AC UNAC

5 We had a nice time at the party. AC UNAC

6 Can I have another helping of dessert, please? AC UNAC

7 I encountered less difficulties than I had expected. AC UNAC

8 Everyone put on their coats and went home. AC UNAC

9 How much money have you got? AC UNAC

10 Due to the storm, all trains are late. AC UNAC

11 She has an awful headache. AC UNAC

12 We only have five left. (position of only) AC UNAC

13 Let's not walk any further right now. AC UNAC

14 We must remember to accurately check each answer. AC UNAC

15 He's one person I simply won't do business with. AC UNAC

16 Go slow. AC UNAC

17 It's me. AC UNAC

18 She acts as if she was my wife. AC UNAC

19 Who did you meet? AC UNAC

20 How are you? Good, thanks. AC UNAC

21 Try and improve your work next time AC UNAC

Adapted from W. Sparke & C. McKowen, *Montage: Investigations in Language*, p. 357.

Share your responses with the group (answers are at end of the chapter).

Variation in written language: different genres

ACTIVITY AND DISCUSSION

Collect samples of writing over several days and categorise them according to purpose and audience.

Q Are there differences in style, word usage, format, handwriting, etc?

Q Why are there such differences?

Q What are the implications for teaching and assessing writing?

Much of the discussion above has focused on speech, but writing, like speech, can be described as varying in structure and form, depending on purpose and audience. The term 'genre' is used to mean the overall structuring of the text (oral and written) that characterises different forms of communication or activities. Written genres can be divided into two main kinds: expressive/imaginative and factual. Expressive/ imaginative types include the recount, narrative, and poetic–literary; factual types include procedure, description, report, and exposition (exploratory, information, scientific). Examples of these will be given later when the structure of language is discussed in chapter 5.

> The term 'genre' is used to mean the overall structuring of the text that characterises different forms of communication or activities.
>
> Written genres can be divided into two main kinds: expressive/imaginative and factual.

Summary

In this chapter we have discussed how language is central to and reflects a culture, how it is used and varies from situation to situation, and the implications of language variation for the teacher.

The language we use is central to all our daily interactions. Apart from reflecting our culture, the language we use can indicate our social standing, gender, and beliefs. To a great extent we are judged and identified by our language. How we use language in relation to other people affects the way they come to see themselves. This is of critical importance to teachers; as teachers we need to consider the effect our language may be having on our students.

> Our language reflects our culture, our social standing, our gender, and our beliefs.

> How we use language towards other people affects the way they see themselves.

Our language varies in form and structure according to different contexts. For effective communication we need to adapt our language to the situation. Hence, we cannot say that there is one correct way of using language, but rather that some ways are more appropriate than others in a particular context.

> For effective communication we need to adapt our language to the situation.

Implications for teaching

1 Students need to be exposed to and encouraged to use a range of language varieties. For this to happen, speakers from different

backgrounds need to be invited to the school to interact with students, and students need to encounter other contexts in which speakers are using language differently. Projects in which students have to interview others in the wider community and perform work experience or community work provide meaningful opportunities for them to hear and use language for different purposes.

2   It is also important that students have the opportunity to reflect on how language is used and consider their attitudes and the attitudes of others to language varieties. Discussion about differences between different dialects and registers can be useful. These differences need to be valued. Drama and role-play activities provide another meaningful context for experimenting with and developing confidence in using different types of speech. For example, students could role-play eating in different types of restaurants, acting as different types of workers or speaking as different news readers. Discussion can be about the speech of the persona or character being role-played, and not the student's speech which is much less threatening.

3   Students come from various backgrounds, using various forms of language. Teachers generally adopt middle-class values and the institution generally maintains middle-class values and speech. Students from backgrounds other than the middle class may feel alienated. The language and values of the school may be strange to them and they may sense rejection. Apart from containing a different variety of language and values, the books that these students are given are often about topics that are alien to them. It is important for teachers to remember that no single type of language or dialect is inherently superior to others, although certain dialects might be more prestigious in a community. As teachers we need to be aware of the values we place on different languages and language varieties, and we should not unjustly prejudge our students and others.

4   It needs to be remembered that language codes are tools used by language users in the process of getting things done, and that language competence develops through use. Language instruction should not be isolated from other curricular areas, but rather should be a natural and functional part of the opportunities selected by students to explore their world, answer their questions, and solve their problems. The basis of a language program should be to provide an environment that demonstrates and demands different uses of language. All the different areas of the curriculum should be used. Language instruction occurs where assistance is needed by students to achieve their purposes.

5   Teaching programs should take into account students' language, the difficulties inherent in the language of instruction, and differences between spoken and written language for all students.

6   Teachers need to:
   • accept the students with their language and culture

- use the students' language in meaningful contexts in all curricular areas
- use the students' language and experiences, particularly as a starting point for reading and writing instruction
- read a wide range of literature to the students and invite a range of speakers to the school to provide other language models
- provide opportunities for students to experiment with different genres and registers in both the oral and written codes
- help students become aware of the appropriateness of different types of language for different purposes and contexts, and become competent in using the language of power
- accept the use of students' dialects in reading and writing, such as using 'Mum' for 'Mother'
- be aware that it is possible for students to misunderstand a teacher's language and the language used in books
- explain the use of terms used in instruction and be precise in the use of these terms
- discuss the language of texts, particularly the structure of texts, which will be discussed in some detail in chapter 5
- be aware of the possibility of inherent discrimination in our language, avoid the use of such language, and help students become aware of sexism and racism in language.

References and further reading

Baker A. & I. *Mathematics in Process*, Eleanor Curtain Publishing, South Yarra, 1990.

*Baker D., Semple C. & Stead T. *How Big is the Moon? Whole Maths in Action*, Oxford University Press, Melbourne, 1990.

Baker S. *The Australian Language*, Angus & Robertson, Sydney, 1966.

Ball P., Gallois C. & Callan V. 'Language attitudes: A perspective from social psychology', in Collins P. & Blair D. (eds) *Australian English: The Language of a New Society*, University of Queensland Press, St Lucia, Qld, 1989.

*Barton D. *Literacy*, Blackwell, Oxford, 1994.

Bernstein B. *Class, Codes and Control*, Vol. 1. Routledge & Kegan Paul, London, 1971.

Cameron D. *Feminism and Linguistic Theory*, Macmillan, London, 1992.

Burridge K. & Mulder J. *English in Australia & New Zealand*, Oxford University Press, Melbourne, 1998.

Cazden C. *Classroom Discourse: The Language of Teaching and Learning*, Heinemann Educational, Portsmouth (NH), 1988.

Clark M. *The Great Divide: Gender in the Primary School*, Curriculum Corporation, Carlton, Vic., 1990.

Collins P. & Blair D. (eds), *Australian English: The Language of a New Society*, University of Queensland Press, St Lucia, Qld, 1989.

Crystal D. *The Cambridge Encyclopedia of Language*, Cambridge University Press, Cambridge, 1987.

Crystal D. *The Cambridge Encyclopedia of The English Language*, Cambridge University Press, Cambridge, 1995.

Davies B. *Gender Equity and Early Childhood*, Curriculum Corporation, Carlton, Vic., 1988.

*Delpit L. 'Language diversity and learning', in Hynds S. & Rubin D. (eds) *Perspectives on Talk and Learning*, National Council of Teachers of English, Urbana, IL, 1990, pp. 247–66.

Downing J. 'The development of linguistic concepts in children's thinking', in *Research in Teaching English*, 1970, Vol. 4, pp. 5–19.

*Eckermann A. *One Classroom Many Cultures*, Allen & Unwin, St Leonards, NSW, 1994.

Eckert P. & McConnell-Ginet S. 'Think practically and look locally: Language and gender as community-based practice', in Roman C., Juhasz S. & Miller C. (eds) *The Women & Language Debates: A Sourcebook*, Rutgers University Press, New Brunswick, NJ, 1994, pp. 432–60.

Eltis K. J. 'Pupil's speech style and teacher reaction', in Collins P. & Blair D. (eds) *Australian English: The Language of a New Society*, University of Queensland Press, St Lucia, Qld, 1989.

*Fromkin V., Rodman R., Collins P. & Blair D. *An Introduction to Language*, 3rd edn, Harcourt Brace & Co., Sydney, 1996.

*Gee J. *Social Linguistics and Literacies*, Taylor & Francis, London, 1996.

*Gilbert P. with Rowe K. *Gender, Literacy and the Classroom*, ARA, Carlton South, Vic., 1989.

*Gilbert P. 'Gender, talk and silence: speaking and listening as social practice', in Bull G. & Anstey M. (eds) *The Literacy Lexicon*, Prentice Hall, Sydney, 1996, pp. 163–89.

Horvath B. *Variation in Australian English: The Sociolects of Sydney*, Cambridge University Press, Cambridge, 1985.

Janks H. *Language, Identity & Power*, Hodder & Stoughton Educational with Witwatersrand University Press, Johannesburg, 1993.

Kamler B., Maclean R., Reid J. & Simpson A. *Shaping up Nicely: the Formation of Schoolgirls and Schoolboys in the First Month of School*, A Report to the Gender Equity and Curriculum Reform Project, Department of Employment, Education and Training, Canberra, 1994.

Kutz E. *Language and Literacy. Studying Discourse in Communities and Classrooms*, Boynton/Cook Pub. Heinemann, Portsmouth, NH, 1997.

Labov W. 'The logic of non-standard English', in Giglioli P. *Language and Social Context*, Penguin, Harmondsworth, 1972, pp. 179–215.

Lee D. *Language, Children and Society*, The Harvester Press, Brighton (UK), 1986, Chapters 7–8.

Lindfors J. *Children's Language and Learning*, 2nd edn, Prentice Hall, Englewood Cliffs, NJ, 1987, Chapters 13–14.

Malcolm, I. 'Aboriginal English: What You Gotta Know', in *Literacy Learning in the Middle Years*, 2002, Vol. 10, No. 1, pp. 9–25.

Maltz D. & Borker R. 'A Cultural Approach to Male-Female Miscommunication', in Gumperz, J. *Language and Social Identity*, Cambridge University Press, Cambridge, 1982.

Mitchell A. & Delbridge A. *The Speech of Australian Adolescents*, Angus & Robertson, Sydney, 1965.

Morris A. & Stewart-Dore N. *Learning to Learning from Texts: Effective Reading in the Content Areas*, Addison-Wesley, North Ryde, NSW, 1984.

Pauwels A. (ed.) *Women and Language in Australian and New Zealand Society*, Australian Professional Publications, Sydney, 1987.

Pearson J. C. *Gender and Communication*, Wm. C. Brown, Dubuque, IA, 1985.

Publications Branch, Education Department of South Australia *Writing: R-7 Language Arts*, Education Department of South Australia, Adelaide, 1979.

Reid J. 'Learning to think about reading', in *Educational Research*, 1966, Vol. 9, pp. 156–62.

Saunders M. 'An investigation of five year old children's knowledge of the reading task and their understanding of terms and concepts involved in learning to read.' Unpublished Master of Education thesis, Monash University, Clayton, 1979.

Saville-Troike M. *The Ethnography of Communication: An Introduction*, 2nd edn, Basil Blackwell, Oxford, 1989.

*Scott J. 'The silent sounds of language variation in the classroom', in Hynds S. & Rubin D. (eds) *Perspectives on Talk and Learning*, National Council of Teachers of English, Urbana, IL, 1990, pp. 285–97.

Sparke W. & McKowen C. *Montage: Investigations in Language*, Macmillan, Toronto, 1970.

*Stubbs M. *Language and Literacy: The Sociolinguistics of Reading and Writing*, Routledge & Kegan Paul, London, 1980, Chapter 5.

Swann J. *Girls, Boys and Language*, Blackwell Publishers, Oxford, 1992.

Swann J. & Graddol D. 'Gender inequalities in classroom talk', in *Researching Language & Literacy in Social Context*, Multilingual Matters/Open University, Clevedon & Philadelphia, 1994, pp.151–67.

*Tannen D. *You Just Don't Understand: Women and Men in Conversation*, Morrow, New York, 1990.

Trudgill P. *Sociolinguistics*, Penguin, Harmondsworth, 1983.

Wardhaugh R. *An Introduction to Sociolinguistics*, Basil Blackwell, Oxford, 1986.

Warlkerdine V. 'Sex, power and pedagogy', in *Screen Education*, 1981, No. 38, pp.14-24.

Wells G. *Language, Learning and Education*, NFER-Nelson, Windsor, UK, 1985.

Whorf B. L. in Carroll J. B. (ed.) *Language, Thought and Reality*, Massachusetts Institute of Technology, Cambridge, MA, 1966.

ANSWER TO THE USAGE TEST

The expressions that are acceptable in your society are the expressions that the majority of the group deemed acceptable.

PART TWO

LINGUISTICS AND LANGUAGE STRUCTURE

CHAPTER 4

AN INTRODUCTION TO LINGUISTICS AND GRAMMAR

FOCUS

This chapter focuses on the understanding that:

- *the structure of language involves a number of different aspects*
- *the context and purpose of language strongly determines the structure of language*
- *speech and writing are different codes, but they possess many similarities*
- *understanding the relationship between speech and writing is important for the teaching of reading and writing*
- *there are different types of grammars to describe language*
- *the term 'grammar' is used by different people to mean different things*
- *teachers need to have a language to talk about language with their students*
- *teachers need to have explicit knowledge of the structure of language to be able to help students learn to use language for different purposes*
- *learning about language in the context of using language can help students' development of language*
- *developing critical language awareness helps students understand the power relationships invested in language.*

PRE-READING ACTIVITIES

1 List the grammatical terms that you know.

2 What do you think we should know about grammar?

Why learn about linguistics?

A major task of the teacher is to engage students in three kinds of learning:
- learning of language
- learning through language
- learning about language.

M. Halliday, *Language Development Project*, Occasional Paper (1979).

This section aims to increase your understanding of language so you can effectively help students learn to use language for an increasing range of purposes. In order to do this, you need to know about language and about how language works to make meaning, and you need to possess a vocabulary to talk about language.

As discussed in chapter 1, language can be viewed from the two perspectives of function and form. Elsewhere we have discussed in some detail the functions of language: how we use language; the power of language; the different ways we use language for different purposes and contexts; and how we learn language. Now, we focus on the form of language—the structure of what we use and students have to learn, and which we have to help students learn. As language users we all have implicit knowledge of the form and function of the language we use. However, as teachers we need explicit knowledge of language. We need to be aware of what students are trying to achieve and learn so we can demonstrate or model aspects of language appropriately, determine what level of understanding they have, and what we can do to help them next.

The feedback or response we give students is critical to their learning process. The quality of this feedback is the key to our professionalism, and this is what distinguishes the professional from the layperson. Students who are learning to read and write (and those who are learning a second language in particular) need our informed responses. In addition, it is fascinating to understand more about something that we use so much and plays such an important role in our lives. Students also find language study interesting if it is related to their interests and needs.

Definitions

As with definitions of language, definitions of linguistics are changing from a narrow focus on isolated speech form or structure to a social perspective of language recognising the context within which it is used: '...in general the study of language is undergoing a revolution, with the dominant views moving away from investigating a system which is described solely in terms of its structure; the study of language is

A major task of the teacher is to engage students in three kinds of learning: learning of language, learning through language, and learning about language.

In order to help students learn to use language effectively, the teacher needs to know about language and how it works, and have a vocabulary to talk about language.

Teachers need explicit knowledge of language and an awareness of what students are trying to achieve and learn.

The feedback or response we give students is critical for their learning process. Students who are learning to read and write, and those who are learning a second language, need our informed responses.

moving towards viewing language as a dynamic social activity which serves people's purposes' (Barton 1994, p. 54).

A recent definition of linguistics is: 'Linguistics thus addresses itself to the fundamental areas of human experience—the mental and the social. Linguists are interested in how language is organised in the human mind and in how the social structures of human communities shape language to their own purposes, reflecting social structures in language use' (Finegan et al. 1992, p. 4).

Linguists traditionally take an objective view of language, making no value judgments about languages; instead they try to describe what they observe. They attempt to formulate explanations to account for language—what meaning is represented and how it is being represented. Linguists seek to develop rules to explain how language is used rather than how it should be used. All linguistic grammars are hypothetical. Thus linguists aim to describe a language (descriptive linguistics) and how it works (theoretical linguistics). Hence we have, among others, a school of linguistics called descriptive or structural linguistics, which studies the observable aspects of the language system; and a school of linguistics called generative transformational linguistics, which studies the rules underlying the language and provides explanations for the structure. We also have functional linguistics, which studies the relationship between function and form, focusing on the choices language-users make and the study of texts in context. Critical linguistics includes the study of the relationship between society and language, in particular how power relations are constructed in and by language.

In the past, linguists studied the sentence, usually in isolation, as the key unit of language; they focused on the form or structure of language and studied the different aspects of language separately from the context. Recently, greater emphasis has been placed on studying larger chunks of language (discourse or text) in context, thus studying the functions and context or 'pragmatics' of the language situation and its influence on the choice of language. In his functional systemic linguistics, Halliday (1985) combines insights from linguistics and sociolinguistics in order to study text in its different forms (genres) in context, involving various factors identified under register. Register includes the influence of subject matter of the text (field), the relationship between participants (tenor), and the channel of communication used (mode). The basis of systemic linguistics is the notion that a language is a system and there is a set of options from which one must choose depending on the purpose and context. These choices are culturally determined. Systemic linguistics has influenced language thinking in Australia, particularly in relation to the teaching of literacy. Many concepts from functional systemic linguistics underlie this book, with more explicit focus on discourse analysis/text structure in chapter 5.

Linguists take an objective view about language and make no value judgements about languages: instead they try to describe what they observe.

The basis of systemic linguistics is the notion that a language is a system and there is a set of options from which one must choose, depending on purpose and context.

In reality, the form and function of language cannot be separated; the purpose and context of language use determines the form. However, for the sake of convenience, each perspective can be viewed somewhat separately. In this part, therefore, we focus on the form or structure of language, particularly the English language.

It should be noted that linguistics has traditionally been concerned with the study of verbal language—particularly speech and, more recently, written language. Sign-language linguistics is a branch of linguistics that has flourished in the past ten to twenty years (in 1960, an American linguist, William Stokoe, established the legitimacy of American Sign Language as a linguistic system and not just a series of gestures as previously thought).

In reality, the form and function of language cannot be separated: the purpose and context of language use determine the form.

Linguistics (other than sign-language linguistics) is concerned with the study of verbal language—particularly speech and written language.

A study of language

Even though we are viewing language from a structural perspective, we want you to keep in mind that language is centred on constructing meaning. All aspects of language are directed to meaning-making. Figure 4.1 illustrates the interactive process between the factors involved and the decisions to be made when using language for different purposes and contexts. The aspects of language traditionally studied by linguists are given in Figure 4.2 (p. 89). For study purposes these aspects are often discussed separately, but in language they all interact to compose or comprehend meaning.

Note that the term 'grammar' is used to cover all the generalisations or conventions of a language, not only the sentence structure and word usage that traditional grammar treated. Figure 4.3 (p. 90) demonstrates how each level is governed by 'rules'; the interaction between the levels is governed by rules, and rules also operate within each level. Language is often described as rule-governed—to learn and use a language we must learn the appropriate 'rules'. We generally do this intuitively, but there are times when specific help in appreciating a 'rule' assists the learning process: for example, in understanding the structure of written texts; how to use language in a specific context; and second-language learning. Hence, as teachers, we need to have explicit awareness of some of these 'rules'. These rules are basic to a language. If we don't know or use the rules, then we don't know the language. This is not to say that some rules don't change as the language changes.

Linguistics frequently deals with conceptual abstractions that may appear to have no direct relevance for teachers. Hence this section uses the insights from different schools of linguistics that we believe are most helpful for teaching. Later you may wish to read further to extend your understanding of language. Terms from traditional grammar are used where possible because many of you will already be familiar with them.

All aspects of language are directed to making meaning.

The term 'grammar' is used to cover all the rules of a language.

The interactions between different aspects of grammar are rule-governed, and rules also operate within each aspect.

These rules are basic to a language. If we don't know or use the rules, then we don't know the language.

Figure 4.1 Language: An interactive process

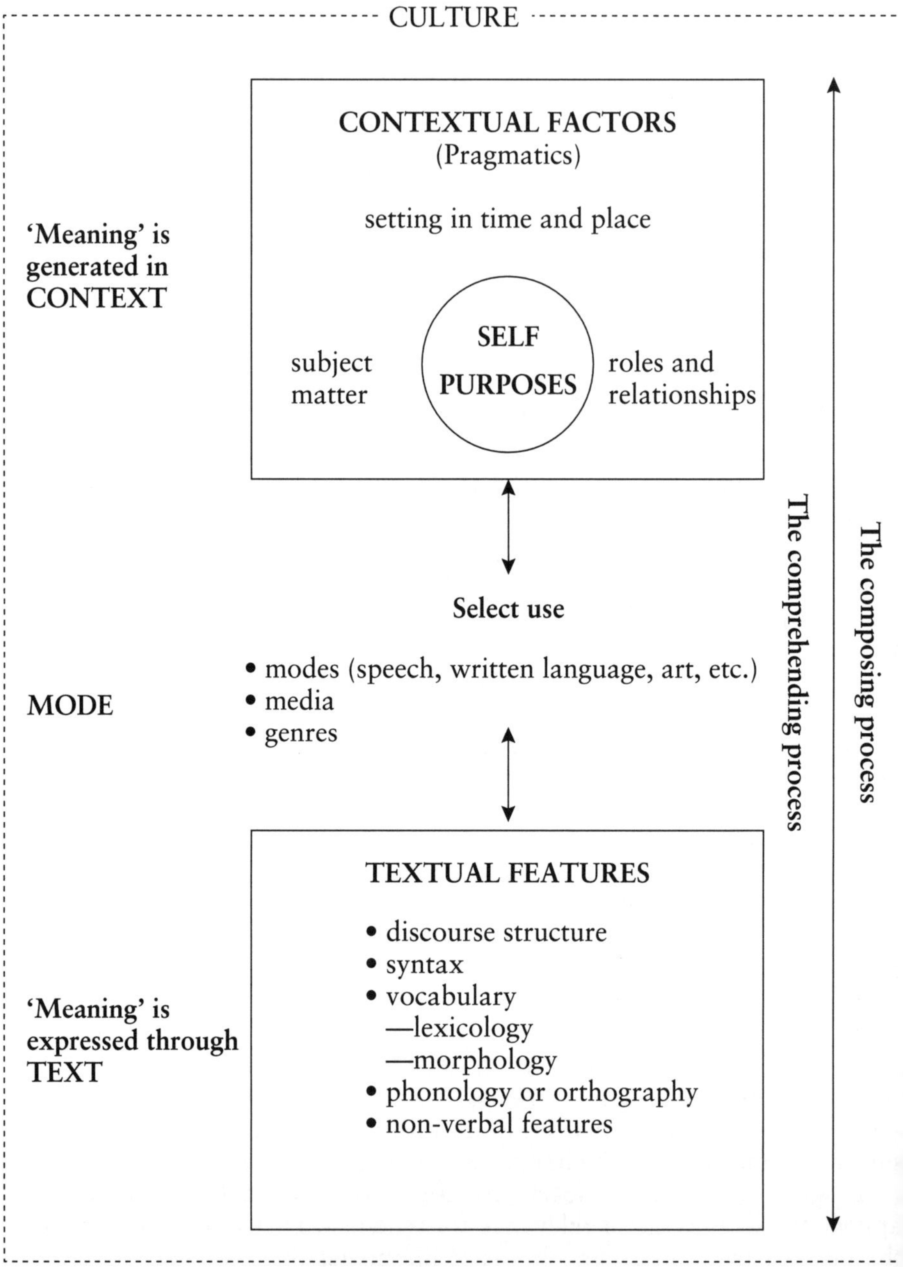

Figure 4.2   Aspects of language studied by linguists

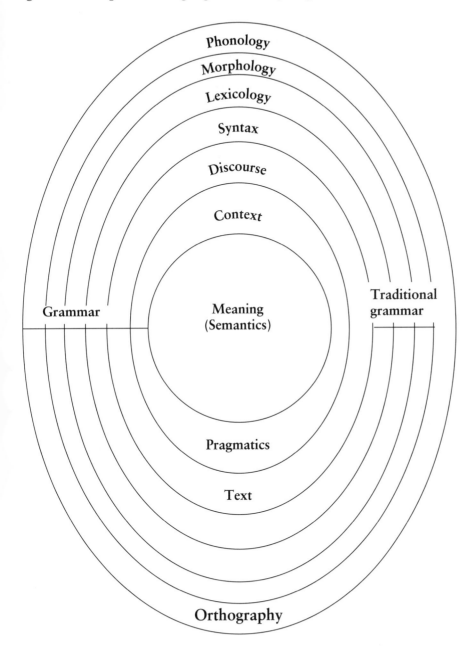

Figure 4.3   Aspects of grammar

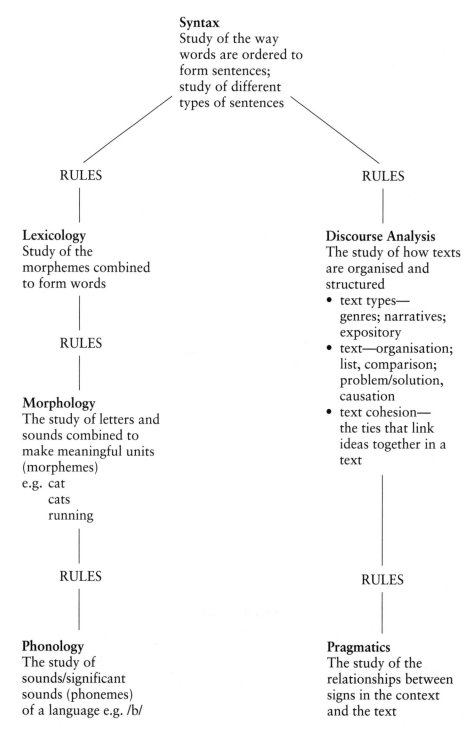

Syntax
Study of the way
words are ordered to
form sentences;
study of different
types of sentences

RULES   RULES

Lexicology
Study of the
morphemes combined
to form words

Discourse Analysis
The study of how texts
are organised and
structured
• text types—
  genres; narratives;
  expository
• text—organisation;
  list, comparison;
  problem/solution,
  causation
• text cohesion—
  the ties that link
  ideas together in a
  text

RULES

Morphology
The study of letters and
sounds combined to
make meaningful units
(morphemes)
e.g. cat
      cats
      running

RULES   RULES

Phonology
The study of
sounds/significant
sounds (phonemes)
of a language e.g. /b/

Pragmatics
The study of the
relationships between
signs in the context
and the text

Grammar today: traditional grammar and functional grammar

There has been much questioning by teachers about the teaching of grammar. Twenty-five years ago, grammar was supposedly discarded from the classroom. However, textbooks on grammar still remain in many classroom cupboards and from time to time are dragged out for use, and new grammar books are being published for classroom use. Literacy standards are still frequently questioned: the catch-cry 'Our children can't write' is frequently heard. Hence, teachers often feel cornered. On the one hand, they are told by researchers that teaching formal grammar is ineffective for improving writing and speech, and, on the other hand, are being pressured to improve literacy standards. There has been pressure for teachers to learn functional grammar. What should be done? What is the place of grammar in the classroom? The following issues need to be considered:

- What do we mean by 'grammar'?
- What should the teacher know about grammar?
- What are the most efficient methods of developing students' language?

> The teaching of formal grammar is ineffective for improving writing or speech.

What do we mean by 'grammar'?

To many, the term 'grammar' means the prescriptive set of rules that dictates how we should use language. In the classroom, rules were taught and students expected to be able to analyse sentences into parts. Based on Latin grammar, this approach was often inappropriate for English usage. In addition, it focused on written language and emphasised the rules of syntax. It is often called traditional grammar. Frequently the term 'grammar' is therefore used to refer to rules of syntax, word usage, and written conventions such as punctuation, abbreviations, and format. You must know what you mean by 'grammar'. There is clearly a place for helping students with punctuation, abbreviation, and word usage when the need arises. But is there a place for the formal teaching of grammar; that is, systematic teaching of grammar, often out of a textbook, removed from context?

> There is clearly a place for helping students with aspects of language, such as punctuation, abbreviation and word usage, when the need arises.

The term 'grammar', as it is used by linguists today, refers to that body of rules that describes or explains how a language operates. It is also used to explain how particular texts are put together. It does not prescribe language usage—as a language changes, its rules must change accordingly. A number of modern grammars have been developed, such as transformational generative grammar, which is best known through the work of Chomsky (1957). It aims not only to describe and explain language structure, but also to investigate the nature of the mind. There is also case grammar that emphasises the functions of units of syntax. More recently, functional grammars have developed, with Halliday's

> Grammar does not prescribe language usage—as a language changes its rules must change accordingly.

systemic functional grammar having the most impact. Functional grammars focus on the purposes and uses of language. They are derived from studying spoken and written language in the contexts of their use. In contrast, traditional grammar aims to describe language as a set of rules for sentence construction, as something we need to know. Functional grammar views language as a resource for making meaning and describes what we do, the choices we have when making meaning. Functional grammar therefore focuses on how meanings are made in texts as well as structures, hence terminology has been developed to describe structures as well as functions. Text is taken as a semantic unit not a grammatical unit with meanings realised through grammar. Functional grammar starts with the general structures and proceeds to more specific features.

Functional grammar focuses on the choices we have in making meaning.

Text is the unit of analysis.

Functional grammar sets out to relate language as a system to how people use language. Three different functions are emphasised:

- action—using language to act upon the world, to get things done; also called interpersonal function
- reflection—using language to reflect on our experiences, to represent the world, to make sense of the world; also called experiential or ideational function
- connection—using language to make connections between a text and its context; also called textual function.

Different functions operate simultaneously in texts.

These three functions operate simultaneously in all texts. When discussing a text, it is interesting to see what structures have been used to achieve a function and how effectively it has been achieved. This provides a useful tool for teachers, particularly in assisting writing development. Collerson (1994, 1997) illustrates how functional grammar describes the features used to achieve these functions. In the following sections aspects of functional grammars are used in discussing the different levels of linguistics; for example, genre and text cohesion at the text level.

Culture, situation, and ideology influence the choices we make in using language.

The context of culture, situation, and ideology are also considered for their influence on the choices we make when using language. The immediate context of situation such as purpose, mode of language, topic or field, role relationships between language users, and tenor all have an influence that is described as register. The context of the culture determines the genre we use—the staged step-by-step structures that have been institutionalised by a culture for achieving certain goals. For example, job interviews have a particular structure. Our ideological position, the beliefs and values we hold, also influence our choice of register and genre. Current thinking emphasises the importance of text analysis, enabling students to identify and question the underlying ideology in texts in order to resist or challenge them.

Figure 4.4 from Collerson (1994, p. 11) demonstrates the relationship between context and text.

Figure 4.4

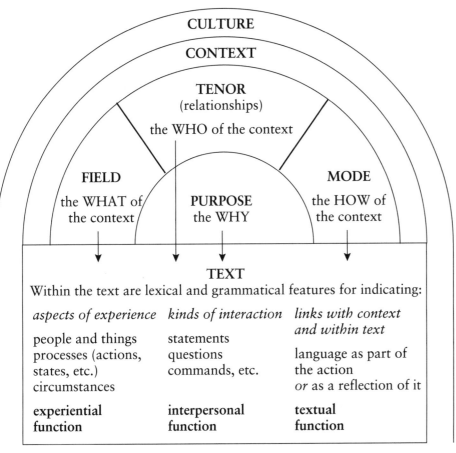

J. Collerson, *English Grammar: A Functional Approach*, p. 11.

Table 4.1 (from Winch & Blaxell 1994) gives terms for both traditional and functional grammars and their meaning.

Hence, the question of whether or not to teach grammar becomes more confusing. You now need to ask: 'Which grammar, if any, do I teach?'

Grammar was basically taught in classrooms to foster students' writing and perhaps their speech. It has been used also to help second-language learners. Wilkinson (1971) summarised the research findings on the usefulness of the formal teaching of traditional grammar. He also questioned the usefulness of the formal teaching of any type of grammar. (Formal teaching means teaching about grammar from a textbook out of context of language in use.) In summary, he concluded that:

Table 4.1   A comparison from traditional and functional grammars

TERMS IN TRADITIONAL GRAMMAR	TERMS IN FUNCTIONAL GRAMMAR	WHAT THEY MEAN
Adjective or adjectival phrase	Attribute	A word or phrase that adds meaning to a noun.
Adverb or adverbial phrase	Circumstance	A word or phrase that adds meaning to a verb, adjective or other adverb.
Auxiliary verb	Auxiliary verb	A part of a verb that makes up the verb group. It shows tense or mood.
Clause	Clause	A group of words with a finite verb.

Connections between different parts of speech, sentences and paragraphs. (cohesion)	Cohesion
	    Reference
	    Substitution
	    Ellipsis
	    Conjunction
	    Lexical
	        (Related Words)
		The linking of ideas in a text.

Conjunction	Conjunction	A joining word in a text.
Finite verb	Finite verb	A verb that has a subject.
Inflection	Inflection	A suffix added to a noun or verb to show number or tense.
Main idea at beginning of clause	Theme and Rheme	The placing of the main idea (theme) at the beginning of a clause for emphasis. The rheme is the remainder of the clause.

Mood
    Indicative
    Imperative
	Mood and Modality
	    Declarative
	    Imperative
	    Interrogative
		Verb forms that indicate statements, questions, commands.

Mood Subjunctive	Modality	Doubts, wishes, possibility, probability, certainty expressed through modal auxiliary (traditional) or modals and modifiers (functional).
Noun	Participant Also represented by pronouns and noun groups.	A name of a person, place or thing.
Participle	Participle	Part of verb in a verb group (or verb phrase), or used as an adjective.

Terms in traditional grammar	Terms in functional grammar	What they mean
Phrase	Phrase	A group of words without a finite verb doing the work of different parts of speech.
Preposition	Preposition	A word that introduces a prepositional phrase.
Principal clause	Independent	A clause that has a single, self-contained message; it can stand by itself.
Pronoun	Participant	A word that stands instead of a noun. In functional grammar, pronouns are regarded as a class of noun.
Sentence	Sentence Clause complex	One or more clauses linked together in meaning. One clause must be a principal clause. Each sentence begins with a capital letter and ends with a full stop, question mark or exclamation mark.
Subject and Predicate	Agent (Participant) and Action (Process) Circumstance is optional	The subject is the subject of the verb; the predicate contains the finite verb and its modifiers.
Subordinate clause	Dependent clause Embedded clause	A clause linked to a principal clause; subordinate because it cannot stand alone.
Tense Present Past Future	Tense Present and Timeless Present Past Future	The form of the verb that indicates when the action occurs.
Verb	Process (Also shown by verb groups including modifiers)	A word in a sentence that states what is happening.
Voice Active Passive	Voice Active Passive	In the active voice, the subject is the doer; in the passive voice, the subject is acted upon (traditional). In the active voice, the doer is the theme, in the passive voice, the receiver of the action is in the theme position (functional).

G. Winch & G. Blaxell, *The Primary Grammar Handbook*, pp. 137–8.

- training in grammar does not improve a pupil's composition
- ability in grammar is more related to ability in some other subject than to that in English composition
- a knowledge of grammar is often taught to children who have not the maturity, intelligence, or knowledge to understand it
- grammar may hinder the development of children's written language because the time spent on grammar may be at the expense of other things—such as actual writing—which may be far more beneficial
- there is no evidence to suggest that written work will suffer if the study of grammar is discarded.

It would appear that the formal teaching of grammar is inefficient in developing writing skills. You are no doubt also aware of the uselessness of teaching rules in order to change speech habits. Rejecting the teaching of formal grammar does not mean that teachers should not use grammar at all in their programs. We now have grammars that are of more practical use in the classroom and greater understanding of language structures and how we use them to make meanings. But there is a significant difference between a teacher learning grammar and the teacher teaching grammar.

Underpinning this book is the belief that teachers need to have explicit knowledge of language in order to help them in their teaching. Students do need to develop a more conscious knowledge of language structures and features so they have better control of them and understand some of the complexities of the relationship between text and context. They need to develop analytical skills to be able to interrogate and question the meanings in texts. They also need a language to talk about language (a metalanguage).

Critical language awareness

Language awareness or knowledge about language has become generally accepted as of value for students. Critical language awareness, which was developed from critical linguistics, goes beyond knowledge about language, emphasising how language conventions and language practices are invested with power relationships (Fairclough 1992). Teachers who adopt a critical view of language pay attention therefore not only to form and function, but also to how power relations affect and are reflected in language. Issues discussed in chapter 1 under ideology, power and language, and knowledge of language differences, are important here. Ivanic (1990, p. 132) gives a checklist that emphasises what she believes should be achieved in a language program. These include:

A. Critical awareness of the relationship between language and power
- Recognize how people with power choose the language that is used to describe people, things, and events

It is important to help students see how power and attitudes influence choices in language, and how they can change their use of language.

- Understand how many types of language, especially written language, have been shaped by more prestigious social groups, and seem to exclude others. That is what makes them hard to understand, hard to use confidently, or hard to write
- Understand how the relative status of people involved affects the way we use a language (for example, a doctor speaks differently from a patient)
- Recognise that when power relations change, language changes too—both historically and between individuals
- Understand how language use can either reproduce or challenge existing power relations.

B. Critical awareness of language variety
  - Recognise the nature of prejudice about minority languages, other languages of the world, and varieties of English
  - Understand why some languages or language varieties are valued more highly than others
  - Understand how devaluing languages or language varieties devalues their users
  - Value your own spoken language
  - Recognise that speakers of languages and language varieties other than standardised English are experts.

C. Turning awareness into action
  - Recognise how language can either be offensive or show respect— and choose your language accordingly
  - Recognise what possibilities for change exist in current circumstances and what the constraints are
  - Learn how to decide whether to challenge existing language practice in particular circumstances
  - Learn how to oppose conventional language practice if you want to.

Useful aspects of grammar

From a traditional grammar perspective Walshe (1980), an experienced writer and educator, suggests that there are five small areas of grammar teaching/learning that can help writers consciously avoid errors.

1   A sentence needs a verb. (This area will require attention to 'What is a verb?', 'What is a sentence?', and 'How is it possible in special conditions to write a verbless sentence?')

2   It is sometimes useful to distinguish between 'sentence', 'clause', and 'phrase'. (In the intermittent classroom discussion of the structuring of sentences, these terms become indispensable.)

3   Subject and verb need to agree. (This area includes the important activity of distinguishing subjects, but it emphatically need not include lessons on the 'predicate'—knowing what a 'predicate' is does not help a writer to write.)

There are five small areas of grammar teaching/learning that can help writers to consciously avoid error.

4   Simple tense differences need to be identified. (This is necessary for securing tense consistency in a composition.)
5   The elements of pronoun case. (Here, especially, written 'correctness' may clash with spoken 'deviation from standard', but the standard form can be taught without invalidating a child's 'home language'.)

R. D. Walshe, *English in Australia* , pp. 39–41.

In his list of five grammatical points, Walshe is not referring to conventions of punctuation, spelling, word usage, or style. These are different aspects of language, which students may need assistance with.

He also suggests that terminology can be introduced incidentally through vocabulary development activities. Terms such as 'noun', 'pronoun', 'adjective', 'verb', 'adverb', 'article', 'preposition', and 'conjunction' are still useful in talking about language. In recent curriculum documents, terms from functional grammar are often used (see Table 4.1 for list of parallel terms). However, a point to remember here is that a word is not a noun or verb unless it is in a sentence. Words are particular parts of speech because of their roles in a sentence. Hence, discussion about the use of these terms must centre on sentences, preferably 'whole' language. Use students' work and examples from literature to highlight the role of words and sentences and other structures.

Even though Walshe suggests that some grammar is helpful for young writers, he does not mean the formal teaching of grammar. Rather he believes that the teacher should encourage lots of interesting writing and, when errors arise, regularly use the student's work to discuss points of grammar. To use his own words: 'I see that minimal grammar teaching taking place only at the point of need, and the need is scarcely ever felt by a whole class simultaneously' (Walshe 1980).

Hence, concepts about language are introduced to students when there is a need. Rules are not taught systematically; rather, students' work is used as a basis for discussion about language. A study of language with students should start with issues of meaning and corresponding issues of text organisation relevant to achieving the purpose of the language. Discussion of the structure of the genre, sentence structure, and word usage may be relevant, but such discussions should not be ends in themselves.

What should teachers know about grammar?

If teachers are to be able to help students when the need arises, they must possess knowledge of the language and be able to explain the concepts simply. Hence, teachers must possess a sound knowledge of their language, not merely the intuitive knowledge that we all possess in order to use our language. They need to know the structures of what it is that they want their students to use so they can highlight key

Terms of formal grammar—such as noun, pronoun, adjective, verb, adverb, article, preposition and conjunction—are useful in talking about language.

Concepts about language should be introduced to students when there is a need.

Discussion of the structure of the genre, sentence structure, and word usage may be relevant, but such discussions should not be ends in themselves.

If teachers are to be able to help students when the need arises, they must possess knowledge of the language and be able to explain concepts simply.

features, if necessary, and be able to demonstrate and/or explain ways of making the language more effective; for example, the role of nominalisation (turning verbs into nouns, see chapter 8) in writing. Teachers need to be able to use their knowledge selectively to assist students rather than teach grammar systematically.

ACTIVITY AND DISCUSSION

Q What do you know about your language? You may like to test your knowledge by responding to the following questions. If you are unsure of the answers see the references listed at the end of the chapter.

- What are the terms given to the different parts of speech? Give an example of each type in a sentence. (Note: words can be classified as a part of speech or having a particular function only when in a sentence.)
- Give examples of different types of nouns.
- Give examples of the different characteristics nouns can possess.
- What role do pronouns play in English sentences?
- Give examples of different types of pronouns.
- Give examples of the different types of adjectives.
- Give examples of the different types of adverbs.
- Give examples to show the differences between transitive and intransitive verbs.
- Morphologically, English has only two tenses, 'present' and 'past', where the words are changed. Show by examples how other verbal categories are achieved.
- Show the difference between the active and passive voice.
- What is a 'gerund'?
- Illustrate the difference between a phrase and a clause.
- English has no gender: the nouns of English cannot be classified in terms of agreement with articles and adjectives as in French. How, do English nouns indicate gender differences?
- In English, number is frequently indicated by adding 's' to nouns, and by changing verbs and pronouns. Give examples of such changes.
- In English, number is closely associated with 'countable' (cat, dog, book) and 'non-countable' nouns (butter, petrol, bread). Give examples that illustrate the differences in usage between countable and non-countable nouns.
- Give examples of some nouns that have no singular.
- What are the different types of punctuation used in English?
- When are capitals used in English?

- What is the difference between contraction and abbreviation?
- Give examples of acronyms.
- Punctuate the following:
  (a) its difficult to know if its right or wrong in its present condition
  (b) the sale of womens and girls clothing was a great success
  (c) the firms bankruptcy was assured by Farmers hopeless leadership
- Correct the following:
  (a) The crowd were a large one.
  (b) Since the cabinet decides such matters we must abide by their decision.
  (c) Neither Jack or Hugh like sandwiches.
  (d) Either you or I are greatly mistaken.
  (e) This racing car is the fastest in the world. They are now being produced in great numbers in Australia.

Summary

This chapter focused on:
- different schools of linguistics
- different uses of the term 'grammar'
- traditional grammar and functional grammar
- place of grammar in the classroom
- importance of knowledge about language.

Implications for teaching

1 Teachers need to have an explicit knowledge of grammar in order to be able to assist their students. For example, a piece of writing may read more powerfully if restructured from a passive sentence to an active sentence. The teacher could demonstrate and discuss this with the students.
2 From children's first years at school, teachers need to introduce terms and labels for thinking and talking about language.
3 Teachers and students should develop a critical awareness of language, how power relationships influence language use, and how to use language respectfully.
4 Students need to hear the grammatical structures of written discourse. It is vital that teachers read aloud to students from a variety of text types.
5 Teachers can draw attention to particular aspects of grammar in the books being read, using them as models of writing that relate to students' personal writing needs.

6 When discussing a student's writing, teachers may need to direct the student's attention to the language structure in order to help the student convey meaning clearly. This is the time for specific instruction on language features, such as sentence structure, word usage, and use of punctuation. Teachers may also wish to use published literature to highlight specific language structures and usage.

References and further reading

*Bain R. *Reflections: Talking about Language*, Hodder & Stoughton, London, 1991.

Barton D. *Literacy*, Blackwell, Oxford, 1994.

*Campbell R. & Ryles G. *Grammar in its Place: Rules, Skills and Practice*, Oxford University Press, Melbourne, 1996.

Chomsky N. *Syntactic Structures*, Mouton, The Hague, 1957.

*Collerson J. *English Grammar: A Functional Approach*, Primary English Teaching Association, Newtown, NSW, 1994.

*Collerson J. *Grammar in Teaching*, Primary English Teaching Association, Newtown, NSW, 1997.

*Derewianka B. *A Grammar Companion for Primary Teachers*, Primary English Teaching Association, Newtown, NSW, 1998.

*De Silva J. H. & Burns A. *Focus on Grammar*, National Centre for English Language Teaching and Research, Macquarie University, Sydney, 1999.

Duffy G. *Teaching Linguistics*, Instructor Handbook Series, Dansville, New York, 1969.

*Eggins S. *An Introduction to Systemic Functional Linguistics*, Pinter Pub., London, 1994.

Fairclough N. (ed.) *Critical Language Awareness*, Longman, London, 1992.

Finegan E., Besnier N., Blair D. & Collins P. *Language: Its Structure and Use*, Australian edn, Harcourt Brace Jovanovich, Sydney, 1992.

*Forrestal P. *Look it Up! A Reference Book for Students of English*, Thomas Nelson, Melbourne, 1987.

Fries P. *The Structure of English*, Longman, London, 1957.

*Fromkin V., Rodman R., Collins P. & Blair D. *An Introduction to Language*, 2nd Aust. edn, Holt, Rinehart & Winston, Sydney, 1990, pp. 204–45.

*Garner M. *Grammar: Warts and All*, 2nd revised edn, River Seine Press, Melbourne, 1989.

*Gerot L. & Wignell P. *Making Sense of Functional Grammar*, Gerd Stabler Antipodean Educational Enterprises, Cammeray, NSW, 1994.

Graddol D., Cheshire J. & Swann J. *Describing Language*, Open University Press, Milton Keynes, UK, 1987.

Halliday M. *Language Development Project*, Occasional Paper, Curriculum Development Centre, Canberra, 1979.

Halliday M. A. K. *A Short Introduction to Functional Grammar*, Edward Arnold, London, 1985.

Halliday M. A. K. *Spoken and Written Language*, Deakin University, Geelong, Vic., 1985.

Hammarström G. & Jernudd B. *Outline of Linguistics*, Monash University, 1968.

*Ivanic R. 'Critical Language awareness in action', in Carter R. (ed.) *Knowledge About Language and the Curriculum: The LINC Reader*, Hodder & Stoughton, London, 1990, pp. 122–32.

*James C. & Garrett P. (eds) *Language Awareness in the Classroom*, Longman, London, 1991.

*Lindfors J. *Children's Language and Learning*, 2nd edn, Prentice-Hall, Englewood Cliffs, NJ, 1987, pp. 48–51.

*Mittins B. *Language Awareness for Teachers*, Open University Press, Buckingham, 1991.

Palmer F. *Grammar*, Penguin, Harmondsworth, 1971.

Pit Corder S. *Introducing Applied Linguistics*, Penguin, Harmondsworth, 1973.

Walshe R. D. 'How much grammar should be taught in the primary school?', in *English in Australia*, 1980, No. 54, pp. 39–41.

Wilkinson A. *The Foundations of Language*, Oxford University Press, London, 1971.

*Williams G. *Using Systemic Grammar in Teaching Young Learners: An Introduction*, MacMillan, South Melbourne, 1994.

*Winch G. & Blaxell, G. *The Primary Grammar Handbook: Traditional and Functional Grammar, Punctuation and Usage*, Martin Education, Cammeray, NSW, 1994.

CHAPTER 5

DISCOURSE ANALYSIS/TEXT LINGUISTICS

FOCUS

This chapter focuses on the understanding that:

- *knowledge of discourse/text structure, in particular the concepts of genre, top-level structure, and text cohesion, is important in assisting the development of writing and reading*

- *teachers need to have knowledge of different types of texts and sentences, and the potential difficulties for those learning to read and write*

- *teachers need to ensure that students are exposed to a range of genres*

- *genres are culturally and functionally determined.*

PRE-READING ACTIVITIES

I   Examine a newspaper or website and list the different types of writing used. Can you think of any linguistic differences in the different structures?
    After reading this chapter you may wish to come back to this activity.

Introduction

There has been much in-depth linguistic study of the sentence, but language is much more than isolated sounds/letters, words, or sentences. Sentences are organised into texts or discourses. A new branch of linguistic and psychological investigation, broadly labelled discourse analysis or text linguistics, has developed that studies the characteristics of texts. It is very much concerned with studying the use of language in social contexts such as conversations, story-telling, and writing for different purposes. Initially the term 'discourse' was used in reference to spoken communication and the term 'text' for written work, but the terms are virtually synonymous now. Spoken discourse has been studied in some depth by sociolinguists (Stubbs 1983), with special significance for second-language learning, and more recently for understanding the dynamics of the classroom (Cazden 1988).

Discourse analysis or text linguistics is a linguistic and psychological investigation of the characteristics of texts. It studies the use of language in social contexts such as conversations, story-telling and writing for different purposes.

Texts are the product of any language event. They can be classified in different ways depending on the interest of those doing the classification. Some may be classed as literary texts, where the interest may be in the use of figurative language, characterisation, selection and ordering of events (as in plot construction), or in any other aspect considered in literary studies. But texts can also be the ordinary spoken and written exchanges between people as they go about their daily business. The productions we see in cinemas and on television can also be thought of, and analysed, as texts.

This section focuses on the analysis of written texts. An understanding of the structure of written texts is important in developing literacy. Comprehension of texts to a large degree depends on a reader's knowledge of the structure of the passage and the use of linking words and phrases. Different books, particularly in different disciplines, use a range of text structures. Unfamiliar structures in texts create comprehension difficulties. Comprehension is more than understanding the meanings of words and sentences: it involves linking ideas across sentences and paragraphs. As a teacher you need to be aware of areas of possible difficulty in the comprehension of written texts, particularly for readers who do not possess a sophisticated knowledge of language. You also need to know how you can assist your students to become aware of different text structures and be able to read them effectively. Maturity in writing involves structuring ideas in a coherent way and using a structure that is appropriate to the purpose and audience. Writing has to be more than a string of sentences. In order to help students extend their writing you need to understand the structure of texts, model different texts and suggest ways of working with texts. Try reading aloud the following sentence:

> *We gave her dog biscuits because she said animals were fed better than humans.*

When reading this sentence do you find that your intonation first reflects an assumption that biscuits are being given to a dog, which you must correct when you read the second clause in the sentence indicating that a female person has been given the dog biscuits? If so, you are experiencing the potential ambiguity inherent in many isolated sentences, just as isolated words tend to be ambiguous. Now read the following passage. Is the above sentence comprehended more easily?

> *Mary is such a chronic complainer about food, we decided to shut her up once and for all. We bought her some dog food although she owns no dog. It came in handy, however, the next day. When we gave her the dog food, she was quite puzzled. We provided her with the following explanation. We gave her dog biscuits because she said animals were fed better than humans.*

(Source unknown)

Comprehension of texts largely depends on a reader's knowledge of the structure of the passage and the use of linking words and phrases.

A teacher needs to be aware of areas of possible difficulties in the comprehension of written texts, particularly for readers who do not possess a sophisticated knowledge of language.

Goodman and Goodman (1977) found that just as words are more easily read in sentences, so sentences are more easily read when embedded within connected discourse. They herald the current trend toward viewing reading as the processing of 'full natural linguistic text' (Goodman & Goodman 1977). This led to the move towards 'whole language' instructional strategies.

Several theorists have examined narratives for structure and developed story grammars. A wide range of stories are read to young children and so they usually become quite familiar with these structures and can use them in their writing. Unfortunately some of the texts we give to beginning readers to assist the learning-to-read process do not possess any recognisable structure. Other theorists are studying the structure of factual texts. Children are generally not as familiar with these structures because their exposure to non-fiction books is limited. There is a trend in schools today to ensure that factual books are part of the reading and writing program from the first years at school. Indeed, children should be exposed to a variety of genres and have opportunities to write for a variety of purposes. As much of later school learning depends on success with textbooks, it is important that students become familiar with the different text structures and can use them for learning purposes. It is important to be aware that different subject areas tend to use different types of text structure.

> As much of later school learning depends on success with textbooks, it is important that students become familiar with the different text structures and can use these structures for different learning purposes.

Genre

We use different types of language in varying contexts for different purposes. The term genre is used by linguists to mean the overall structuring of the text (oral or written) that characterises different forms of communication; for example, in a court hearing, a church service, a party, or the classroom. There are lots of variations in language use in a context at different times, but there are also predictable elements and accepted sequences of events. These predictable elements and sequences form the basis of the structure of the genre. Different cultures and societies develop different structures or genres to suit the needs of the group. (Traditionally, the term 'genre' was used, and is still used, to refer to different types of literature such as poetry, drama, and the novel, and also to refer to more specific literary genres such as historical fiction and science fiction. It is also applied to different types of films and music, all of which can lead to some confusion in understanding the concept of genre.) Linguists use the term 'genre' to refer to the structure of the language used for a specific purpose in a particular social context.

> We use different types of language in varying contexts for different purposes.

> Different cultures and societies develop different structures or genres to suit the needs of the group.

Martin (1985), who has focused on written language, divides genres into two main kinds—expressive/imaginative and factual. Expressive/imaginative types include recount, narrative, and poetic-literary. Factual types include procedure, description, report, exposition (exploratory, informative, scientific), and explanation. You could also include the common classroom types of picture description and observation/comment. An early form that appears in children's writing is the label, for example, 'This is a dinosaur'. Other types of writing can be listed such as play scripts and posters. Obviously there are many different types of writing, but it is proposed that those mentioned above are the most common in schools.

Another way of looking at genres is to think about the processes involved in the text, such as describing, explaining, instructing, arguing, and narrating. In order to perform these processes, certain structural and grammatical knowledge has to be applied to produce appropriate texts. Hence genre can be seen both as product (text type) and process (Knapp & Watkins 1994).

Teachers have to determine what types of language they will focus on—what types of writing will empower their students. The purpose, content, and context for each genre must be authentic, otherwise understanding the use of the genre will be very limited. The teacher needs to know the structure of different genres in order to demonstrate them explicitly and provide specific help to a writer. It needs to be remembered, however, that genres are not static, fixed structures. They are formed through social interactions providing guidelines for using language and, as such, change over time with the needs of the culture.

> The purpose, content, and context for each genre must be authentic, otherwise understanding the use of the genre will be very limited.

ACTIVITY

Examine some books that are used in different curriculum areas. Identify and list the different structures you locate.

Recent studies have focused on the genres commonly found in schools, including observation/comment, recount, narrative, procedure, report, explanation, and exposition. Examples are given below with some of the significant language features for the different genres (Callaghan & Rothery 1988).

Observation/comment

This is a dinosaur.
The baby is crying.

The above is a common genre used by teachers when labelling young children's drawings and writing.

Recount

We went to the zoo. We saw lions and tigers. We had lunch at the zoo. We had fun.

The text structure of recounts generally involves an orientation providing relevant background information, such as 'We went to the zoo'; a series of events, such as 'We saw lions and tigers'; and personal comments are often included, such as 'We had fun'. Significant language features include focus on individual participants, use of past tense, temporal sequence of events, and use of action processes (verbs). This form is very common in young children's writing.

Narrative

Narrative involves a series of events in a time sequence, normally in past tense, with some kind of orientation, that tells us about the who, where, and when of the story. The setting may be quite elaborately detailed, as in an historical novel, or may be implied rather than overtly stated, as in some science fiction or fantasy stories. The events are usually arranged so that there is a problem or complication that is subsequently solved in a resolution. It is obvious that there are many different types of narratives, such as adventure stories, science fiction, crime fiction, fairy tales, myths, legends, and popular romance.

There are many types of writing other than the story. We should be precise in our use of the term 'story' otherwise we could confuse young writers.

The following is an example of story-writing by a Year 2 boy.

A Boat Story

When my father went to the shop he bought a boat. The boat was beautiful. Then we went in the boat. Then we went to the sea and we went very deep. I was very scared.

My father and I fell in the sea. My mother and sister were crying because we did not come home. My mother called the police and the police said 'They are dead'. They started to cry very much. We got out of the water and came back home. Everyone was very happy.

J. Collerson (ed.), *Writing for Life*, pp. 15–46.

Procedure

Procedures include sets of instructions and directions as in recipes, science experiments, how-to-do-it kits, and the rules of games. The structure of procedures usually consists of a goal, often indicated in the main heading and/or diagram; materials listed in order of use, such as the ingredients of a recipe; and a method section, where steps are given for achieving the goal. Some key language features are: focus on generalised human agents; use of simple present tense and sometimes the imperative; and use of action processes (verbs).

Report

This genre provides a way of describing what some aspect of the world is like, but it also involves classification, relating the topic to a broader category. The structure of a report generally includes an opening with a general statement or general classification about the topic of the report, and facts about various aspects of the subject, which form the centre part of the report. These facts are often grouped around topic areas in separate paragraphs, each possessing a key topic sentence. The ending is often provided by some general statement about the topic. Diagrams, maps, and photographs are often used to illustrate points. Key language features are: focus on generic participants (groups of things); use of simple present tense; use of 'being' and 'having' processes; and use of pronouns to refer to nouns. The following example was written by a girl in Year 4.

Koalas

Koalas are a tree marsupial. Koala means 'No drink' given by the aborigines. Koalas feed at night. Koalas feed on gum leaves. Because gum leaves are juicy they don't have to drink water. Out of the variety of gum leaves they only eat about twelve kinds including Blue gum, Grey gum and Manna gum. Some koalas can live to twenty years of age. When the koala is just born it looks like a fat worm. Lots of people think that koalas are harmless animals, but they can bite and scratch. People call the koala a bear but it isn't. Koalas spend most of their time in a tree and rarely come to the ground. Female koalas have one baby each season.

J. Collerson (ed.), *Writing for Life*, p. 18.

Explanation

This is a factual text that gives reasons. Initially there is some statement about the topic to orient the reader, often in the form of a heading or question, followed by a sequenced explanation of why or how something occurs. Key language features are: focus on the generic; non-human participants; use of simple tense; use of temporal and causal conjunctions; and the use of action processes and some passives. The next example was written by a student in Year 6.

How do Animals Survive?

Many animals that were once alive are now extinct. Some extinct animals are the dodo and the moa bird. Other animals like whales, koalas and buffalo nearly died out but man has tried to save them. For animals to survive nature and their enemies they need protection. Some types of protection they have are:
1. *hard shells*
2. *teeth*
3. *spikes*
4. *claws*

5. tusks
6. fur.

J. Collerson (ed.), *Writing for Life*, p. 19.

Exposition

This contains an argument that puts forward a case for something, at the same time recognising that there are other positions. The focus of the text is generally on ideas rather than things. At the beginning there is some statement of position with some background information, followed by a 'logical' series of points and evidence to support the argument or position taken. Finally there is a summing up of the position or arguments, sometimes with a recommendation for action. Some key language features are: focus on generic human and nonhuman participants; use of simple tense; and few temporal conjunctions. The following example comes from a student in Year 5. The children had been asked the question: 'Should children in special units be integrated into everyday classes?'

> *No, I do not think children in special units should be integrated because they need special services and their teachers have been specially trained and they wouldn't let their training go to waste. They would also need the teacher more than ourselves. It would be very hard to cope without having our teacher. At times we would have to help without getting on with our own work.*

J. Collerson (ed.), *Writing for Life*, p. 20.

ACTIVITIES

Collect and examine samples of students' writing.

Q Can you determine what genre they are? Working with a friend use a highlighter to mark the different structural features of the writing samples.

Q Can you see how you could help the writer be more precise in expressing meaning?

To become a competent and confident language user you need to be able to select the appropriate genre for your purpose. Students need to be exposed to a range of language genres in authentic contexts and able to experiment and use them for their own purposes. One of the key challenges for a teacher is to provide an environment that demonstrates and demands different uses of language. Assistance may need to be given to make explicit the underlying structures of the different genres. Talking to students about the different features of their and others' writing will give them a metalanguage to talk about writing and assist their awareness of what is involved in effective writing.

Students need to be exposed to a range of language genres in authentic contexts and be able to experiment and use them for their own purposes.

It needs to be remembered, however, that many texts do not have structures as clearly defined as described here. Sometimes a text may have a mixture of genres, done deliberately for effect or done carelessly because the writer was unclear about the purpose. A good example of the use of a range of genres is the picture book *The Jolly Postman* by Janet and Allan Ahlberg.

As the needs of the culture change, new genres or variations of old genres are developed. Language is dynamic and must not be treated as something rigid with set rules, but there are certain conventions that need to be considered. We should help our students regard language as a powerful tool to serve their purposes. Knowledge of the structural features of different types of writing provides us with tools to write more powerfully to achieve our purposes. Similarly, such knowledge enhances the power of our speech.

Top-level structure

Another way of looking at the structure of a text is to determine the type of overall structure that best describes the relationship among ideas in a written or spoken text. This overarching structure is called the top-level structure.

In order to learn from a text, it is useful to determine its top-level structure and use that as a coat hanger on which to hang ideas. (If there is no clear structure you can impose one.) Understanding the relationship between ideas is critical for learning. It is useless if a student remembers two ideas from a text, but misses the relationship between them—a response at the meaning level has not really been made. A student may recall the content items—the words—but they are likely to be forgotten if the relationship has not been understood at the same time.

Bartlett et al. (1988) described top-level structure in the following way.

> *Like the ideas themselves, there is an order of importance among their interrelationships. They fan out like branches of a tree. Minor ones are like twigs joining leafy words, which are small details. More important ones are branches joining clusters of twigs and their leaves. In that way, they are interrelating chunks of information that together play fairly significant supporting roles for critical message content. Key relationships are the sturdiest of the branches. They set a framework for the critical message information and usually span many different parts of the communication. At the very core is one relationship—the top-level structure. It is like the tree trunk, a key to the whole structural scaffold.*

B. Bartlett et al., *Knowing What and Knowing How*, Book 1, p. 148.

As the needs of the culture change, new genres or variations of old genres are developed.

Understanding the relationship between ideas is critical for learning. It is useless if a student remembers two ideas from a text, but misses the relationship between them—response at the meaning level has not really been made.

Four types of relationships are commonly found in text (there are subtypes within each category):

- comparisons
- problems and solutions
- causes and effects
- descriptions and lists.

Comparisons are where ideas are built upon a comparative framework. Researchers have found this structure to be the most useful for remembering information.

Problems and solutions are where ideas cluster around a predicament (for example a problem, question, or issue) and a response of some sort (solution, answer, or reaction).

Causes and effects are structures where ideas cluster around effect(s) and cause(s). This structure is very similar to that of problems and solutions, but not all causes are problems nor are all effects solutions.

Descriptions and lists are where ideas are grouped as an ordered or non-ordered set of descriptions. This structure has been found to be least helpful for learning, but is most frequently used in textbooks.

Bartlett et al. (1988) then go on to say: 'Any or all of the four types can be found throughout the structural scaffold. As 'middle-level structures', they bind major supporting ideas to the main one at top level. As 'bottom-level structures' they link the detailed, highly specific information to the rest of the message. But, it is as 'top-level structures' that they provide an identity for the organisational pattern that runs through the whole text' (Bartlett et al. 1998, p. 148).

It is the top-level structure that we need to focus on with our students. When reading texts, certain signal words and word groups may alert us to which top-level structure the text has, for example:

- comparisons—contrast, have in common, different, share, on the other hand, the same as, whereas, compared to/with, however, but, instead, unlike, alike, other
- problems and solutions—the problem was, my query is, to fix this problem, to clarify the situation
- causes and effects—because ... therefore, as a result, since, owing to, well, so, then, the outcome, suppose, in order to, the result, the effects, the purpose of, the reason why, the consequence was
- descriptions and lists—each of the following, this particular, the characteristics are, there are ... ways to, first, to begin with.

Patterns in specialised texts

The above structures tend to occur in different subject/discipline areas in the following ways:

Comparisons

Comparisons and contrasts are used to organise information in a range of subject areas. This pattern occurs in science, mathematics, social

Four types of relationships are commonly found in text: comparisons, causes and effects, problems and solutions, and lists and descriptions.

studies, history, and second-language learning. Unlike other patterns, adversative arguments are of unequal weight—usually one side is given prominence.

Problems and solutions

Problem–solution dominates the social and behavioural sciences, including economics, social studies, geography, and psychology, as well as mathematics. Readers must be able to see the problem and consider specific solutions. Sometimes various solutions are explored before the problem is fully explained; sometimes various problems are presented before full solutions.

Causes and effects

Cause–effect is vital to the reading of science. It also appears, but functions differently, in narratives and history. Unskilled readers at all levels have difficulty with cause–effect relationships in texts.

Descriptions and lists

Temporal order using description is vital in narratives. Skilful readers know how to work with author manipulation of order such as foreshadowing and flashback. Knowledge of temporal order is also essential for reading history, as readers look for the order of events and interpret information on the basis of this order. Time-lines, graphs, or charts are often included in history texts to illustrate the order of events.

Listing information has been related to spoken discourse and narrative. Some scholars believe that list-making may be a prerequisite to literacy and a characteristic of the earliest use of writing. Many students resort to list structure in their recall of information when they lack familiarity with or sensitivity to other text patterning.

All of these patterns also occur in texts used in everyday life and work situations. Business and industry use many forms of communication, all of which can be organised around the above patterns. Companies may prepare advertising text that points to the advantages of new products using compare–contrast arguments. By demonstrating how a new product solves a problem, they also use the problem–solution structure. A critical reader must recognise the arguments and build counter-arguments.

The advantages of the use of top-level structure in reading and writing can be summarised in terms of:

- recall—more information is recalled in a more organised way
- memory—the information is remembered for longer
- understanding—the meaning of a passage, text, or examination question is more likely to be understood
- the ability to read more critically
- the main idea can be found more easily

- summaries and note-taking are made easier
- written assignments can be organised better
- the use of the strategy can be verbalised.

ACTIVITIES

Go through a newspaper or website and find examples of different types of top-level structures. Examine textbooks and try to determine the top-level structure of the texts.

Rewrite the following using an appropriate top-level structure to make the meaning of the passage clear.

> When comparing acids and alkalis it is important to accent their differences.
>
> Acids are corrosive. They act chemically on the surface of metallic substances eating away towards their inner space. Most acids are sour but dangerous to taste. They have a pungent odour. They neutralise alkalis and turn all bases to salts. All acids are compounds of some other element with hydrogen. Alkalis belong to the family of bases.

B. Bartlett & M. J. Usher, *An Inservice Package for Secondary Teachers About Top-Level Structure*, p. 18.

Text cohesion and cohesive ties

One of the priorities of discourse analysis or text linguistics has been the study of text cohesion; that is, the study of the way in which text 'hangs together'. Authors achieve cohesion in their text by relating different ideas using a range of language devices or cohesive ties. The comprehension of a text depends on understanding the different ideas and relating them. The interpretation of one idea in the text depends on the successful interpretation of another. In order to comprehend the text, the reader must understand how the ideas are related. It has been shown that skilled readers can detect the property of cohesion and use it to assist comprehension. They can also, when presented with mutilated text (a text in which the sentences have been disconnected), reassemble it in more or less the same order intended by the author. Students whose reading has begun to develop beyond the initial stages can reassemble texts at their own level quite satisfactorily. When reviewing students' written work, teachers can determine that one piece of writing hangs together, or coheres, better than another. Hence, it appears that there are linguistic signals within sentences that act as clues to their ordering within the whole. Two linguists, Halliday and Hasan (1976), determined an inventory of linguistic mechanisms that they suggest give texts this quality of cohesion. A glance at the detailed tables they provide highlights that a considerable degree of development is required to become a really proficient reader–writer.

The comprehension of a text depends on understanding the different ideas and relating them.

When reviewing students' written work, teachers can determine that one piece of writing hangs together, or coheres, better than another.

There are five types of cohesive ties: reference, substitution, ellipsis, conjunction, and lexical cohesion.

Halliday and Hasan developed an elaborate system for analysing and describing the semantic relations in a text. Their framework consists of five different types of cohesive ties:

1 **Reference** pertains to items that make references to something else for their interpretation. The three types of reference are personal, demonstrative, and comparative. Examples of references are:
   - *exophoric*: the interpretation of references lies *outside* the text and is situated within a particular context, the relationship between the text and its references is said to be exophoric, the references playing no direct part in textual cohesion. For example:
   Look at that.

   (that = ☀)

   - *endophoric*: the interpretation of references lies *within* the text, the relationship between them is called endophoric and the references form cohesive ties within the text. Endophoric relations are of two kinds:
     — *anaphoric*: those that link back to something already introduced in the text; for example, 'Look at the sun. It's going down quickly' in which 'It' refers back to the sun.
     — *cataphoric*: those that look forward in the text for their interpretation; for example, 'It's going down quickly, the sun' in which 'It' refers forward to the sun.
2 **Substitution** refers to the replacement of one item by another. The three types of substitution are nominal, verbal and clausal.
3 **Ellipsis** (the omission of an item) is similar to substitution, and is sometimes referred to as 'substitution by zero'; that is, something is left unsaid.
4 **Conjunction** serves as a cohesive device by linking what is to follow with what has gone before. Four types of conjunctive relations are additive, adversative, causal, and temporal; examples of conjunctions by type are:
   - *additive*: and, or, furthermore, similarly, in addition
   - *adversative*: but, however, on the other hand, nevertheless
   - *causal*: because, consequently, as a result, therefore
   - *temporal*: when, while, during, after.
5 **Lexical cohesion** involves the use of vocabulary that is in some way related to previously occurring items. The two basic types of lexical cohesion are *reiteration* (repetition of a word) and *collocation* (using a word from the same semantic field). Lexical relationships include:
   - *hyponymy*: the inclusion of a more specific term within a general one (daffodil is a hyponym of flower; gum and wattle are hyponyms of tree.)
   - *metonymy*: part/whole (arm is a part of a body)
   - *collocability*: (Monday relates to Tuesday)

- *synonymy*: (sad/unhappy)
- *antonymy*: (big/little)

Some cohesive ties have been researched in detail. Chapman (1979) charted the ability of children aged 8, 11, and 14 years to perceive these ties while reading. Reference and conjunction have been explored in some detail with the finding that the ability to cope with cohesive ties was still being acquired beyond 14 years of age. Furthermore, the ability to process the reference group of ties distinguished the reader who was becoming fluent at eight years from the reader who was not yet fluent.

Other examples of cohesive relationships are:

- *Clausal substitutions*: 'Sarah is very fond of Rachel. So am I.'
- *Comparison*: 'My thumb is stronger than that hammer.'
- *Syntactic repetition*: 'We came in. They came in.'
- *Consistency of tense*: 'We ate as we watched TV.'
- *Stylistic choice*: 'The gentleman encountered an acquaintance' versus 'The guy met up with a bloke he knows'.
- *Pronouns*: including personal pronouns (I, me, we, you, she, he), demonstrative pronouns (this, that, these, those) and pro-verbs (do, can, will, would, could, should) and many nouns that serve the function of pronouns.

Most texts will reveal cohesive structuring. Some texts can be confusing because cohesive ties have been used inappropriately or because a beginning reader or second-language learner is unfamiliar with the structures. Consider the difficulties in the following:

- 'Some spiders are hairy all over. They are called wolf spiders.' Some inexperienced readers do not realise that 'they' refers to the spiders in the previous sentence. They don't realise that they have to link ideas across sentences.
- 'Then the cloth is put into different liquids. One cleans the cloth. Another makes the cloth stronger.' The reader has to know that 'one' and 'another' refer to liquids.
- 'He was not very smart, but he knew he could not stop. If he were to do so, the tiger would eat him up. So he continued.' The reader has to know that 'do so' means 'stop'.
- 'The horse arrived at the barn door just before feeding time. The building, however, was locked.' The reader has to know that building refers to 'barn'.
- 'The pin was set with precious jewels. Each gem glistened in the sunlight.' The reader needs to know that 'gem' refers to 'jewels'.
- 'As the group approached, Bill could recognise the three who had visited him last night—Mr Smith, Mr Jones, and Mr Collins.' The reader has to know that 'Mr Smith, Mr Jones, and Mr Collins' refer to the three' in the preceding clause, and also that they comprise either all or part of the 'group'.

- 'When you talk and sing or shout, the air passing between your vocal cords makes them vibrate. This is what makes the sound of your voice.' The reader has to realise that 'this' refers to the air passing between your vocal cords.

Pearson's (1974–75) experiments with nine-year-olds demonstrated that:

- a person has a better understanding of a communication if it is expressed in one sentence, with linking words, rather than in two sentences with no expressed linkages
- language signals or cueing link words, such as 'because' and 'so', improve the subjects' memory of the sentences that contain them
- the subjects, when asked about their preferences, selected the most cohesive and grammatically complex forms.

To understand the relation between sentences, we need to understand such things as how causal relations, sequences, and main ideas are signalled, as well as the role of anaphora (backward references).

Difficulties may arise in understanding causal relations, such as when no causal signal is explicit or when causality is signalled by a conjunction; for example:

The soil was too arid to cultivate. The pioneers left the valley.
John mowed the lawn and his mother said he could go out.

Furthermore, many causal relations are disguised as time relations; for example:

After John mowed the lawn, his mother said he could go out.
When John mowed the lawn, his mother said he could go out.

Asking children to list events in a sequence often causes difficulties. Children have problems in doing this successfully. Clark (1971) found that young children use temporal order in speech (and probably spatial order in text) as the only indicator of sequence. Hence, a sentence where the sequence is not listed in temporal or spatial order is frequently misinterpreted. For example, 'Before John ate lunch, he mowed the lawn' would be interpreted as 'John ate lunch and then he mowed the lawn'. Researchers have looked at the difficulties created by anaphora for children's comprehension of texts. One finding is that intermediate grade children are only 60 to 80 per cent accurate in determining the relationship between the pronoun and the reference (Pearson & Johnson 1978). Research (Gardner 1975) has been carried out on the use of terms such as 'because', 'actually', 'moreover', 'either', 'or', 'if', and 'then' in secondary science texts, and has demonstrated that many secondary students have difficulty understanding these terms. Hence, instruction with and discussion on the use of such terms, and other devices that are used to relate different ideas in a text, may be beneficial. At the very least, the teacher needs to be aware that these terms may create problems of comprehension.

To understand the relation between sentences, we need to understand such things as how causal relations, sequences and main ideas are signalled, as well as the role of backward references.

ACTIVITIES AND DISCUSSION

Examine the passages below.

Q Which passage would be easier for a student to understand? Why?

(1) In the 1800s, Hawaii was an independent republic. (2) The Hawaiians had settled there from all over the world. (3) but most of them spoke English. (4) Because of this, Hawaiians wanted to become part of the United States. (5) In 1900, Hawaii was made a US territory. (6) This resulted in increased trade with the United States, (7) and this brought great prosperity.

(1) In the 1800s Hawaii was an independent republic. (2) English was the dominant language. (3) In 1900, Hawaii was officially made a territory. (4) Increased trade with America brought prosperity.

A. Moe & J. Irwin, *Cohesion, Coherence and Comprehension*, p. 6.

Read the passage below.

Q Can you determine to whom all the pronouns refer?

Note the difficulty that inexperienced readers might have in fully understanding this text. In particular, determine to what or whom 'they' in the last sentence refers.

John's father asked him to go to the hardware store to buy a box of nails. On his way there he (1) saw his friend Sam. He (2) was on his way home from a little league baseball game. He (3) liked to build things with his hands. John asked Sam to go to the store with him (4). They walked around the store talking about the expensive tools. As they were leaving, John noticed a bulge in Sam's jacket. The jacket was tight. The zipper slipped down. Out came the nails, right in front of the owner. He (5) was arrested for stealing. John's father was very angry when they (6) called him.

C. Clark, *Instructional Strategies to Promote Comprehension of Normal and Noncohesive Texts*, p. 127.

Summary

In summary, discourse analysis is a relatively new area of linguistic investigation. So far we have some insights into varying structures of texts and the importance of a reader's knowledge of these structures for comprehension. It is also important that the writer understands different structures in order to write effectively for different purposes. If we are to help our students become competent in using writing to fulfil a range of purposes, however, much more research is necessary to detail: (i) the specifics of discourse; (ii) the development of knowledge of text structures by readers and writers; and (iii) the role of the teacher in fostering students' knowledge of the nature of the structure of different genres.

Implications for teaching

1   We must ensure that our students are exposed to a range of texts, fiction and factual, and have the opportunity to discuss them.

2   We know that our students must see and hear language being used for a range of purposes—to entertain, to inform, to persuade—and that the classroom must be structured so that students have the opportunity to experiment with and explore different types of language, and use different types of texts for real purposes. To do this the classroom needs to be enquiry-based, where students have lots of questions and are encouraged to explore and experiment, read, write, and make meaning in the process of answering their questions and sharing their answers.

3   As teachers we must know about the various structures and features of different texts in order to be able to select a wide range of them for our students' reading and to model different aspects of genres to help students write more effectively.

4   It is not necessarily essential for students to know about structural matters such as text cohesion, but if it is obvious that some students are experiencing difficulties comprehending larger texts, activities such as co-operative cloze (Pulvertaft 1982) and sequencing of sentences and paragraphs will increase their understanding of the role of specific language features.

5   In the early stages of learning to read and write a particular genre, select texts that are generically simple, that is, texts that have clear purpose and consistent use of genre.

References and further reading

Ahlberg J. & A. *The Jolly Postman*, Heinemann, London, 1986.

Bartlett B. L. 'Putting Text Structure Before Content to Improve What Young Children Remember and Comprehend from Reading', in Burnes D., French H. & Moore E. (eds) *Literacy: Strategies and Perspectives*, ARA, Adelaide, 1985.

Bartlett B., Barton B. & Turner A. *Knowing What and Knowing How*, Book 1 Lower Primary, Thomas Nelson, Melbourne, 1988.

Bartlett B. & Usher M. J. An Inservice Package for Secondary Teachers About Top-Level Structure, Unpublished, 1987.

Callaghan M. & Rothery J. *Teaching Factual Writing: A Genre-based Approach*, Disadvantaged Schools Project (DSP) Literacy Project, Sydney, 1988.

*Campbell R. & Ryles G. *Grammar in its Place*, Oxford University Press, Melbourne, 1996.

*Cazden C. *Classroom Discourse: The Language of Teaching and Learning*, Heinemann, Portsmouth, NH, 1988.

Chapman J. 'Confirming children's use of cohesive ties in text: pronouns', in *The Reading Teacher*, 1979, Vol. 33, No. 3, pp. 317–32.

Chapman J. 'Reading: prospects for the eighties', in Bessell-Brown T., Lathman R., Reeves N. & Gardiner E. (eds) *Reading into the '80s*, ARA, Adelaide, 1980, pp. 1–9.

*Christie F. et al. *Language: A Resource for Meaning* (series), Harcourt Brace Jovanovich, Sydney, 1990.

Christie F. & Martin J. (eds) *Genre and Institutions: Social Processes in the Workplace and School*, Cassell, London, 1997.

Clark C. 'Instructional strategies to promote comprehension of normal and noncohesive texts', in Irwin J. (ed.) *Understanding and Teaching Cohesion Comprehension*, IRA, Newark, DE, 1971.

Clark E. V. 'On the acquisition of meaning of before and after', in *Journal of Learning and Verbal Behaviour*, 1971, Vol. 10, pp. 266–75.

*Collerson J. (ed.) *Writing for Life*, Primary English Teaching Association, Rozelle, NSW, 1984.

Cope B. & Kalantzis M. 'Literacy in the social sciences', in Christie F. (ed.) *Literacy for a Changing World: A Fresh Look at the Basics*, ACER, Melbourne, 1990, pp. 118–42.

*Derewianka B. *Exploring How Texts Work*, Primary English Teaching Association, Rozelle, NSW, 1990.

Furniss E. 'Getting the most out of the text', in *Reading Education*, 1980, Vol. 5, No. 1, pp. 43–8.

Furniss E. 'Schemes for reading text differing in organization: a study of sixth grade proficient readers', in Bessell-Brown T., Lathman R., Reeves N. & Gardiner E. (eds) *Reading into the '80s*, ARA, Adelaide, 1980, pp. 11–23.

Gardner P. L. Logical Connectives in Science: a Preliminary Report. Paper presented at the Sixth Annual Conference of the Australian Science Education Association, Adelaide, May, 1975.

Goodman K. & Goodman Y. 'Learning about psycholinguistic processes by analysing oral reading', in *Harvard Educational Review*, 1977, Vol. 47, No. 3, pp. 317–33.

Halliday M. A. K. *A Short Introduction to Functional Grammar*, Edward Arnold, London, 1985.

Halliday M. A. K. & Hasan R. *Cohesion in English*, Longmans, London, 1976.

*Harrison A. & McEvedy M. *Speech to Writing, Modelling, Evaluating and Negotiating Genres*, Robert Andersen & Assoc., Malvern, Vic., 1987.

Horowitz R. 'Text patterns: Part 1', in *Journal of Reading*, 1985, Vol. 28, No. 5, pp. 448–54.

*Knapp P. & Watkins M. *Context—Text—Grammar: Teaching the Genres and Grammar of School Writing in the Infants and the Primary Classroom*, Text Productions, Broadway, NSW, 1994.

*Martin J. 'Literacy in science: Learning to handle text as technology', in F. Christie (ed.) *Literacy for a Changing World: A Fresh Look at the Basics*, ACER, Melbourne, 1990, pp. 79–117.

*Martin J. R. *Factual Writing: Exploring and Challenging Social Reality*, Deakin University, Geelong, Vic., 1985.

Moe A. & Irwin J. 'Cohesion, Coherence and Comprehension', in Irwin J. (ed.) *Understanding and Teaching Cohesion Comprehension*, IRA, Newark, DE, 1986.

*Morris A. & Stewart-Dore N. *Learning to Read from Text: Effective Reading in the Content Areas*, Addison-Wesley, Sydney, 1984.

Pearson P. D. 'The effects of grammatical complexity on children's comprehension, recall and conception of certain semantic relations', in *Reading Research Quarterly*, 1974–75, Vol. 10, pp. 155–92.

Pearson P. D. & Johnson D. *Teaching Reading Comprehension*, Holt Rinehart & Winston, New York, 1978.

*Pulvertaft A. *Let's Breed Readers*, Ashton Scholastic, Gosford, NSW, 1982.

Reid I. (ed.), *The Place of Genres in Learning: Current Debates*, Centre for Studies in Literary Education, Deakin University, Geelong, Vic., 1987.

Stubbs M. *Discourse Analysis The Sociolinguistic Analysis of Natural Language*, Basil Blackwell, Oxford, 1983.

CHAPTER 6

SYNTAX, MORPHOLOGY, AND LEXICOLOGY

FOCUS

This chapter focuses on the understanding that:

- *teachers need to have a language to talk about language with their students*
- *teachers need to have explicit knowledge of the structure of language to be able to help students with their writing*
- *words are formed in a number of ways*
- *knowledge of the structure and origins of words has implications for the instruction of spelling and word recognition strategies.*

Introduction

The great expansion of linguistics as a discipline in the 1960s and 1970s was associated with advances being made in theories of grammar. The term 'grammar' here means a theory of language. Noam Chomsky, a key figure in this field, revolutionised beliefs about language and stimulated great activity in the study of children's language with his theory of transformational grammar. Chomsky and his contemporaries tended to base their work on the study of the sentence at the syntax level. Despite new approaches we still use many traditional and familiar concepts and categories to describe the structure of the sentence.

The term 'grammar' can be taken to mean a theory of language.

Syntax

The linguistic knowledge that we have about our language is often termed our 'linguistic competence'. The rules underlying our decisions about what is acceptable usage are part of this competence and constantly being applied in daily life when we read or listen to speech. These are abstract rules that govern the organisation of words into sentences, and the organisation of sentences into larger stretches of discourse. Syntactic analysis tries to formalise the rules that are part of a native speaker's linguistic competence. As users, we do not need to be

The linguistic knowledge we have about our language is often termed our linguistic competence.

consciously aware of these rules, but as teachers, we must have explicit knowledge of them to assist students in their writing and in second-language learning.

In the past, syntax has often been referred to as 'grammar', but we prefer to use 'grammar' in the wider sense to refer to the whole structure of a language code. Syntax, therefore, may be defined as a set of rules that is used to describe and/or explain the way in which words are related within a sentence. But what is a sentence? According to Fries (1952) there are more than 200 different definitions of a sentence. Intuitively we feel that we know what a sentence is, but find it difficult to explain this knowledge. Many have said that a sentence expresses a complete thought. There are, however, many exceptions to this. When listening to speech it is not always easy to discern the sentences. Frequently there are no clear pauses. However, in structural/descriptive linguistics the nature of a sentence was assumed, and techniques for analysing the sentence were developed.

Sentences are more than words strung together in random order. Speakers of a language know the principles that govern the organisation of sentences though they may not necessarily be consciously aware of their linguistic knowledge. For example, we can judge whether sentences are grammatically acceptable or not, or whether different sentences possess similar meanings, as in 'My dog was hit by a car' and 'A car hit my dog'. We can also judge whether sentences have similar structures or not, as in 'The firefighter phoned up the station' and 'The firefighter rushed up the road'. Intuitively we know that these examples do not have similar meaning structures, although their word structures are alike.

English syntax

ACTIVITY

Write the following nonsense words on cards and arrange them to make a seventeen-word sentence. Use each word only once:

    sallipesh, morked, had, his, lampix, blites,
    when, baslurker, the, the, ciptally, plony, and,
    up, felmed, coofed, the.

If you completed this activity you would have demonstrated your knowledge of English syntax. English syntax is based on word order, use of structure words and, to a lesser degree, inflections (word endings). There are some words and parts of words in this sentence that will be meaningful to you. The smallest unit of meaning, called a morpheme, provides information not only about the meaning of the word but also its function within the sentence. For example, the suffixes

Syntax can be defined as a set of rules that is used to describe and/or explain the way in which words are related in a sentence.

Sentences are more than words strung together in random order.

English syntax is based on word order, use of structure words, and inflections.

–ed, –er, and –ly may have led you to use 'morked', 'felmed' and 'coofed' as verbs; 'baslurker' as a noun; and 'ciptally' as an adverb. Try this activity with friends or students working in small groups and listen to the discussion that goes on. It is usually rich with explanations of why particular words should be used in particular positions in the sentence. The following two sentences indicate the importance of word order:

John hit the ball. The ball hit John.

The same four words are used in both sentences but because of the change in word order the two sentences possess different but acceptable meanings. Contrast these sentences with the same words used in a different order.

Hit ball John the.

This group of words is neither syntactically nor semantically acceptable according to our intuitive knowledge of English. To arrive at this assessment, we must use some criteria. Word order would appear to be one such criterion. Now look at this sentence:

Education hit the ball.

The word order is acceptable, but the sentence is not, because the word 'education' possesses attributes that do not allow it to be used with the other words making up the sentence.

Further evidence for underlying word patterns is the possibility of:
- substituting single words for any given word in the sentence, for example in the sentence 'The dog can run', 'run' can be replaced by a number of other words such as 'sleep', 'eat', 'drink'
- substituting a group of words for any one word in a sentence without altering the basic sentence pattern; for example, in the sentence 'The man who was sick lost his money', the group of words 'the man who was sick' may be replaced by a single word such as 'he' or 'John'.

Furthermore, non-verbal elements, such as intonation in speech and punctuation in writing, may also influence the interpretation of the sentence structure. For example, the sentence: 'You are going' with a rising intonation would indicate a question, while the same sentence with a falling intonation would indicate a statement. Consider also the effects of stressing particular words: 'You are going' ('you' is being distinguished from anybody else); 'You are going' (you are going and that's that); 'You are going' (you are not doing anything else, you are going). Similarly, different punctuation alters the meaning; compare the following: 'You are going?', 'You are going.' and 'You are going!' It is obvious that word order is very important in English, but it is only one of several factors that determine the meaning assigned to a sentence.

English sentences

Traditionally, English sentences were described in terms of their form and function. On the basis of form, sentences were divided into:

- simple: 'The boy sat'
- compound: 'The boy sat and cried' or 'The boy sat and he did his work'
- complex: 'The boy who was lonely sat down'
- compound-complex: 'The boy who was lonely sat down and cried', with an embedded sentence or clause 'who was lonely'.

On the basis of function, sentences were divided into:

- statements: 'It is a dog'
- exclamations: 'Will he be surprised!' (with a specific intonation)
- imperatives: 'John, do that'
- questions: 'What is this?' or 'Is this a dog?'.

Sentences were further described by reference to them being:

- either active or passive: for example, 'John hit the ball' (active) and 'The ball was hit by John' (passive)
- positive or negative: for example, 'Sue is working now' (positive) and 'Sue is not working now' (negative).

A more recent concept of syntax postulates that there is one underlying form. For English this underlying form is thought to be something like a simple, declarative, active, positive sentence. For example:

John hit the ball.

Sentences such as:

The ball was hit by John.
John did not hit the ball.
John didn't hit the ball.
Did John hit the ball?
The ball wasn't hit by John.
Who hit the ball?

all possess a close relationship to the postulated underlying form, 'John hit the ball'.

It is suggested that—through processes of addition, deletion, rearrangement, substitution, and contraction—these sentences have been derived from the underlying form. Linguists and psycholinguists postulate that users of a language code employ rules or processes similar to those outlined above.

A sentence is often referred to as a structured string of words. As has been discussed previously, this structure depends partly on the position of words in the sentence, the relationship between words, the type of words used, affixes and non-verbal elements.

Part of the structure of a sentence is formed by the grouping of words or the phrase structure of the sentence. Phrase structure may be

A recent concept postulates that there is one basic form underlying any variations of a particular sentence.

Part of the structure of a sentence is formed by the grouping of words or the phrase structure of the sentence.

described in a variety of ways. One of the simplest ways is to divide a sentence into segments or constituents; for example, the sentence:

The boy bought lollies.

may be divided into two parts roughly corresponding to the subject ('the boy') and predicate ('bought lollies'). Intuition will not allow the sentence to be divided in a way that would group 'boy' and 'bought' together: the constituents 'The boy' and 'bought lollies' go together. The constituents 'The boy' and 'bought lollies' may be further divided, and the breaks would occur in the following way:

the boy bought lollies
the boy / bought lollies
the / boy / bought / lollies

The accuracy of the divisions may be tested by substitution; for example, in the sentence, 'The boy bought some lollies', 'The boy' may be replaced by one word ('John'), and 'some lollies' may be replaced by one word ('food').

Each constituent is assigned a label; in the sentence (S) 'The man bought a car', the constituent 'the man' is referred to as a noun phrase (NP), and the constituent 'bought a car' is referred to as a verb phrase (VP). The VP may be further divided into verb (V) and the noun phrase (NP). NP may be further divided into determiner (Det) and noun (N).

Most sentences may be described by using phrase structure rewrite rules. For example, the sentence 'the man bought a car' can be described in the following way:

S: NP_1 + VP	where: V = bought
VP: V + NP_2	N_1 = man
NP_1: Det_1 + N_1	N_2 = car
NP_2: Det_2 + N_2	Det_1 = the
	Det_2 = a

A tree diagram is another way of illustrating the constituents of a sentence. The above sentence may be shown in the following way:

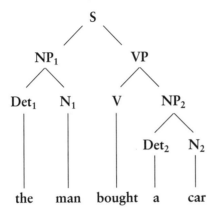

The ambiguity of some structures can be demonstrated via tree diagrams. Consider the following examples:

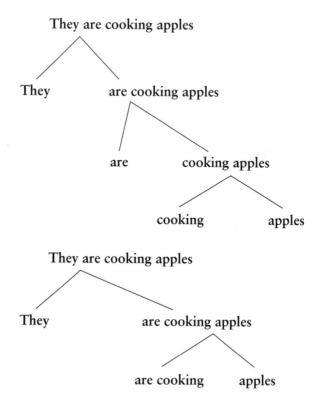

All sentences possess the two basic constituents of NP and VP. These basic constituents can be expanded. For example the NP 'the man' can be expanded to 'the man who lives next door' and 'a car' can be expanded by the addition of another NP 'and a house'.

The rules of syntax for speech and writing differ. Complete sentences are relatively rare in speech, whereas in writing they are the expected norm. Some structures are more common in one than the other. Some of these differences are discussed in more detail in chapter 8.

Summary

This section focused on:
- the nature of English syntax, showing the significance of word order and use of structure words in English syntax
- the nature of English sentences, the different types of sentences, and the relationship between the different parts of a sentence.

Morphology and lexicology

PRE-READING ACTIVITIES

I List any words you know of that have been borrowed from another language.

2 List any word games you have played such as crossword puzzles and Scrabble. What knowledge do you need to play these games?

3 Think about the spelling of English words and your spelling. What factors influence your spelling?

4 What strategies do you use when you spell? Share your responses.

Some definitions

Morphology is the study of the smallest meaningful units in speech and writing. Words are formed by one or more meaningful units (morphemes).

Lexicology is the study of words. As morphology studies the structure of words and lexicology extends this study to examine the role of words, the origins of words etc., it is useful to discuss these two closely related aspects together. These aspects are also frequently studied under the heading of syntax as they play a major role in understanding sentence structure. A study of words and word meanings is also very much a part of semantics, the study of meaning. Both the syntactical and semantic aspects of words are discussed in this section.

An understanding of morphology and lexicology is of great relevance to the teacher. Morphology has implications for understanding strategies of word recognition and spelling. Your understanding of words can greatly enhance students' excitement about language and words.

Morphology is the study of the smallest meaningful units (morphemes) in speech and writing.

Lexicology is the study of words.

What do you know about our words?

Language is more than words, but words are an integral part of speech and writing. As labels for concepts, words are tremendously influential in facilitating thinking. Each word is rich in different meanings and the information it conveys. For example, consider the word 'shovel': as well as telling you the name of the object, it gives you information on how it can be used, what it isn't, and you immediately think about what it is related to. In addition, the effective use of verbal language is characterised by the use of appropriate vocabulary. The mark of a good speaker or writer is the use of words—the types of words and how they are used to create vivid images and convey precise meanings.

Language is more than words, but words are an integral part of speech and writing. In their role as labels for concepts, words are tremendously influential in facilitating thinking.

Students' fun with language needs to be encouraged.

The effective language-user needs extensive listening, speaking, reading, and writing vocabularies. Students' interest in words needs to be fostered so their vocabularies can be expanded continually and their use of words refined. Also, students' fun with language needs to be encouraged. Students are renowned for creating riddles and puns outside the school environment. This needs to be legitimised and expanded as a valuable learning activity within the classroom.

To be able to foster an interest in words a teacher needs to demonstrate an interest in:

- new words
- interesting words
- different uses of words
- origins of words
- play with words.

The teacher can stimulate interest in words and their uses by sharing stories about the origins of words, encouraging students to investigate the origins of words, and fostering fun with words.

The teacher needs to know about the structure and formation of words in order to help students learn to spell and use effective word recognition strategies, and to use words effectively in their language.

The teacher also needs to know about the structure and formation of words in order to help students learn to spell, use effective word recognition strategies, and use words effectively in their language. We can study words from various perspectives such as:

- the structure of words, that is, morphology—the study of the smallest meaningful units of words
- the functions and roles words play in sentences (part of syntax)
- the characteristics of different words, such as the semantic features or properties of words (part of semantics)
- the origin of words
- the use of different types of words, such as contractions and abbreviations
- the relations between words, such as homophones, homographs, and synonyms
- uses of words in puns, metaphors, idioms, riddles, proverbs, euphemisms, colloquial expressions, and slang.

Some of these aspects are discussed below.

Morphology

Morphology is the study of the smallest meaningful units in speech and writing—morphemes. Words are formed by one or more morphemes. Each meaningful unit belongs to a morpheme; for example, the word 'cats' possesses two morphemes, 'cat' and the plural 's'.

In English there are two main types of morphemes: free and bound. Free morphemes can be used on their own in a sentence, for example 'cat', 'tree', 'hand'. A bound morpheme cannot exist on its own: it must be used in conjunction with another morpheme—bound or free: for example 's' in the word 'cats' is a bound morpheme. A word may have two or more meanings simultaneously, for example 'took' possesses two simultaneous meanings—'take' plus 'past'—which represent two morphemes. Further examples of this are the irregular past tense verbs in English, for example 'ran', 'went', 'stood'. Some morphemes have several different sounds and/or visual representations, but they all belong to the same morpheme because the same meaning is assigned to each; for example, the different variants of plural morphemes for nouns. Different representations of morphemes are called allomorphs—a subclass of the morpheme. For example the plural morpheme has a number of allomorphs: /s/ as in the word 'cats', /z/ as in the word 'dogs', /əz/ as in the word 'horses', and changes in the word itself—'mice' for 'mouse'.

Evidence of children's acquisition of morphemes is provided when they overgeneralise and make mistakes, and say 'footses', 'mouses', or 'runned'.

Free and bound morphemes can be used in the following ways to form words:
- one free morpheme, for example 'house'
- two or more free morphemes, for example 'blackboard', 'greenhouse', 'jack-in-the-box'; these are often called compound words
- one or more free morphemes and one or more bound morphemes, for example 'houses', 'blackboards', 'deschooling'.

Creating words

From the above examples it can be seen that bound morphemes are the same as affixes. There are two types of affixes—prefixes and suffixes. Prefixes act as initial markers for a change in meaning of the base word, for example 'un' indicates the negative, 'not' the opposite of. Suffixes also assist as end-markers of changes in meaning, but often they also change the class of the word; for example, an adjective ('sad') can be changed to a noun by adding 'ness' ('sadness').

Compound words are formed by joining together two or more free morphemes. These morphemes may come from the same word class—for example, two nouns or two verbs—or from different word classes—for example, verb and noun, or adjective and verb, as illustrated in Table 6.1.

Table 6.1 Compound words formed by combining adjectives, nouns, and verbs

	-adjective	-noun	-verb
Adjective	bittersweet	poorhouse	highborn
Noun	headstrong	rainbow	spoonfeed
Verb	carryall	pickpocket	sleepwalk

V. Fromkin et al., *An Introduction to Language*, p. 52.

New words are continually being created this way, especially in advertising. List any you can think of. Your students can create lists of known compound words and create new words.

Some words are formed by blending two words together. For example, 'smog' from 'smoke' and 'fog'; 'motel' from 'motor' and 'hotel'; and 'brunch' from 'breakfast' and 'lunch'. These are sometimes called portmanteau words. Other words are formed by clipping the original word; for example, 'ad', 'bike', 'gas', 'bus', 'gym'. There is a common rule regarding the length of a word and its frequency, which is that words used frequently are shortened.

Some words are formed by using the initials of a number of words; for example, 'scuba' is from 'self-contained underwater breathing apparatus'. Other examples include laser, radar, jeep, posh, AIDS and Anzac. These are called acronyms. Acronyms are different from abbreviations (ABC, NSW, i.e., Vic.,) and contractions (Mr, St, Rd) in that the acronym is pronounced and functions as if it were a word in its own right. Other words are coined or invented for new discoveries and concepts, such as 'nylon' (developed originally from the idea of 'no run'). Yet others that are derived from people's names—such as pasteurisation, cardigan, and sandwich—are called eponyms. Sometimes words originate from place names, such as 'dalmatian', or are developed from old Latin or Greek roots, for example 'vitamins' from the Latin vita meaning 'life'.

The function of words in sentences

Words in a language may be assigned to word classes on the basis of their role in a sentence, that is, their syntactic role and morphological structure. Some of the terms used for traditional parts of speech can be used as names of classes when categorising words according to their function, such as noun, verb, adjective, adverb, determiner, negative, preposition, conjunction, and pronoun. These classes may be determined through an examination of the role that words play in sentences. In the following sentences words from only certain classes can be inserted sensibly in the spaces:

The................was good (noun)
The boy................to the party (verb)

Words are assigned to word classes partly on the basis of their syntactic function. As a result, some words may be classified under more than one class, such as the word 'round' in the following:

One round is enough (noun)
You round the bends too quickly (verb)
A round tower (adjective)
He came round (adverb)
He wandered round the table (preposition)

Hence it is useless to classify words as parts of speech in isolation.

Words can also be classified according to the kind of meaning they carry. Some words possess meaning even when used alone, such as 'boy', 'run', and 'beautiful', and are often referred to as 'content' words. Other words have meaning only when used with content words. These are referred to as 'function' or 'structure' words, such as 'and', 'the', 'a', and 'not'. These words play an important part in providing syntactic structure to the sentence. Children sometimes have difficulty learning to recognise these words in reading, especially if they have been taught in isolation. They need a context to have meaning and hence to be learnable.

Words can also be classified according to the kind of meaning they carry.

Semantic features or properties of words

All words possess certain attributes, and rules operate as to which words can be used together. Consider the nouns that could fill the space in this sentence:

All words possess certain attributes, and rules operate as to which words can be used together.

> The.....................was good

all possess at least the following attributes:

- they are common nouns as opposed to proper nouns, that is, not a proper noun such as a name of a person or place
- they are concrete as opposed to abstract, that is, something you can see, hear, feel
- they are 'count nouns' as opposed to 'mass nouns', that is, they can be counted individually, like peas, whereas a mass such as water cannot.

Words can also possess other features. They can be animate or inanimate, human or non-human, male or female, young or old. As in other levels of linguistic study, there are rules about how different nouns are used. Nouns that are abstract cannot be used with verbs that possess concrete, animate features; for example, it is not sensible to say 'loneliness walks fast'. Common errors made by people when they substitute one word for another usually share common semantic features, which indicates something about how we process words; for example, referring to 'blond eyes' instead of 'blond hair'.

Origins of words

History of the English language

To appreciate the origins of a large proportion of English words, it is necessary to understand the history of the English language. A language is continually in a state of flux and any significant event influences the introduction of new words, makes some words more prominent, and changes the meaning of some words (for example, 'space race', 'Watergate').

A language is continually in a state of flux and any significant event influences the introduction of new words, makes some words more prominent, and changes the meaning of some words.

English belongs to the Indo-Hittite language group. This family covers languages in most or all of Europe and parts of Asia, great sections of Africa, and all of North and South America and Australia. Modern English developed from an old Germanic language and there have been major influences from French, Latin, and Greek. See Table 6.2 for an overview of the influences on English.

Table 6.2   A history of the English language

Date	Historical events	Influence on the language
1st–4th centuries	First Roman invasion of England by Julius Caesar 55–54 BC	No English, only Celtic languages
5th century	Anglo-Saxon invasion; Angles, Saxons, and Jutes settled, bringing Germanic dialects to different parts of England	**Old English** The low west Germanic dialects fused to make Old English, very little borrowing of Celtic words; runic alphabet for magic spells and inscriptions; oral literature
6th–7th centuries	Second Roman invasion; the coming of Christianity to England	Extended writing introduced by monks
787–886	Viking raids; some Danes settled; King Alfred the Great made a treaty with Vikings	Books destroyed; many books translated into Old English
1066–1200	Norman Conquest; rulers were French	French became the language of power; French words were assimilated into English; English people learn French
1150–1500	Universities established; extension of education; Middle English used in schools; Chaucer's *Canterbury Tales* (1387–1400); in 1476 Caxton set up the printing press in London	**Middle English** By late 1200s French ceases to be the dominant language; many English dialects; London English becomes the standard form of English
15th–16th centuries	The Renaissance; great expansion of learning	**Modern English** Borrowings of words from Latin, Greek, French, etc.

Table 6.2   cont'd

Date	Historical events	Influence on the language
16th–18th centuries	Colonising and trade movements; Johnson's *Dictionary* (1755); Latin-based grammar books	Many new words introduced from the Americas and West Indies; spelling standardised
19th–20th centuries	Interaction of colonial forms of English with British English; major events, wars, the space race, technology	Development of American English and Australian English; formation of new words
1950s	Fries—descriptive grammar	
1957–1965	Chomsky—syntax, transformational grammar	Research into children's grammar
1970–1990	Halliday—language in context; functional grammars	Research into language use, language of power

The Anglo-Saxon conquest of Britain late in the sixth century resulted in a whole new group of people settling there. Their language became dominant, with very few traces of the Celtic language remaining in old English or modern English.

The Viking invasion of England during the ninth century also left its mark on the language. Modern words that have Viking origins include 'by-law', 'crave' and 'riding' (as in the electoral division). Many common, frequently used words originated from the Vikings, such as:

Nouns		Adjectives	Verbs	Pronouns
sister	dirt	wrong	give	they
leg	skill	low	call	them
neck	bag	loose	want	
window	cake	odd	take	
sky	fog	flat		
knife	fellow			

The Norman conquest of 1066 heralded a strong French influence on English. For some centuries English ceased to be the language of the governing classes and, when it did again become the language of the country, it had changed greatly because of the French influence. Hence, many of our words to do with government and law are French loan words, for example:

There have been three major phases of Latin-based influence on English: the time of the Roman invasions and conversions; the Norman conquest during the eleventh century; and then during the Renaissance, from the fourteenth to the sixteenth centuries.

sovereign	duke	chancellor	prison
prince	government	nation	verdict
punish	crown	people	sentence
marquis	state	county	attorney
count	parliament	justice	plea
baron	council	judge	accuse
crime			

As French was the language of the ruling class, many French loan words were also concerned with religion, war, fashion, and art:

religion	abbey	armour	dress	column
service	friar	battle	costume	paint
saviour	clergy	castle	apparel	music
virgin	parish	tower	art	chant
saint	prayer	war	beauty	poem
relic	sermon	cruelty	colour	romance
mercy	charity	fashion	courtesy	obedience

Many French loan words and old English words that possess similar meanings are still in use today:

English	French loan	English	French loan
king	sovereign	hearty	cordial
queen	prince	holy doon	saint
lord	peer	stench	perfume
lady	count	bill	beak
knight	baron, duke	help	aid
house	manor, place	begin	commence
man, maid	butler, servant	end	terminate
*calf	*veal	feed	nourish
*ox	*beef	hinder	prevent
*swine	*pork	deed	action
*sheep	*mutton	dale	valley
folk	people		

It is interesting to note that the old English words for animals ('calf', 'ox', 'swine', 'sheep') have survived while the French words have been retained for the dressed flesh ('veal', 'beef', 'pork', 'mutton'). This was probably due to the fact that the farmers spoke English and the upper class spoke French. A somewhat similar distinction can be found for terms that refer to body parts and functions—old English words are frequently taboo words today, whereas the French and Latin words for the same body parts and functions are acceptable as polite alternatives.

Early in its history, the English language was influenced by Latin in two different ways: by the Roman invasion of Britain; and by the contact of English people with the European continent. Our modern words 'street', 'mint', and 'wine' have Latin origins, entering the English language during the Roman invasion. The following words also have Latin origins, but entered the language during the Middle English period (1150–1500):

requiem	recipe	adoption	species
gloria	dissolve	conflict	radius
client	distillation	dissent	apparatus
executor	concrete	imaginary	pollen
conviction	comet	implication	
memorandum	equator	genius	

During the Renaissance, the Latin influence on English was considerable. Although Latin was the main source of new words at the time, a number were borrowed from other languages. Quite a few were from classical Greek, although in many cases they entered the language via Latin or French. Many of them were technical terms of literary criticism, rhetoric, or natural science, such as: 'pathos', 'phone', and 'rhapsody' (direct from Greek); 'irony', 'drama', 'rhythm', and 'climax' (via Latin); and 'ode', 'elegy', and 'scene' (via French). Some scientific terms came direct from Greek, for example 'cosmos', and others came via French, for example 'cube' and 'acoustic'. However, the majority of scientific terms came via Latin, including 'anemone', 'caustic', 'cylinder', 'stigma', 'python', 'electric', and 'energy'. Virtually all medical and anatomical terms have come from Latin. Essentially, Latin was the language of scholars and academia.

Quite a number of words were also borrowed from Italian and Spanish. Italian has contributed such words as 'madrigal', 'opera', 'sonnet', 'fresco', 'cornice', 'squadron', 'parapet', 'bandit', 'traffic', 'contraband', and 'frigate', whereas 'cash', 'cargo', 'anchovy', 'sherry', 'armada', 'parade', 'guitar', 'mosquito', 'potato', and 'cannibal' have come from Spanish. In some cases, it is difficult to determine which language contributed which words because French, Italian, Spanish (and Romanian) are 'Romance languages', which means that they have descended from Latin, and consequently have many words (or forms of words) in common.

Widespread colonising by the British, and growth of world trade, has brought English into contact with many new objects, experiences, cultures, and languages. Hence many new words have been borrowed and created. This is an ongoing process.

Widespread colonising by the English, and the growth of world trade, has brought the English language into contact with many new cultures and languages.

The nature of English spelling

As the above discussion demonstrates, there have been many influences on English, which has implications for English spelling. It is of interest to explore further the nature of English spelling.

The English writing system is alphabetic (that is, it uses a set of letter symbols which make words when combined). In contrast, Chinese is logographic (that is, it uses signs which represent entire words). The alphabet possesses twenty-six letters, which can be used to represent more than forty English phonemes. As stated previously, there is no way that a one-to-one relationship exists between sound and letter in our current spelling system, although at one time more words were spelled in a more regular way. Pronunciations have changed over years, while spellings have remained relatively static. Furthermore, the many borrowings from other languages have introduced words that possess different spelling patterns.

There are many appeals for spelling changes, but even if we had an alphabet of forty letters there would still be many problems in representing speech in a phonetically regular way. Which English dialect would you represent—British, American, or Australian? As it is, the spelling of English represents no particular dialect and any attempt to make English spelling a closer reflection of one particular dialect would make it more difficult for everyone else who did not speak it. Not only can written English be read by speakers of a wide variety of dialects around the world, it can be written by speakers of a wide variety of dialects.

Today, spelling is very consistent and conventional, although that was not always the case. Shakespeare repeatedly spelled his name in different ways. However, widespread publishing and literacy has fostered a very strong community belief in a fixed conventional way of spelling. Great value is placed on correct spelling today.

Factors influencing English spelling

Before about AD 1500, English words were spelled as they were pronounced; that is, spellings varied from place to place according to the variation of their dialect pronunciations. Over the years a number of factors have been important in providing us with our present spelling system:

- Professional scribes disliked the confusing repetition of up-down strokes in words like 'wimin', 'munk', 'wunder', 'muney', and 'luv'. To facilitate rapid writing the scribes changed the spellings to 'women, 'monk', 'wonder', 'money', 'love', thereby creating the first irregular English words.
- Typing and publishing (with the invention of the printing press) created a need for consistency in spelling and led to a gradual standardisation of spellings.
- Many early printers were Dutch who were unsure how English speakers pronounced certain words, thus they put 'ch' in 'yacht' because the equivalent Dutch word contained a consonant similar to that in the Scottish pronunciation of the word 'loch'.
- Influential spelling reformers in the 15th and 16th centuries wanted to alter spellings to reflect the Latin or Greek origins of words at the expense of phonetic regularity. Thus 'dette' became 'debt', 'doute' became 'doubt', and 'sutil' became 'subtle'. Sometimes the reformers got it wrong. For example, they introduced a 'c' in 'scissors' and 'scythe' because they thought (wrongly) that both words derived from the Latin word scindere

There are many appeals for spelling changes, but even if we had an alphabet of 40 letters, there would still be problems in attempting to represent speech phonetically because of the many different dialects.

Today, spelling is very consistent and conventional, although that was not always the case.

There are a number of factors that have influenced English spelling, and these include the appearance of the written word, the growth of typing and publishing, the application of spellings from other languages, the desire to reflect the origins of the word, and pronunciation changes.

(to cleave); similarly 'anchor' ('h' introduced from 'anchorite' although there is no 'h' in ancora, the Latin). Other examples are 's' in 'island' (iland) and 'h' in 'hour' (oure). None of these letters has ever been pronounced in English.

- Creation of dictionaries led to greater consistency and conventional use. In Britain, Dr Samuel Johnson's *Dictionary* (1755) reflected current educated usage. In the USA Noah Webster wrote his *Dissertations on the English Language* in 1789 in which he proposed a standard language for the newly independent nation. When he compiled his *American Dictionary of the English Language* (1828), he eliminated 'u' in 'our' words, such as 'favour' and 'colour', and he abolished a few double letters in words, transforming 'waggon' to 'wagon'.

- There have been pronunciation changes since the move to consistent spelling, which have led to greater numbers of irregularly spelled words. For example, 'k' was originally pronounced in 'knave' and 'knife'; 'l' was originally pronounced in 'would' and 'should'; and the 'gh' in 'right', 'light', 'bought' and 'eight' was pronounced something like the 'ch' in 'loch'. Rather than change the spelling to match the altered pronunciation, we are left with certain anomalies: we have 't' in 'often' (which is frequently pronounced [ɒfən]) and the spellings of 'anthem' and 'theatre', which were originally pronounced using [t] not [θ] or 'th' (the 'h' was introduced to match Greek spelling, and pronunciation eventually altered to reflect the changed appearance of the words). In Chaucer's time (14th century), 'meet' and 'meat' were pronounced differently.

- There are orthographic rules, which are concerned solely with the internal structure of the orthography, the spelling system itself. The trend of consistency in spelling brought with it rules about spelling that had nothing to do with sound. Certain letter combinations are not allowed: for example, 'ie' in 'lie' and 'die' is changed to 'y' in front of 'ing' to make 'lying', 'dying', to avoid the 'iei' combination; and 'y' is changed to 'ie' when adding 's' as in 'party' and 'parties' because 'consonant-ys' is not a conventional ending in English words. Words such as 'nave', 'love', 'move' all have a non-functional 'e' at the end because English words do not end with 'v'. Origins of words have been a major factor in our spelling, as discussed above. English possesses words from many languages and, although words are anglicised, they frequently retain some characteristics of the original spelling. Teachers should have an understanding of the history of English and the origins of words, and be able to share some of this with students.

- Morphographic structure, that is, the meaning base of words, has great influence on English spelling. Written English represents poorly the sounds of English mainly because the representation of the sounds of speech is of a relatively low priority for spelling.

There are two other considerations that are more important: consistency (as discussed above) and the representation of meaning. A basic principle operates: words, or parts of words with similar meanings, should be spelled alike. Understanding this principle is an important strategy for spellers. For example, if you are unsure whether 'muscle' has 'c' in it, think of other related words, such as 'muscular'; similarly, the 'g' in 'signature' means that there is a 'g' in 'sign'. Meaning would be much less clear if we allowed spelling to follow the idiosyncrasies of speech—for example, plurals would be more irregular, as would past tense. This is one facet of spelling that makes life easier for both the reader and writer.

ACTIVITIES AND DISCUSSION

1 A morpheme is the smallest meaningful unit of speech or writing. Two types of morphemes are free and bound morphemes. Give an example of a word with:
   • three morphemes
   • three syllables but one morpheme
   • three syllables but two morphemes.

2 How many morphemes are represented in each of the following words?

   children   detrimental   furniture   went

   Give the meaning and origin of each morpheme
   Note: Remember, you are dealing with meaning units not syllables.

3 Give an example of a word that possesses the following attributes

   +noun   +common   -animate   +count

4 What attributes does the word 'education' possess?

5 What do the following groups of words have in common?
   (a) pasteurisation   (b) posh   (c) telly
       cardigan   scuba   phone
       sandwich   radar   petrol
       pavlova   laser   caf
       lamington   snafu   uni
       mackintosh
       volt

   (d) smog   (e) Baker   (f) blackboard
       motel   Clerk   bittersweet
       urinalysis   Butler   corkscrew
       brunch   Butcher   pickpocket
                             Taylor
                             Smith

(g) cottage
beak
terminate
valley
manor/palace
veal/beef
pork

(h) house
bill
end
dale
hut
cow
pig

(i) denim
dalmatian
bikini

(j) xerox
kleenex
thermos
primus

(k) nylon
dacron

(l) strafe
blitz
panzer

(m) unlikely
denationalise
prewar
anti-uranium
vaporise

(n) oxygen
uranium
benzene
vitamin

(o) passed away
visit the bathroom

(p) it's raining cats
and dogs
slip of the tongue
pay through the nose
bury the hatchet
spill the beans
open a can of
worms

(q) bottom of the
harbour

(r) Jackson
Adamczyk
MacAdam
Cohen

(s) Bruno
Reid
Rosen
Stalin
Weiss
Armstrong

(t) Echols
Romero
Brook
Stone
Mill

(u) guppy
lynch
boycott
bloomer

(v) Ballarat
Canberra
Dandenong
Kalgoorlie

(w) dingo
boomerang

Can you think of other words for the different lists?

Summary

By now you will be aware of:
- the importance of understanding the meaning components of words
- the importance of using your insights about the structure of words to help students become aware of the meaning bases of words for their reading and spelling

- the value of the concept of allomorphs to explain variations in word structures, such as plural endings
- the attributes of words, which again can assist you in helping students understand the use of words
- the value of understanding the origins of words as a means of explaining the reasons for differences in spelling patterns, and as a language study which enables you to capitalise on the interest and knowledge of students with different cultural/language backgrounds.

Implications for teaching

1   Using the words that students meet in their reading and writing, help them to see why words are spelt in particular ways in the English language and that spelling is related to the meaning of words.

2   Draw attention to the relationship between words in the same word families, based on derivations, and how new words can be formed by adding prefixes and suffixes in semantic groups (for example, success, successful, successfully, unsuccessful). Students can have fun making up their own words. A study of the use of language in advertising and the environment also highlights how words are created and given new meanings, such as the use of the words 'down' and 'up' in many expressions.

3   A study of changes in vocabulary over the years (for example, comparing the differences in vocabulary when students' parents were children), develops an interest in language, as well as developing an awareness of the dynamic nature of a language and an understanding of the nature of meaning as represented by words.

4   Do not expect words to be learnt in isolation, particularly the structure words such as 'a', 'and', 'as', 'an', 'in', 'not', and 'but'. These words will be learned only by lots of exposure in meaningful contexts.

References and further reading

Artman J. *Language: Activities and Ideas on the History and the Nature of Language*, Good Apple, Carthage, IL, 1980.

*Bean W. & Bouffler C. *Spell by Writing*, Primary English Teaching Association, Rozelle, NSW, 1987.

*Burridge K. *Blooming English: Observations on the Roots, Cultivation and Hybrids of English*, ABC Books, Sydney, 2002

*Burridge K. & Mulder J. *English in Australia and New Zealand*, Oxford University Press, Melbourne, 1998.

Crystal D. *The Cambridge Encyclopedia of the English Language*, Cambridge University Press, Cambridge, 1995.

Fries P. *The Structure of English*, Longman, London, 1957.

*Fromkin V., Rodman R., Collins P. & Blair D. *An Introduction to Language*, 3rd Aust. edn, Harcourt Brace, Sydney, 1996.

*Halliday M. A. K. *Spoken and Written Language*, Deakin University, Geelong, Vic., 1985.

*Lindfors J. *Children's Language and Learning*, 2nd edn, Prentice-Hall, Englewood Cliffs, NJ, 1987, pp. 35–51.

Palmer F. *Grammar*, Penguin, Harmondsworth, 1971.

*Primary English Teaching Association of NSW 'A Sense of History', Primary English Notes, Primary English Teaching Association of NSW, Rozelle, NSW, 1981.

Roberts P. *English Sentences*, Harcourt, Brace & World, New York, 1962.

*Scraggs D. G. *A History of English Spelling*, University Press, Manchester, 1974.

*Stubbs M. *Language and Literacy: The Sociolinguistics of Reading Writing*, Routledge & Kegan Paul, London, 1980, Chapters 2, 4.

ANSWERS TO ACTIVITIES AND DISCUSSION

1 Three morphemes: blackboards; three syllables, one morpheme: elephant; three syllables, two morphemes: elephant-s.

2 Children: two morphemes; detrimental: two morphemes in modern English (in the original French it had four); furniture: two morphemes; went: in modern English 'went' has two morphemes (to go and past).

3 Attributes of +noun +common -animate +count: table

4 Education has the following attributes: + noun + common -animate, -count.

5 (a) Names of people; (b) acronyms; (c) shortened words; (d) blended words; (e) occupations to surnames; (f) compound words; (g) French words; (h) old English words; (i) words formed from place names; (j) brand names; (k) coined words; (l) German war words; (m) words with affixes; (n) words coined from Latin or Greek roots; (o) euphemisms; (p) idioms; (q) recently coined idioms; (r) equivalent of son affixed to surname; (s) surnames formed from adjectives; (t) surnames formed from names; (u) historical incidents that have led to words with specific meanings; (v) place names formed from Aboriginal words; (w) Aboriginal words.

CHAPTER 7

PHONOLOGY AND THE RELATIONSHIP BETWEEN LETTERS AND SOUNDS

FOCUS

This chapter focuses on the understanding that:

- *understanding the relationship between speech and writing is important for teaching reading and writing*
- *there is not a one-to-one relationship between sounds and letters in English, and this has implications for assisting people to learn to read and write*
- *different languages possess different sounds and use sounds differently, and this has implications for the learning of a second language.*

PRE-READING ACTIVITIES

1 List all the English speech sounds that you can think of. How many did you get?

2 List the reasons why a teacher should know about the relationships between letters and sounds. Share your responses.

Why study phonology and letter–sound knowledge?

It is important to understand the relationship between sounds and letters in order to assist learners at the early stages of literacy development.

It is very important to understand the relationship between sounds and letters in order to assist learners at the early stages of literacy development. For example, to be able to read students' invented or temporary spellings you need to appreciate their linguistic backgrounds and what they are trying to learn. As we become literate we tend to think of words as being made up of letters rather than sounds, and we tend to assume that letters represent sounds on a one-to-one basis. This contrasts with beginning reader/writers who have competent knowledge of the sounds of words, but minimal knowledge of the spelling. They have to match whatever letters they know with the sounds they can hear in the word. To help learners develop appropriate phonic (letter–sound) knowledge, you, the teacher, must have accurate, explicit knowledge of these relationships. Too frequently learners are given misleading information that clearly does not assist their learning and often creates confusion. For example, teachers sometimes teach that the letter 'a' is pronounced /æ/ (as in 'cat'), but the letter 'a' can represent a number of different sounds (for example, 'father', 'make', or 'rare').

In addition, in order to help second-language learners, it is important to understand the sound system of English and appreciate how it may differ from other languages. Furthermore, if you have an appreciation of the production of sounds you may, in co-operation with a speech pathologist, be able to help a student with an articulation problem.

> Too often, learners are given misleading information that clearly does not assist their learning and often must create confusion in their minds.

Phonetics and phonology

The sounds of speech are studied in phonetics and phonology. Phonetics is the study of articulation and acoustic phenomena, which make it possible to produce and perceive speech sounds. It provides us with tools and descriptive terms to describe as minutely as is necessary any speech sound, regardless of the language system. It uses insights from anatomy, physiology, physics, and psychology.

> Phonetics is the study of the articulate and acoustic phenomena that make it possible to produce and perceive speech-sounds.

Phonology is more strictly linguistic. It is the study of the sound systems of particular languages and develops general principles that are applicable to sound systems of all languages.

> Phonology is more strictly linguistic than phonetics, being the study of sound systems of particular languages.

Phonology in speech and graphology in writing are the study of the smallest set of sounds, called phonemes. It appears that there is a bank of human speech sounds. Different languages use some of the sounds and not others, and sometimes they use these sounds differently from other languages. For example, in some Aboriginal languages there are six nasals whereas English has only three; in the Aboriginal languages /r/ cannot normally occur initially, and there are three vowels which usually don't occur initially in a word. In New Zealand English there is very little difference in the pronunciation of the words 'six' and 'sex'. In Australian English, where the vowel sound in 'six' is represented [ɪ] and that in 'sex' is [e], in New Zealand English they would both be [ɨ].

> It appears that there is a bank of human speech sounds and different languages use some of the sounds and not others.

Among other factors, the use of different phonemes makes it difficult to learn another language, especially for adults who find it difficult to hear new sounds and produce them. For example, because the sounds /r/ and /l/ are not distinctive phonemes in Japanese, native Japanese speakers often interchange the letters that represent them when writing in English.

This section examines the sounds of English, how they relate to the letters of English, and the implications for the teacher.

How are speech-sounds produced?

The sounds of English are made when we expel air (in some languages speech sounds can be made when inhaling). It is a little like blowing through a tube. If you change the shape of the tube you obtain different sounds. If you open your mouth and make a sound, you will produce a vowel sound. If you change the shape of your mouth, you will produce the different vowel sounds. If you block the airflow in any way, for example by closing and then opening your mouth, you will produce a consonant sound.

The sounds of a speech code can be described by referring to how the sounds are produced. Generally speech sounds are produced by air being expelled from the lungs, passing through the vocal folds (cords) and out through the mouth and/or nose.

Modification to the airflow produces the different sounds of a language. Figure 7.1 shows where different types of speech sounds are produced.

Figure 7.1   Place of articulation of English consonants

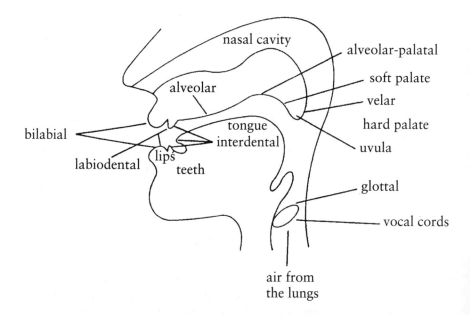

Definitions of some common terms

A number of terms are used to describe different patterns of letters and sounds. These are generally a part of the teaching vocabulary and should become part of your vocabulary. Some of these terms are:

blend: a combination of two or three consonants pronounced so that each sound keeps its own identity, for example scrap.

digraph: two letters representing a single sound; for example 'th', 'ph', 'ng', 'ee', 'ea'.

diphthong: a vowel blend sound where one vowel sound glides onto another, producing only one vowel sound, for example in Australian English the vowel sounds in 'day', 'coin', 'side'.

schwa: also known as the reduced or indistinct vowel, a common sound in English and is the cause of many spelling errors. For example, in speech, the first vowel in the word 'above' is a schwa. Can you think of other words where there is an indistinct vowel? It is represented by the symbol /ə/.

syllable: a sound pattern with a vowel as a nucleus; for example, 'at', 'hum', 'un'.

phonics: a teaching term for referring to sound–letter relationships.

Different types of sounds

There are two broad categories of speech sounds—vowels and consonants. Vowels are produced with minimal obstruction to the flow of air from the lungs. Changing the shape of the mouth produces the different vowels. In English there are approximately twenty vowels and diphthongs, but we have only five vowel letters—a, e, i, o, u.

Consonants are sounds that are produced with some obstruction to the airflow. Figure 7.1 indicates the different places where obstruction can occur. Sounds are classified according to the place and name of articulation. When first attempting to spell, young children use place of articulation as a clue as to what letters to use. For example, sounds with similar articulation may be represented by the one letter.

Sounds can be classified according to the place and manner of articulation. The place of articulation may be the use of two lips (known as *bilabial*), use of the upper teeth and lower lip *(labiodental)*, use of the upper and lower teeth and tongue tip *(interdental)*, point at which the tongue tip contacts the roof of the mouth *(alveolar)*, point at which the blade of the tongue contacts the roof of the mouth *(alveolar–palatal)*, point at which the back portion of the tongue contacts the rear portion of the roof of the mouth or soft palate *(velar)*, or opening when the vocal cords are apart *(glottal)*. The manner of articulation or quality of sound produced (or phonemes) can be voiced or unvoiced. We have voiced and unvoiced phonemes. All vowels are voiced, and phonemes of similar voicing status tend to go together; for example, *plosive* (complete stop and then explosion of air), *nasal* (using the nasal cavity), *fricative* (friction occurring when some air still passes, not a complete stop), *lateral* (air passing round the side of the tongue), or *rolled* (tongue is rolled, obstructing airflow).

The variety of sounds in spoken English are produced by combining place and manner of articulation (see Table 7.1).

Vowels are produced with minimal obstruction to the airflow from the lungs.

Consonants are sounds that are produced with some obstruction to the airflow.

There are voiced and unvoiced phonemes. Phonemes of similar voicing status tend to go together.

Table A.1   Classification of English consonants

		Bilabial	Labiodental	Interdental	Alveolar	Alveolar-palatal	Palatal-velar	Glottal
Plosive	vl	p			t		k	
	vd	b			d		g	
Nasal	vd	m			n		ŋ	
Lateral				l				
Rolled					r			
Fricative	vl		f	θ	s	ʃ		h
	vd		v	ð	z	ʒ		
Semi-vowels	vd	w					j	

θ as in *thin*
ð as in *thine*
ʃ as in fi*sh*
tʃ as in *choke*
dʒ as in *job*
ʒ as in azure
ŋ as in si*ng*

EXERCISES

1 Make the /s/ and /z/ phonemes while placing your fingers on your
larynx (throat). You should feel a vibration when you produced the /z/
sound that was absent when you produced the /s/ sound. This
vibration indicates voicing. Voicing or the absence of it is the difference
between these pairs of phonemes.

2 Consider the plurals of words such as 'cot' and 'dog'. The word 'cot'
ends in /t/ which is voiceless. To make it plural we add /s/ which is also
voiceless. In contrast, the word 'dog' ends in /g/ (voiced); when we
make the word plural we add /z/ (voiced). The same phenomenon
occurs when transforming some verbs, such as 'jump' and 'drag', into
past tense. The word 'jump' ends in /p/ which is voiceless and we make
it past tense by adding /t/, which is also voiceless. In contrast, the word
'drag' ends in a voiced sound /g/ so we add a voiced sound /d/.
Children's early spelling attempts such as 'jumpt' and 'dogz' reflect their
accurate hearing of the words. We need to appreciate this and
respond accordingly, not simply criticise their attempts.

3 In any speech code the phonemes are combined in certain ways. In
English some consonants never occur together in certain positions, for
example 'tl' at the beginning of the word. Similarly, certain letter
patterns do not occur in English in writing. As users of a language we
come to know what sounds or looks right. This knowledge of how
English words look is an important part of learning to spell. List other
sound combinations that do not occur in English.

In any speech code the
phonemes are combined in
certain ways.

4 It is important to be clear about the relationship between sounds and
letters if you want to give accurate feedback to beginning readers and
writers. Test your awareness on the following activities. Remember you
are thinking of phonemes—distinctive sounds—not letters.

- How many phonemes are represented in the following words?

    elephant   giraffe   school   bomb   sang

- How many syllables are in the following words?

    dereliction   flora   houri   June
    skein   treacherous   corruptibility   barked

- Which of the following words ends with a consonant sound?

    piano   baby   relay   pencil   below

- In which of the following words does the letter 'c' represent a less
  frequently used sound?

    city   cat   chair   Chicago

- In which of the following words does the letter 'g' represent a less
  frequently used sound?

    great   go   ghost   rig   none of these

- If 'tife' were a word, the letter 'i' would probably sound like the 'i' in:

  if   beautiful   find   ceiling   sing   I

- An example of a reduced vowel is found in:

  cotton   phoneme   stopping   preview   grouping

- A diphthong is found in which of the following spoken words?

  coat   boy   battle   retarded   slow

5 Using the list of Australian English phonemes in Appendix 1 do the following:
   — choose three consonant phonemes and write down all the letters that can be used to represent each phoneme: for example /f/ can be represented by 'f', 'ft', 'ph', 'gh', 'ff'
   — choose a vowel letter and give examples of words in which this letter represents a different phoneme; for example 'a' represents different sounds in each of these words: bat, mate, car, aisle, dawn, mortgage, sugar.

Suprasegmental phonemes

Besides the phonemes discussed previously, other sound features are important in speech. These are stress, pitch, and juncture. Together they make up the intonation pattern of speech that enables our speech to have great flexibility and indicates grammatical features such as mood, modality, and so on.

Stress

Technically, it is not easy to describe stress, but few native speakers of a language have difficulty in recognising it when they hear it. They can tell you that in 'forget' the second syllable is stressed and in 'later' the first syllable is stressed. If asked how they know, most people will say that the relevant syllable is louder. Apart from a few words like 'controversy', where usage tends to vary (*controversy* and contro*versy*) there is a normal stress pattern in each word that is recognised and followed by all native speakers. In English, however, there is no one uniform place for the stress, which causes difficulties for second-language learners of English. Stress differences can be heard in pairs of words; for example, compare 'a present' with 'to present' or 'your conduct' with 'to conduct'.

In English there is no one uniform place for stress.

Pitch

Pitch is caused by the varying rapidity of vibration of the vocal cords. The more rapid the vibration, the higher the pitch. Changing the pitch frequency results in a change of tone. Pitch and tone are important in tonal languages, such as Chinese. Here, by changing the tone of a word, the meaning is changed. It is usually considered that English speakers use four tones. They are used, however, within a sentence, not within an individual word as in Chinese.

Pitch is caused by the varying rapidity of vibration of the vocal cords.

Juncture

Juncture is the slight pause between elements of speech (syllables, words, sentences), which is usually more anticipated than heard by the native speaker. The native speaker senses the difference between: 'It's a nice house' and 'It's an ice house'. Clearly, interpretation is assisted by the context.

Juncture is the slight pause between elements of speech, which is often more anticipated than heard by the native speaker.

Paralinguistic features

In speech there are other features that play an important part in conveying and receiving meaning. As you no doubt are aware, gestures, facial expressions, and voice features (such as quality of the voice and other non-speech sounds) all play a part in communication. These are called paralinguistic features.

Other features of speech that are important in conveying and receiving meaning include gestures, facial expressions, and voice features.

ACTIVITIES

1   Try saying the following words, which are examples that illustrate the use of *stress* to carry meaning (in this case, to differentiate between nouns and verbs):

Noun	*Verb*
incense	incense
permit	permit
insult	insult
reject	reject

2   The following sentence can be said as a statement declaring a fact or as a question:

She is a singer.

Think of two more examples of sentences that differ in the use of pitch.

3   Try saying the following words:

night rate	nitrate
an aim	a name

Think of two other pairs of words that show the use of *juncture* in spoken English

The activities you have undertaken here should have made you appreciate the complexity of the relationship between sounds and letters. Obviously there is not a one-to-one relationship, as we have 26 letters of the alphabet and more than 40 phonemes. Some letters can represent a number of phonemes, and a phoneme can be represented by different letters. However, there are basic principles that can be described:

There is not a one-to-one relationship between sounds and letters. Some letters can represent a number of phonemes, and a phoneme can be represented by different letters.

- Certain phonemes can be represented by putting together two existing letter symbols. This forms digraphs such as 'th', 'ch', 'sh', which are used to represent single phonemes. This may lead to a minor problem, since readers do have to distinguish between the digraph and the sequence 't' and 'h' as in lighthouse, but these confusions rarely occur, and it is usually possible to recognise them on other grounds—such as the fact that the digraph does not occur over a morpheme (meaning) boundary
- One letter symbol is made to represent more than one phoneme; for example, 'th' represents /θ/ as in 'thin' and /ð/ as in 'thine'
- One letter symbol is made to represent more than one phoneme, but exactly which phoneme will depend on the context of the other letters. One of the most familiar examples of this is the so called magic 'e' which indicates the nature of the preceding vowel, but which is not sounded itself; examples include 'pane' versus 'pan', 'pine' versus 'pin'.

This last principle is very widespread in English and many attempts have been made to identify the different contexts and sequences that indicate how the letters represent sounds. Studies inform us that although they are complex, there are patterns—certain sequences go in certain positions. George Bernard Shaw once suggested that /fish/ could be spelled as 'ghoti'—'gh' as in 'rough', 'o' as in 'women', 'ti' as in 'nation'. But this is impossible, because there are 'rules' that indicate which sequences in particular positions can represent which sounds. The suggested 'ghoti' will never occur because 'gh' never represents /ʃ/ in the initial position 'o' for /ʃ/ is extremely rare, being an orthographic convention (see p. 137 for further details) and would not occur before 't'; 'ti' to represent /ʃ/ is also contextually determined, and 'ti' (or more accurately 'tion') represents /ʃ/ only at the beginning of a syllable.

It is important, therefore, that we do not talk to learners as if there is a one-to-one relationship between letters and sounds. Generally it is more effective to refer to the relationship between clusters of sounds and letters, for example, 'ing', 'hum', 'str'. Furthermore, teachers should be careful about their use of terms—the terms 'letter' and 'sound' are not interchangeable: a letter only represents a phoneme in a word or sentence. For example, compare the word 'present' in the sentence: 'We gave the cat a present' with the word 'present' in the following sentence: 'We will present him with a medallion'.

Phonic knowledge (sound–letter knowledge) should be discussed only in a meaningful context. From the discussion above you may think that phonics has no place in a literacy program, but phonic knowledge is important in learning to read and write. The issue is what the learner needs to know and how this knowledge is best learned. As speakers we know the sounds of our language, but in order to read and write we have to map these sounds to letters and letter patterns. This is not an easy task. Research (Oglan 1997) demonstrates that beginning writers

Teachers should be careful about their use of terms—the terms 'letter' and 'sound' are not interchangeable: a letter represents only a phoneme in a word or sentence.

Phonic knowledge should be discussed only in a meaningful context.

The teacher needs to determine what the learner needs to know and how this knowledge is best learned.

go from sounds to letters. They attempt to spell words using whatever letter knowledge they possess. These strategies include:

1 Letter name: Each letter of a word says the name of the letter. Vowels are usually absent, e.g. *first/frst, letter/ltr, elephant/lfnt*

2 Spelling as it sounds: Students rely on the sounds they hear that are close to the actual sound, e.g. *uncle/uncul, feather/fethir, jumped/jumpt*

3 Placeholder: When spelling words with vowels, students will replace one vowel with another that is similar in sound, e.g. *went/wont, video/vedio*

4 Representations: Students sometimes know that a vowel is needed but insert a random vowel, e.g. *misery/maziry, sometime/semtim*

5 Overgeneralizations: When students discover a new structure such as the silent *e* at the end of words, they use it exclusively, e.g. *won/wone, from/frome*

6 Transpositional: Words are spelled using all of the correct letters but in the wrong order, e.g. *tried/tride, watch/wacht*

7 Visual: Words have a visual likeness to the conventional form, e.g. *school/scool, teacher/techer*

8 Articulation: Vowels and consonants are close in sound and are usually used interchangeably, e.g. *combat/kmbat, graphics/grafics, tried/chid*

9 One-letter misses: The word is close to the conventional form with the exception of a letter, e.g. *snowed/snowd, waiting/wating*

10 Multiples strategies: Combinations of the strategies, e.g. *neighborhood/nebrhode, retirement/ritearment.*

G. Oglan, *Grocery lists, shopping, and a child's writing and spelling development,*
pp. 3–4.

Phonic knowledge is important in reading because it provides a basis for initial predictions, for confirming predictions, and, as a last resort, a word recognition strategy. However, as phonic knowledge is the weakest cue possessed by beginning readers (skilled readers rely more on semantic cues and syntactical knowledge), an over-reliance on phonics through the texts we provide or the advice we give may not be helpful. Instead, the emphasis can be on prediction, drawing from the context, meaning, and structure of language and allowing students' phonic knowledge and visual image of words to be acquired gradually.

Phonic knowledge is best learned at the point of need through reading and writing for real purposes, and activities that highlight the structure and patterns within words. Activities that isolate letters and sounds from whole texts are meaningless tasks. They have nothing to do with language and make learning difficult; whatever is learned is often not transferred to reading and writing. The strategies for using phonics in reading and spelling need to be taught. An examination of the beginning writer's spelling will demonstrate knowledge of phonics and what assistance, if any, is needed.

Research demonstrates that beginning writers go from sounds to letters. They represent the spelling of words with whatever letter knowledge they possess.

Phonic knowledge is important in reading because it provides a basis for initial predictions, for confirming predictions, and as a word-recognition strategy.

Phonic knowledge is best learned through reading and writing for real purposes and activities at the point of need that highlight the structure and patterns within words.

Summary and implications for teaching

Summary	Implication for Teaching
• Letters do not have sounds, but they can represent sounds in words. — A letter in isolation possesses no sound.	• Teachers should use letter names to refer to letters and discuss how a letter represents a particular sound in specific words. Informally, throughout the day, teachers can draw the attention of beginning reader–writers to sound–letter patterns and ask for other words that fit the pattern.
• There is not a one-to-one correspondence between letters and sounds; rather, it is more appropriate to consider the relationship between clusters of sounds and letters.	• The teacher must be accurate when talking about sounds and letters with beginning reader–writers, emphasising that a letter is not a sound and that a sound can be represented in more than one way. Attention needs to be drawn to patterns.
• The phonemes/sounds of a language can be classified according to distinctive features; studies in language acquisition indicate that children learn sounds by learning their distinctive features and probably learn the letters of the alphabet in a similar way.	• Learners must be exposed to the different letters of the alphabet, rather than receive instruction on one letter at a time in order to learn the differences between the letters.
• The formal teaching of phonics to young children is of dubious value. Sound–letter relations are complex, as the activities above have shown, and many children are cognitively immature for such a task. — Phonic knowledge, however, is important for word recognition and confirming predictions in reading, and for spelling. Research indicates that initially children perceive sounds at the syllable level and beginning reader–writers use their phonic knowledge for spelling; this is very obvious when we examine 'invented' spellings.	• Phonic knowledge is probably best learned through lots of reading and writing, and activities that grow out of reading and writing, such as discussion of words in shared reading of big books and wall charts, and discussion of spelling attempts. • For students to be able to use phonics in reading and for spelling, strategies need to be taught. That is, phonics needs to be taught in context. Phonics in isolation is a meaningless task and learners often do not transfer any learning to their reading and writing.
• There appears to be a common bank of phonemes used by human languages. A particular language possesses a certain number of phonemes and uses them in a particular way; therefore, different languages do not possess identical phonology systems. This may create difficulties for a second-language learner, firstly in hearing the different sounds and then being able to produce them.	• A phonic approach to reading for second-language learners is not appropriate as the knowledge of the English sound system will be their weakest information system.
• The use of phonemes in a language is controlled by rules, as is the use of letters in writing.	• Beginner reader–writers need lots of exposure to words in real reading and writing to become familiar with patterns and generalisations.

References and further reading

Adams M. J. *Beginning to Read: Thinking and Learning about Print*, MIT Press, Cambridge, MA, 1990.

Clay M. *An Observation Survey of Early Literacy Achievement*, Heinemann, Auckland, 1993.

Corder S. Pit. *Introducing Applied Linguistics*, Penguin, Harmondsworth, 1973.

Duffy G. *Teaching Linguistics*, The Instructor Publishing Co., Dansville, NY, 1969.

*Emmitt M. & Hornsby, D. 'Phonics in Early Literacy', in *Practically Primary*, June 1996, p.11–17.

*Ericson L. & Juliebo M. *The Phonological Awareness Handbook for Kindergarten and Primary Teachers*, International Reading Association, Newark, DE, 1998.

Fromkin V., Rodman R., Collins P. & Blair D. *An Introduction to Language*, 3rd Aust. edn, Harcourt Brace, Sydney, 1996, Chapters 5, 6.

*Goodman K. *Phonics Phacts*, Scholastic, Richmond Hill, Ontario, 1993.

Goswani U. & Bryant P. *Phonological Skills and Learning to Read*, Lawrence Erlbaum, Wheatons, Exeter, UK, 1990.

Graddoll D., Cheshire J. & Swann J. *Describing Language*, Open University Press, Milton Keynes, 1987, Chapter 2.

Hammarström G. & Jernudd B. *Outline of Linguistics*, Monash University, Clayton, Vic., 1966.

*Hill S. *Phonics*, Eleanor Curtain, Armadale, Vic., 1999.

*Hornsby D. *Sounds Great: Learning Graphophonic Connections in a Whole Language Classroom*, Martin Education, St Leonards, NSW, 1993.

*Lindfors J. *Children's Language and Learning*, 2nd edn, Prentice-Hall, Englewood Cliffs. NJ, 1987, pp. 52–8.

*Moustafa M. *Beyond Traditional Phonics: Research Discoveries and Reading Instruction*, Heinemann, Portsmouth, NH, 1997.

Oglan G. *Parents learning and whole language classrooms*, Urbana, IL: NCTE, 1997.

Oglan G. 'Grocery lists, shopping, and a child's writing and spelling development' in *Talking Points*, 2001, Vol. 12, No. 2, pp. 2–6.

*Powell D. & Hornsby D. *Learning Phonics and Spelling in Whole Language Classroom*, Scholastic, New York, 1993.

*Strickland D. *Teaching Phonics Today: A Primer for Educators*, International Reading Association, Newark, DE, 1998.

Weaver C. *Reading Process and Practice: From Socio-psycholinguistic to Whole Language*, Heinemann, Portsmouth, NH, 1994.

*Wilde S. *What's a Schwa Sound Anyway? A Holistic Guide to Phonetics, Phonics, and Spelling*, Heinemann, Portsmouth, NH, 1997.

Answers and discussion for workshop activities

Phonemes

3 Some non-English sound patterns are /ng/, /ʒ/ and /r/ /l/ in the initial position.

4 Phonemes in
e/l/e/ph/a/n/t = 7
g/i/r/a/ffe = 5
s/ch/oo/l = 4
b/o/mb = 3
s/a/ng = 3

The word elephant commences with a vowel, represented by 'e'. If there were no vowel sound you would pronounce the word like the beginning of 'lemon'. In fact, this is how many beginning writers do commence to write the word elephant; 'lfnt' is a common spelling for elephant: they use what they know about letter names to help them for example 'el' for the letter l.

Giraffe has a vowel as its second sound. If there were no vowel, there would be an initial blend (as there is in school).

- Syllables in:
  de/re/lic/tion = 4
  flo/ra = 2
  hou/ri = 2
  June = 1
  skein = 1
  trea/che/rous = 3
  cor/rup/ti/bi/li/ty = 6
  barked = 1
- Word(s) ending with a consonant sound: pencil.
- Less frequent sound for the letter 'c': /sh/ in Chicago.
- Less frequent sound for the letter 'g': none of these.
- The letter sound i as in 'find' and 'I'.
- A reduced vowel is often found in 'cotton'.
- A diphthong is found in: 'coat', 'boy', 'slow'.

5 Consonant phonemes; for example:
/k/ = 'c', 'k', 'q'
/s/ = 's', 'c', 'sc', 'ss', 'ps'
/d/ = 'j', 'g'

Vowel letters of the alphabet; for example:
o = cot, coat, boil, cook, town, four, do, port.

CHAPTER 8

DIFFERENCES BETWEEN SPEECH AND WRITING

FOCUS

This chapter focuses on the understanding that:

- *speech and writing are different codes but they possess many similarities*
- *teachers need to have knowledge of the differences between speech and writing*
- *teachers need to be aware of possible difficulties in texts for students learning to read and write.*

PRE-READING ACTIVITY

I List any differences you can think of between speech and writing. Share your list with others and add to it as you read this chapter.

Introduction

Speech is generally considered of primary importance compared with writing. In the course of human evolution speech developed first and the individual normally learns to speak before learning how to write. However, written language is often accorded a higher value than speech. When people criticise an individual's speech, they often use knowledge of writing as the basis of their criticism. For example, some will chastise 'don't drop your g's' (as in going), although there is no g sound in 'ing'. Speech and writing are two different codes of language, although obviously there are similarities between them. They share similar syntax and morphological bases, but there are key differences: some syntactic structures occur in writing and not in speech; and there are differences in uses and discourse structures. In conversation small amounts of information are provided at a time (to avoid density of content and not appear to assume total ignorance on the part of the listener), while in writing much more detail is provided. Exaggeration is much more acceptable in speech than in writing. Writing is characteristically planned and, unlike speech, has the advantage of

Speech is generally considered of primary importance compared with writing. In the course of human evolution it developed first and, in the individual situation, speech normally develops prior to writing.

Speech and writing are two different codes of language, although obviously there are similarities between the two codes.

allowing revision and polishing. For many speakers the commonality between speech and writing is close because they spend so much time engaged with the written code that it influences their speech.

The differences between speech and writing can be viewed from different perspectives:

- uses and contexts
- degrees of formality
- grammatical and text structure.

Some obvious differences between speech and writing, on the basis that they operate as different channels of communication, have been summarised by Czerniewska (1985), shown in Table 8.1.

Table 8.1 Differences between speech and writing as different channels

The oral channel	The written channel
1 Sounds	Letters
2 Intonation patterns, changes in pitch and stress to convey attitudes and some grammatical distinctions	No direct counterpart though underlining words, parentheses, punctuation (e.g. exclamation marks) and capital letters can convey similar meanings
3 Non-verbal gestures, eye contact	No direct counterpart though different types of handwriting might express similar meanings
4 No direct equivalents though changes in pitch and speed may express equivalent meanings	Punctuation marks such as dashes, question marks and dots; different types of handwriting or type faces
5 Pauses and silence	Gaps and dashes
6 Expressions to indicate topic changes, e.g. 'right then', 'now'	Headings, new chapters, paragraphs, etc. Words like 'firstly'; 'in conclusion'
7 No direct equivalent	Capital letters for names and beginning of sentences
8 Gap-fillers, e.g. 'you know', 'er'	Hesitations not shown in final form of writing
9 Checks on listener attention and to maintain interaction such as 'do you know what I mean?'	Perhaps less common but checks on reader involvement employed, e.g. 'try to bear in mind ...', 'if you have followed my arguments so far ... '

P. Czerniewska, in D. Graddol et al., *Describing Language*, p. 180.

One of the main reasons for the differences between speech and writing is that these two codes traditionally perform different functions. Speech is generally used in everyday social interactions, the here and now of getting things done. On the other hand, writing is generally used for more permanent communications, such as instructions and records. In the past, another distinction was the fact that writing could transcend space and time. With advances in technology the clear, functional differences have been blurred, but we can still look at different types of speech and writing on a continuum of characteristics (Hudson 1984) shown in Table 8.2.

One of the main reasons for the differences between speech and writing is that these two codes traditionally perform different functions.

Table 8.2 Different types of speech and writing

1. Transitoriness

Permanent record	Printed book	Note for milkman	Ephemeral
	Recording of a parliamentary debate	Conversation	

2. Degree of formality

Formal	Act of parliament	Shopping list	Informal
	Queen's speech	Informal conversation	

3. Use of standard English

Standard	School textbook	Poem in local dialect	Non-standard
	BBC News	Parent–child conversation	

4. Degree of interaction between producer and receiver

Low interaction	Telephone directory	Notes passed between children in classroom	High interaction
	Radio talk	Telephone conversation	

5. Type of interaction between producer and receiver

Message-oriented	Recipe	Christmas card	Socially-oriented
	Football commentary	'How do you do?'	

6. Dependence on context

Context-independent	A story	Instructions for self-assembly kit	Context-dependent
	Poetry recitation	Oral directions	

R. Hudson in D. Graddol et al., *Describing Language*, p. 183.

Text density

Written texts are generally described as being more dense than spoken texts—that is, written texts contain more words that carry meaning, known as lexical items such as nouns, adjectives, verbs, and some adverbs. It may be useful to occasionally calculate the lexical density of texts you typically make available in your classroom by using the following formula:

1 count the number of clauses in the text (a clause is a group of words with a finite verb, that is a verb that has a subject)
2 count the number of lexical items in the text (nouns, adjectives, verbs, and some adverbs)
3 divide the number of lexical items by the number of clauses (this gives you the mean lexical density).
   Example (clauses are underlined and lexical items bolded):

During the **day, Leonie** *was a* **schoolgirl.** *At* **night,** *she was a* **cat-burglar.** *While the* **world** *was* **asleep,** *she* **put** *on her* **cat costume,** *and* **prowled** *the* **alleyways** *by* **moonlight. Nothing** *was* **safe** *when* **Leonie** *was about. The* **police** *were* **baffled,** *and* **said so. Newspapers printed stories** *about her.* *They* **called** *her The* **Paw.**

N. J. Prior & T. Denton, The Paw p, 1–5.

Number of clauses: 11
Number of lexical items: 24
Lexical items divided by number of clauses: 24/11 = 2.18

This formula can be used to demonstrate the difference in lexical density between two or more written texts, and between oral and written texts on the same topic.

Nominalisation is a characteristic of formal written texts, in particular bureaucratic or legal language. It is the conversion of verbs or verbal groups into nouns. As a result, actions become things and the content seems more abstract. The agent (the individual or entity doing the action) is removed and the focus is on the concept. Policy documents are frequently written in this way. Use of nominalisation is a sign of more mature writing but the effect of removing the subject (and therefore the person or thing undertaking the action) needs to be considered. 'Amusement' in the following sentence is an example of nominalisation:

Amusement is expressed at the mention of the Emperor's name.

Other examples are 'development' (instead of 'develop'), 'initiation' (instead of 'initiate'), 'action' (instead of 'act') and so on.

Possible difficulties with the written language

As many of the structures in written language are different from those in speech, students must be exposed to them through fiction and factual texts being read to them. Often reading a text is made difficult because the structures used are not as easy to predict and/or to chunk together; sometimes they place a heavy burden on short-term memory or are simply unfamiliar.

Perera (1984) summarised the possible difficulties that students may experience with written language. Difficulties can be experienced at:

- *the sentence level*
  —with structures that are difficult to predict; for example, late-acquired structures and/or structures that are rare in speech, and open-ended structures
  —with structures that are difficult to segment, such as constructions without function words, constructions with ambiguous function words, constructions with grammatically uninformative lexical words, and ambiguous strings
  —with structures that place a heavy burden on short-term memory, such as interruptions and long subject–noun phrases
- *the discourse level*
  —at the local/micro level within and between sentences, such as misleading or ambiguous use of pronouns, use of synonymy, use of ellipses (omissions), use of unfamiliar connectives, and minimal use of connectives.
  —at the global/macro level with an unfamiliar structure or poorly structured text.

Structures that are most frequently found to be difficult are:

- interrupting constructions where phrases and clauses intervene between the subject and verb and object
- long subject–noun phrases, and in subject nominal clauses where a clause is used as the subject
- 'advanced' relative clauses
- non-finite (verbs that cannot stand on their own) and verbless clauses
- elliptical constructions where words are omitted.

Interrupting constructions

Examples that Perera (1984) has taken from children's own textbooks include:

It then became possible to make polymethylmethacrylote in commercial quantities, and its toughness and transparency—in

As many of the structures in written language are different from those in speech, students must be exposed to them through fiction and factual texts being read to them.

Potential difficulties with the written language can be experienced at the sentence level and at the discourse level.

sheer form it is as clear as glass—made it suitable for applications such as aircraft canopies.

John visited Bill who was in the house in order to give the gift.

Because plastics need heat to soften them, the barrel (that is the part of the extruder between the hopper and the hole at the end, which is called a die) must be made so that it can be heated and controlled at a steady temperature.

These sonatas, owing much to the structural methods of C. P. E. Bach, Hayden, and Mozart and to the distinctive and influential piano style of Muzio Clement (1752–1832), an Italian who made his home in England, are familiar.

Housewives and, in big houses, sewing women made all the clothes.

Long subject–noun phrases

These are common in non-fiction. Examples from Perera (1984) include:

Differences in water temperature, the abundance of food supplies and the availability of the right places to breed or spawn are the main reasons for the migration of animals.

The conversion of the products obtained from the crackers of the old refineries into the basic raw materials of the plastics industry occupies a large section of the world's chemical industry.

(It is difficult to determine the head noun conversion when six nouns are present.)

The customer that the broker planned to cancel the illegal transaction for had often engineered some shady deals.

Subject nominal clauses

An example from Perera (1984):

The exploration and charting of the coastlines of these new lands was the work of an English seaman.

Compare this structure with the following structures:

(a) *An English seaman explored and charted the coastlines of the new lands.*

(b) *It was an English seaman who explored and charted the coastlines of the new lands.*

(c) *The coastlines of the new lands were explored and charted by an English seaman.*

The first sentence as it appeared in the text is more difficult for inexperienced readers to understand. The words 'exploration' and 'charting' are examples of nominalisation. Nominalisation is much more common in writing than in speech and adds to text density.

'Advanced' relative clauses

'Whom', 'whose', preposition + relative pronoun, and a series of relative pronouns within one sentence are included in the following example from Perera (1984):

> 'From his cradle, he was filled with the love of wisdom above all things', wrote a friend, the Welsh monk Asser, whom, like many others, he brought to Wessex to restore learning.

> Polythene is a tough solid material. Ethylene, from which it is made, is a gas.

Non-finite and verbless clauses

Non-finite verbs cannot stand on their own in a sentence. Example from Perera (1984):

> Returning from its feeding sojourn in the Antarctic Ocean, the emperor penguin leaps to a height twice its length.

The relationship of the clause 'Returning from its feeding sojourn ...' to the rest of the sentence is not explicit, which may cause confusion. The meaning of the sentence would be more explicit if the sentence read: 'When the emperor penguin returned from its feeding sojourn ...'. In the following example, meaning can only be constructed if the missing words are mentally inserted.

> When quite close they spring on it.

Elliptical constructions (ellipsis)

> Alice showed the girls which thread to use for the silk dresses that had been given to them and taught the girls how to use it.

> A camel is well equipped to survive in the desert, and the polar bear in the Arctic.

ACTIVITY AND DISCUSSION

Consider the difficulties in the following paragraphs that were originally published in a junior science book.

> The fact that the monomers, and similar chemicals that are the starting materials for the manufacture of plastics, can now be made fairly cheaply and in large quantities, is a result of all the research and development that has been carried out in recent years.

The conversion of the products obtained from the crackers of the oil refineries into the basic raw materials of the plastics industry occupies a large section of the world's chemical industry. Some of the products of the oil refineries (such as ethylene, propylene, butadiene—all known as petrochemicals) can be polymerised directly into plastics, but sometimes several steps are needed to convert the petrochemicals into the chemicals needed by the plastics industry.

Cited in K. Perera, Children's Writing and Reading, pp. 316–17.

Can you find examples of difficult constructions in texts you use with students? Share these examples with your colleagues.

Writing for children

Sometimes the simplistic rules and advice about writing given to children and second-language learners are inappropriate. Three rules that are often given are: (1) use familiar vocabulary; (2) use short sentences; and (3) keep subordination to a minimum. However, consider the application of these rules in the following examples given by Perera (1984).

Use familiar vocabulary

A boat was approaching the island.
A canoe was approaching the island.
A submarine was approaching the island.

The more unfamiliar words contain more precise and probably more relevant meaning.

Use short sentences

John slept all day. He was lazy.
Because John was lazy he slept all day.

The link between ideas is made obvious in the longer sentence.

Keep subordination to a minimum

The engineer's delight at the messenger's delivery of the urgently needed equipment was visible to everyone.

Everyone could see that the engineer was delighted when the messenger delivered the equipment that was urgently needed.

The relation between the ideas is clearer in the second sentence.
When writing or selecting books for inexperienced readers the following should be considered:
- the text should be well organised and systematic
- movement within the text from one section to another needs to be signalled explicitly

- whenever possible, grammatical subjects of sentences should be agents of the verb, that is, they should be in the first part of the sentence
- links between ideas need to be made explicit (use a main clause plus a subordinate clause, rather than badly juxtaposing two simple sentences)
- avoid texts with a dense use of difficult structures.

Factors such as layout, subject matter, and interest level should also be considered.

Writing instructions and examination questions

Be wary of the use of the following if you want to avoid any possibility of misunderstanding:

- concealed negatives, for example 'The gibbon is rarely seen; soon there may be few left'
- two or more negatives in one sentence, for example 'Of the million or so different kinds of animal there is hardly one that doesn't astonish us with a special characteristic, evolved through millions of years'
- fronted constructions, where objects are placed first in the sentence, for example, 'The thread and the screwdriver we hid'
- nominalisations, where verbs are turned into nouns, for example 'The exploration and charting of the coastlines of these new lands was the work of an English seaman' ('An English seaman explored ...', 'It was an English ...', 'The coastlines of these new ...')
- reversible passives, such as 'The dog was chased by the cat' and 'The cat was chased by the dog'
- adverbial clauses introduced by 'although', 'unless', and 'provided that'. For example 'The meal was good although the pie was lukewarm'; inexperienced readers might not understand the meanings of the linking words
- inferential 'if' clauses
- misleading, ambiguous, or inconsiderate pronominal references
- difficult connectives, for example 'consequently', 'hence', 'moreover', 'similarly', 'that is', 'thus'.

Summary

In this section we discussed some of the key differences between speech and writing. The purpose for using the language determines the mode of language used—oral or written, and the genre and degree of formality. Because of the differences in uses and structure of the oral and written language codes, there are syntactic structures that tend to be used only in written language.

Implications for teaching

1 Teachers need to be aware of differences in written language. They should read and discuss lots of different texts with students of all levels of education so that they can become familiar with these written patterns.
2 The teacher needs to consider the complexity of the language used when (1) selecting texts for students to learn from, and (2) writing for students (tasks or tests).
3 When selecting texts for students to read, teachers should be sure that they have a well-organised structure, and should not be misled by thinking the vocabulary must already be familiar or the sentences must be short and simple. These factors do not necessarily make the text easier to read.

References and further reading

*Graddol D., Cheshire J. & Swann J. *Describing Language*, Open University Press, Milton Keynes, UK, 1987.

*Halliday M. A. K. *Spoken and Written Language*, Deakin University Press, Geelong, Vic., 1985.

*Hammond J. 'Is learning to read and write the same as learning to speak', in F. Christie (ed.) *Literacy for a Changing World*, ACER, Melbourne, 1990, pp. 26–52.

Perera K. *Children's Writing and Reading: Analysing Classroom Language*, Basil Blackwell, Oxford, 1984.

Prior N.J. & Denton T. *The Paw*, Allen & Unwin, St Leonards, NSW, 1993.

PART THREE

LANGUAGE AND LEARNING

CHAPTER 9

LEARNING LANGUAGE

FOCUS

This chapter focuses on the understanding that:

- *learning to talk means becoming a social being*
- *language learners act as scientists who learn the rules of language*
- *different theories have been used to explain young children's language learning*
- *interaction with significant others is the most influential factor in children's language development*
- *children still have much to learn about language and language use when they come to school*
- *language learning is very successful in the pre-school environment and has many implications for teachers*
- *second-language learning involves many processes and strategies similar to first-language learning.*

PRE-READING ACTIVITY

1 Write down how you think we learn to talk. Compare your answers with others.

Learning speech

The most impressive intellectual achievement that any of us ever accomplishes is learning our first language. What seems more remarkable is the fact that we do it all without being directly taught.

The most impressive intellectual achievement that any of us ever accomplishes is learning our first language. The process begins and makes its most spectacular progress in our earliest years, at an age when commonsense might suggest that we were least able to do something that at first glance seems to be so intellectually demanding. What seems even more remarkable is the fact that we do it all without being directly taught. How we do it has interested people from ancient times to the present.

Of course not all of the interest in children's language development has had the same focus or concern. Some researchers have been interested in establishing the claims between fundamentally different theories about the nature of human intelligence. Others, as we shall show, seem to have been motivated by what is now seen as nothing more than idle curiosity. This chapter assumes that our readers are interested in the development of children's language because they are teachers or training to be teachers. Knowledge of how language has developed before children start school and what to expect during the school years will be useful when we come to think about how children's language might be developed after they start school.

An interest in assisting children's development has not always been at the heart of child language studies. The Greek writer Herodotus, who set out to write a history of the world, included the following tale about what may have been the first experimental study of children's language development.

The Natural Language of Man

The Egyptians before the reign of Psammetichus used to think that of all races in the world they were the most ancient. Psammetichus, however, when he came to the throne, took it into his head to settle this question of priority, and ever since his time the Egyptians have believed that the Phrygians surpass them in antiquity and that they themselves came second. Psammetichus, finding that mere enquiry failed to reveal which was the original race of mankind, devised an ingenious method of determining the matter. He took at random, from an ordinary family two newly born infants and gave them to a shepherd to be brought up among his flocks, under strict orders that no one should utter a word in their presence. They were to be kept by themselves in a lonely cottage, and the shepherd was to bring in goats from time to time, to see that the babies had enough milk to drink, and to look after them in any other way that was necessary. All these arrangements were made by Psammetichus because he wished to find out what word the children would first utter, once they had grown out of their meaningless baby-talk. The plan succeeded; two years later the shepherd, who during that time had done everything he had been told to do, happened one day to open the door of the cottage and go in, when both children running up to him with hands outstretched, pronounced the word 'becos'. The first time this occurred the shepherd made no mention of it; but later, when he found that every time he visited the children to attend to their needs the same word was constantly repeated by them, he informed his master. Psammetichus ordered the children to be brought to him, and when he himself heard them say 'becos' he determined to find out to what language the word belonged. His inquiries revealed that it was the Phrygian word for 'bread', and in consideration of this the Egyptians yielded their claims and admitted the superior antiquity of the Phrygians.

Aubrey de Selincourt (Trans.) *Herodotus, The Histories*, pp. 102–3.

ACTIVITIES AND DISCUSSION

Make a list of criticisms of King Psammetichus' research study.

Q What assumptions or beliefs about language does his alleged experiment reveal?

Q What motivated his study?

Q If you were to study children's language development, what would you do? Make a plan.

Several problems may have occurred to you as you attempted to plan a research study into children's language development. When did you plan to start? Did your plan include the development of bilingual children? What did you decide to observe? How did you plan to interpret the observations you made? These questions are important because your answers would reveal your assumptions and beliefs about language, and if you set them out more or less systematically they would add up to something like a theory of language. Your theory might not be very complete, or very consistent, and for most of the time you might not be self-consciously aware of it, so it is probably a little presumptuous to call your personal views on language a theory. However, once you begin to undertake a research enquiry or a career to expand and extend children's language, a theory becomes crucial because theory directs the questions to be asked, decides what counts as evidence, and finally provides the framework for interpreting the evidence and planning a program.

Problems with language development research

A problem in interpreting the educational consequences of language development research is that, while researchers are interested in the practical application of their findings, they are also very careful to qualify their discoveries. Findings are often derived from small groups of subjects within specific cultural groups and the research may be conducted within a theoretical framework that does not focus on educational issues. Researchers are interested in describing what is, and how and why it came to be so. For this reason, theories and explanations are often tentative and incomplete and, as we have seen, have had to be abandoned or modified as further research was conducted. On the other hand, teachers are obliged to act before theorists and researchers have written the last word.

The difficulty in educational planning that acknowledges theory and research is not an excuse to ignore the insights they provide. We've already suggested that what we do in classrooms will reflect our personal theories anyway. Teachers can ensure they are as informed as possible about language-learning theory and research so that their

The findings of language development research are often derived from small groups of subjects from within specific cultural groups. The research is often conducted within a theoretical framework that does not focus on educational issues.

practices reflect or can be described in terms of what is known, rather than what is imagined or taken for granted.

Several theories have guided research into children's language and few of them have had much to do with a teacher's practical concerns with planning and implementing classroom programs. Despite this, however, there has been significant influence on language education from research based on theories not directly focused on education. Many of the materials and teaching methods used in classrooms over the past fifty years have reflected theories that were not based on education and are now outdated.

> Many of the materials and teaching methods used in classrooms over the past fifty years were not based on education and are now outdated.

Learning language

What is to be learned?

Let's start by making clear what we think is meant by the phrase 'to learn language'. Children must learn the systems of speech used in communicating with others, but learning a first language involves more than learning the patterns of sounds, words, and sentences that make up speech. When children learn language they learn to use the most powerful and pervasive system humans have available for making and sharing meaning. This is because language shapes our thoughts and makes shared meanings possible. Our interest in language learning is to describe the way children learn how to make and share meanings with others in their communities for a range of purposes.

> Our interest in language learning is to describe the way children learn to make and share meanings with others in their communities for a range of purposes.

Different theories

Not everyone who has studied language development has approached the question from the same point of view, and as a result the questions to be answered have varied depending on the initial assumptions. Some have been interested in using language development to test learning theories, discover the 'rules' that seem to underlie a mature speakers' ability to create and understand an infinite variety of sentences, and find evidence of the biological foundations of human knowledge. Others have been interested in describing the nature of interactions between adults and children in which children come to learn the language of their parents and the way children discover the function of language. In all, researchers' interests and questions have been quite varied.

Behaviourism and language

For most of last century the discipline of psychology claimed as its own the task of discovering the basis of human perception, learning, and those activities that in ordinary conversation are called thinking. A powerful tradition in psychology that guided this task rejected the

Behavioural psychology focuses on aspects of the operation of the brain that could be observed in an individual's behaviour.

notion of 'mind' or 'mental states' because they could not be observed or measured directly. Instead, psychologists who followed this tradition concentrated on aspects of the operation of the brain that could be observed. This kind of psychology focused on behaviour rather than thinking, because behaviour could be observed and thinking could not. Although interested in perception, learning, and memory, behavioural psychologists chose to observe, describe, and measure behaviour that indicated the operation of perception, learning, and memory, which were unobservable in any direct way.

It may seem strange that theories about human language learning could have been influenced by theories derived from experiments performed on animals, but this is in fact what happened. A series of experiments on dogs carried out and reported by a Russian psychologist, Ivan Pavlov (1849–1936), provided a powerful base on which behavioural psychologists built learning theories. Pavlov's experiments were based on the fact that in 'natural' circumstances a dog salivated (produced saliva) when presented with food. Pavlov reasoned that a psychological mechanism existed that connected the presentation of the food with the production of saliva and he set about exploring the nature of this connection. He began by arranging for a bell to be rung each time the food was presented and by doing this established an 'association' for the dog between the ringing of the bell and the presentation of food: the dog 'learned' to salivate when it heard the bell. In a further set of experimental trials the dog learned to associate a flashing light with the ringing bell and, in time, came to salivate when the light was flashed.

How was a theory of learning constructed from something that seems only a little more systematic than a dog owner's attempts to teach a pup a new trick? The theory was gradually built on the notion that learning should be thought of as developing associations between stimuli and responses. Thus, in this theory, learning was the establishment of habitual new responses to particular stimuli.

A great deal of experimentation, often with animals, was undertaken to extend, develop, and test the theory of learning as the formation of habit. Elaborate applications of the theory were assumed necessary to explain the achievement of complex behaviours such as language or other complex learning. However, the general principles of learning language were held to be essentially the same as those demonstrated by Pavlov's dogs.

An American psychologist, B. F. Skinner, developed the most clearly articulated description of what is called behaviouristic (after its focus on behaviour) language learning theory. In his book *Verbal Behavior*, published in 1957, the basic learning process he identified was a variation on the classical conditioning model of learning first outlined by Pavlov.

Skinner set out to describe how an association already established between a sensory stimulus (such as a seen object or a spoken word) and a particular response (such as a name) could come to be conditioned to a new stimulus and a new response. That is, among other things, he wanted to show how words and their meanings were learned.

The theory of behaviouristic learning certainly seemed to do some of the things required of a theory. It explained aspects of language development and predicted that children could be taught by conditioning. Experimental studies showed that children could be trained to make particular verbal responses to satisfy needs and naming-type verbalisations in appropriate situations.

QUESTIONS FOR DISCUSSION

It seems a good place to pause for a while in this very brief review of Skinner's approach to explaining language learning in children.

Q What problems can you see arising from this explanation?

Q Can you make a list of possible problems?

Q Can you think of ways these problems could be tested?

Behaviourism and teaching

Throughout the 1950s and 1960s, the behaviourist theory was very significant in education, particularly in guiding approaches to the teaching of reading and writing. The key concepts of motivation, reinforcement of correct responses, and repetition of associations until the conditioning was established all showed up in teaching methods and materials. Learning to read was thought of as matching the correct verbal response to the appropriate visual stimulus, that is, saying the right word when the word was shown. Words and single alphabetic letters were printed on cards and rapidly displayed or flashed at children. This was intended to establish an association between the stimulus (the flash card) and the response (the word called out aloud by the children or the supposed sound the alphabetic letter was meant to represent). Correct responses were praised and errors supposed to be ignored. Teaching was organised so that complex tasks were broken into simple tasks to be mastered before the more complex tasks were attempted. It has to be said that some children learned to read in classrooms that followed this approach, and some children didn't. The question that arises is: if this empiricist approach to explaining language learning was successful, why was it substantially rejected?

The influence in education of the behaviourist approach was reflected in the key concepts of motivation, reinforcement of correct responses, and repetition of associations until conditioning was established.

The cognitivist view of language learning

Another American, the linguist Noam Chomsky, provided a comprehensive criticism of behaviourist approaches to language when he reviewed Skinner's *Verbal Behavior* in 1959. Chomsky explicitly rejected the behaviourist position that language should be thought of as

Chomsky explicitly rejected the behaviourist position that language should be thought of as verbal behaviour, arguing that it should be thought of as knowledge held by those who use the language.

verbal behaviour. He argued, on the contrary, that language should be thought of as knowledge held by those who use the language. This is no trivial difference. Remember that Skinner and other behaviourists rejected approaches to the study of human thinking based on unobservable human characteristics like knowledge. They held that only what we could see, and measure, could be discussed sensibly.

Chomsky argued that the language overheard by infants wouldn't provide enough complete data for children to develop the kind of language that they soon develop. In other words, he argued that unless children were already predisposed to learn language, the environment in which they overheard and participated in talk wouldn't give enough examples to develop the kind of associations that behaviourist theories needed.

An even more telling argument of Chomsky's was that behaviourist accounts couldn't explain how children learned to say things they had never heard. Furthermore, the behaviourists could not explain how children could understand sentences they had never heard uttered before. Chomsky suggested that the learner of any language has an inbuilt capacity for acquiring language that enables each learner to construct a kind of personal theory or set of rules about that language on the basis of very limited exposure to it. Central to Chomsky's approach was the idea that our 'knowledge' of language was different from the particular examples or occasions on which we actually used speech. He called this knowledge 'competence' in order to distinguish it from what we actually might say on some occasion when our speech might contain false starts, mistakes, and stumbles. The point he was making was that even though our speech performance (or language behaviour if you incline to Skinner's approach) is sometimes fragmented and flawed, it rests on a more abstract competence or knowledge. For Chomsky, the abstract knowledge of language consisted of a limited set of rules that enabled an infinite number of sentences to be uttered and understood. A key notion in Chomsky's argument was the fact that children and adults can produce and understand sentences they have never heard before.

Skinner had attempted to explain language as behaviour caused by the individual's interaction with the environment, but Chomsky (1959) pointed out that this was a premature claim because there was little point in explaining the processes of language learning if there was no clear idea of what it was that was being learned. Skinner had used language learning as a demonstration of the operation of a theory about learning in general, and his account had focused on the learning process rather than on what was being learned. Chomsky argued that Skinner's conception of language, or what was being learned, was quite inadequate because it couldn't explain how language users learned to discriminate between sentences that were superficially similar, but that were at heart quite different. If language learning was a process of

Chomsky suggested that the learner of any language has an inbuilt learning capacity for language that enables each learner to construct a kind of personal theory or set of rules about language based on very limited exposure to that language.

Chomsky distinguished between language competence and performance, where our competence is a measure of our abstract knowledge of rules of language, and performance is a measure of the speech that we actually use.

associating words and strings of words with meanings, how could we learn to recognise, and resolve, the ambiguity of sentences like:

Visiting relatives can be boring.

Chomsky's solution to this problem was to illustrate that seemingly different interpretations of the same sentence were in fact two sentences with quite different underlying structures. These structures, he suggested, were not learned, but rather reflections of the way human thinking was organised. In his view human beings are predisposed to language, and the minimal examples of language heard by infants are sufficient to set a process of language development into action.

He proposed that the human capacity to develop language from limited data could be thought of as a Language Acquisition Device or Language Acquisition System. He suggested that, just as physics students were sometimes given problems in which they had to infer the circuitry of a 'black box' from given electrical inputs and outputs, the problem for linguists and psycholinguists was to describe the circuitry of the Language Acquisition System (Chomsky 1961, 1965; Katz 1966; McNeill 1966) and in doing so the nature of language and language learning would, at last, be understood.

Results of language learning research since Chomsky

Chomsky's suggestion that learners acted as theory builders, testing their theories against language that was overheard or used each day, was soon tested by an extensive research effort. Individual children and their parents were observed, tape-recorded and analysed in numerous languages in order to discover evidence of an emerging system of rules underlying children's language and whether children could be considered theory constructors as they learned language.

Previous research into child language development had taken many forms. From the story recounted by Herodotus to carefully recorded case studies, many had attempted to document and explain the progress made by children as they learned to talk. However, Chomsky's claim that there was a specific learning capacity for language that reflected the structure of human intelligence gave researchers a new impetus. It seemed that if the nature of language and language learning could be explained, then profound insights into the nature of human cognition might be very close.

After a flurry of research into and theorising about children's language learning over twenty-five years, our current understandings present us with some mixed conclusions. This is because each new research approach or theory often turned out to provide only part of the story. Just as Skinner's application of behaviourist learning theory to language turned out to be inadequate, so problems began to emerge for a theory of language that took language to be a system of rules for generating and interpreting sentences.

Since the late 1970s, researchers' explorations into children's language learning have been framed by a number of theoretical perspectives. As the research has attempted to get closer to what it is that children learn to do when they learn to use language, a rich and complicated picture has begun to emerge.

The beginnings of language as interaction

At birth children cry. If this is considered to be the starting point in the development of language, it is because it is the first articulation made by the child on the way to developing speech and the resources of language that underpin speech. The first cries seem to take their pattern of rising and falling tone from the breathing cycle and we would be hard pressed to find evidence of language in them. Even so, many parents of very young children claim to be able to distinguish between the cries of hunger and those of other kinds of discomfort.

Whether or not parents or others can distinguish between cries, there seems to be little doubt that the infant is especially tuned to speech. Experiments in which newly born infants can activate tape recordings of human speech and other sounds by sucking on an artificial nipple have demonstrated that infants are much more responsive to human voices than other sounds (de Villiers & de Villiers 1979). These same experiments have shown that infants respond differently to the very small acoustic differences that mark distinctively different sounds in what will be their mother tongue. Other experiments with three-week-old infants have shown that they are disturbed if they see their mothers through a glass screen, but hear their voices displaced from the same visual location by a loudspeaker located a metre to the left or right (Dale 1976). Of course being sensitive to differences in speech sounds does not mean the same as knowing what the differences mean, or even which differences are important and which can be ignored because they are not 'phonemic' or 'distinctive' in the language. By the end of the first three months, a new range of vocal sounds have been added to the cries of hearing infants. The infant now begins to produce vowel sounds that are sometimes called 'back vowels' because they are produced with the tongue raised towards the back of the oral cavity. These sounds are often rounded by the shape of the mouth and give the characteristic 'cooing' sounds made by children of this age. Within the next month or two the child begins to produce speech-like sounds by alternating these vowel sounds with a range of consonants, or sounds produced by the total or partial stopping of the airstream. The first consonants to appear are those made at the back of the oral cavity such as /g/ and /k/ and these are soon replaced by the consonants /b/, /p/ and /d/, which are produced by stopping the airstream at the lips and the teeth. At this point the child is said to have reached the babbling stage.

Whether or not parents or others can distinguish between infants' cries of hunger and cries of other kinds of discomfort, there seems little doubt that the infant is especially tuned to speech.

Babbling provides some puzzles for researchers of children's language. There may well be a process of biological maturation involved in its development because it seems to be independent of the language culture into which the child is growing. Russian, Japanese, and Australian children at five months of age all sound the same. Deaf infants begin to babble too, so the process doesn't seem to be initiated by the hearing of speech. Deaf children do not continue to babble beyond eight or nine months, however, so there must be some kind of learning process taking place at this time. Deaf babies immersed in an environment in which native sign language is used will acquire sign language by the same age as a hearing child has acquired speech. The particular language a child acquires, whether it is a spoken language or sign language, will depend on the language to which she is exposed (for example, English, Russian, Japanese, Auslan, Russian Sign Language or Japanese Sign Language and so on).

What might a child learn through babbling? There have been various suggestions. One relates to the fact that although human beings can produce about 200 separate speech-sounds, only about 50 become phonemes or distinctive speech-sounds in any particular language. Soon after the beginning of the babbling stage, infants seem to produce a considerable part of the whole range of speech-sounds. Towards the end of this period there is some evidence that the range of sounds begins to resemble more closely the set of sounds used in the language community into which the child is growing. At this stage it can be said to be babbling in the characteristic sounds of English or Japanese, or whatever.

A further development that gives these babblings a language-like quality is the emergence of the intonation patterns of the language the child is about to start speaking. An intonation pattern or contour is the recognisable rise and fall in tone of the voice that marks the difference between questions, declarations, and assertions. Children's babblings acquire these contours, although there is some debate about whether they represent for the child the consistent meaning that they have for mature speakers.

The question of meaning in this early babbling is something of a problem because, as Gordon Wells (1986) points out, adult responses to infants are shaped by the adult's culture. The infant's vocalisations are therefore given cultural meanings that are responded to in culturally significant ways, thereby shaping the infant's behaviour towards what is culturally acceptable and relevant. This is an important realisation because it warns us against imagining that one family's way of responding to its infant members will be the way other families respond to infants. The kind of language users that children ultimately grow into will have been shaped by this kind of response, if not in a way that can be called imitation, then at least in terms of what sort of things the child chooses to do with its language. This point will be taken up again shortly.

Russian, Japanese, and Australian children at five months of age all sound the same.

Although human beings can produce about 200 separate speech-sounds, only about 50 become distinctive speech-sounds in any particular language.

An intonation pattern or contour is the recognisable rise and fall in tone of the voice that marks the difference between questions, declarations, and assertions.

The kind of language users that children ultimately grow into will have been shaped by the culture-based responses of the family, if not in a way that can be called imitation, then at least in terms of what sort of things the child chooses to do with its language.

The first words

It had long been believed that children's first recognisable language was the single-word utterance and there is no doubt that this is regarded as a significant event for many parents. While this occurs around twelve months of age (earlier for deaf infants acquiring sign language), for some time before this children show that they can partially understand what others around them are saying.

The emergence of the one-word utterance has been labelled 'holophrasis' because it seems to be a one-word phrase. If you've been with young children from about twelve months of age you'll know the phenomenon. The child says 'ball' (or at least that's what it seems like) and adults who are present will interpret the meaning to be something like: 'I see a ball' or 'Give me the ball' or 'Where's the ball?' Questions of meaning are really very difficult to resolve. How do we know what the infant means? Parents and others may behave as though they know the meaning and may respond in a range of ways that could be seen as seeking to confirm the meaning:

Oh you see the ball do you?
Yes that's the ball ...
Do you want the ball?
The ball is on the floor.

The list could go on to cover almost any possible context in which the interaction occurs. Some researchers believed that these responses to children's one-word sentences provided an expansion of what the child wanted to say and thus became a model that stimulated further development. It would have been a good theory because it would have provided us all with a neat teaching strategy. In fact research has shown that the real story is more complex than this. Expansions by adults don't seem to change children's language in any direct way at all, but more will be said of this later.

What does the child mean by these one-word sentences? Comments, directions, and requests, sometimes demands, seem to be the range of the holophrastic utterances, but it is often difficult to specify exactly what the child might mean by them. This is one reason why adults often respond with an apparent expansion. It serves to check on whether the adult has understood the child's intention. There seems to be little doubt that the utterance means a great deal more than what the word on its own might mean for an adult.

Studies of children's first words have suggested that the words may well name objects that the child can easily act on or use to identify specific individuals. A common feature of word use at this stage is the overextension of meaning of the words to wider categories or classes of objects than permitted by adult language. Thus 'papa' may be used appropriately to identify the child's father, but may then be applied to other adult males.

Some researchers believed that expansions of children's one-word sentences articulated what the child wanted to say and thus became a model that stimulated further development.

There seems little doubt that the single-word utterance means a great deal more than what the word on its own might mean for an adult.

A possible explanation of this overextension, or overgeneralisation, of meaning is that the child learns to apply the particular word on the basis of only one or two defining characteristics. Thus, 'papa' or 'dada' come to be applied to any humans who are adult and male. Similarly, words like 'dog' or 'cat' may be misapplied from an adult point of view, yet for the child the defining characteristic for the use of one or the other may be four-leggedness or a furry coat.

The first sentences: a grammatical approach

For many linguists, however, the really interesting stage in the development of language begins sometime around the child's second birthday. We hesitate to specify a date because it immediately gives rise to concerns about the development of children who arrive at this point more slowly and encourages smugness about those who may get to it sooner. The plain fact is that there is great variability between children in the precise age at which two-word sentences first appear, even if there is little variation in the fact that the two-word stage seems to be universal.

What was the result of the enquiry into two-word sentences? Linguists and psychologists and a group of researchers sharing insights and methods from both disciplines (who called their field 'psycholinguistics') all began to study the utterances of two year olds with intense professional interest. Sentences like 'Allgone milk', 'More milk', 'Byebye car', and 'Mommy sock' became the subject of the most careful analysis. One researcher, Martin Braine, seemed to have made an important discovery in 1963 when he proposed that these children seemed to be using a grammar in which the first words fell into either one of two classes. One class of words was relatively small in number but seemed to be used frequently. These were labelled 'pivot' words because a growing number of other words, called 'open' words, were attached to them as the following two-word sentences illustrate.

It was suggested that two-word sentences were comprised of two classes of words: pivot and open words, where the pivot class of words expanded only slowly while the child's repertoire of open class words was extended rapidly.

Allgone milk
Allgone car
Allgone Daddy

It was suggested that the pivot class of words expanded slowly while the child's repertoire of open class words was extended rapidly. What gave the description some appeal was the fact that it implied a regular set of structural rules being applied by the child. The pivot words, it was argued, could only be used in given positions in a sentence. Some words were first-position words and others were second-position words, and they were not interchangeable. However, open words could be attached to pivot words or to other open words.

At first glance it seemed a plausible way of describing what young children do with their first sentences, but there were some serious problems with the whole approach. By the beginning of the 1970s, the idea that children at the two-word stage were using a regular grammar of pivot and open words had to be abandoned, because not all children's two-word sentences could be described in this way. Examples were noted of apparent pivot words occurring either alone or in first or second positions. For example, 'bye-bye' was noted (Brown 1973) in the following constructions:

Bye-bye
Bye-bye man
Papa bye-bye

So the grammar, or structural rules, didn't seem to fit the way in which children spoke. Even more importantly, they didn't come anywhere near capturing the capacity of children at this age to understand the language of those around them. A grammatical description of children's language would have to do more than merely describe the rules they might use in putting two-word sentences together.

An even more telling criticism arose because this structural description of children's language couldn't account for differences in meaning between sentences that were superficially similar but in fact quite clearly different. Lois Bloom, a prominent researcher at the time, provided the destruction of the emerging theory in 1970. Her research subject, Kathryn, uttered the same sentence twice on the same day to make quite different meanings. On the first occasion her sentence, 'Mommy sock', was a comment as she picked up one of her mother's socks; and on the second occasion it was uttered as her mother was putting a sock on Kathryn's own foot. If the structural description of pivot–open class grammars couldn't distinguish between these two uses of the same utterance, then they weren't very useful at all. You might remember that a central point in Chomsky's argument for a description of the rules of language was that there had to be a means of showing that sentences with similar surface structure, but different meanings, had a different underlying structure. Pivot–open class grammars failed the test.

Now why should we tell you about a theory that didn't work? One reason is that the exercise pointed out the pitfalls involved in trying to explain children's language as a set of structural rules without reference to meaning. Alternative descriptions and explanations of children's language development focused on the child's growing capacity to construct and share meanings with others. Even when children begin to use more than two-word sentences, an approach that looks at both structure and function proves to be more helpful than the strict consideration of structure alone.

The first sentences: meaning and function

The first thing to be said about the function of children's early language use is to point out that, even though children may be growing into a wider speech community than the one provided by the immediate family, it is the immediate daily contact between the child and significant others in the child's life that sets the scene for the kind of language the child subsequently comes to speak. That is to say, even in a community where a particular language is dominant, as English is in Australia, the English that is learned will reflect the particular functions that the language serves for the family into which the child is socialised. For example, some fairly general differences have been noted in the ways care-givers talk to children. The differences are not so much of absolute usage as they are of probability. All care-givers use language in referential ways and expressive ways. Referential uses are those in which language is used to point out objects in the child's environment, such as 'See the dog' or 'Oh, there's the pin'. Expressive uses are those in which comments are made about the speaker or the child, as in: 'Mummy's very pleased' or 'You're a good boy'.

It has been argued (Nelson 1973) that in some families one or the other type of utterance predominates in parents' language and this is reflected in the child's early sentences. Serious consequences should not be drawn from this difference, but it does point out that children learn to do what others demonstrate for them. Not every family provides the same sort of demonstrations of the purposes and functions of language; therefore; conclusions drawn from data obtained in one family may not hold true for others.

There is some convincing research that points out the kinds of variations that can occur across cultures and what these variations mean for young language learners when they come to school. Shirley Brice Heath spent almost ten years studying two small, working-class communities on the edge of a larger town in the south-eastern United States of America. She found considerable variation in the ways each community responded to and therefore shaped the developing language of its children. We will return to this important study when we look at the role of adults in language development.

Another ten-year study of language development carried out in England by Gordon Wells (1981, 1986) noted variations in the kinds of language encounters and interactions provided by different families for their infant members, and these too seemed to have powerful consequences for children's prospects of success at school.

If nothing else, these studies ought to put us on our guard against the idea that all children experience the same practices and follow the same developmental path as they grow into their language. This wariness can lead us to more careful interpretation of existing or future

It is the immediate daily contact between the child and significant others in the child's life that sets the scene for the kind of language the child subsequently comes to speak.

Not every family provides the same sort of demonstrations of the purposes and functions of language, thus conclusions drawn from data obtained in one family may not hold true for others.

Heath found considerable variation in the ways that two different American communities responded to and thus shaped the developing languages of their children.

Wells also found that these variations had powerful consequences for children's prospects of success at school.

We should be wary of the idea that all children experience the same practices and follow the same developmental path as they grow into their language.

research. For example, a great deal of misinterpretation has been applied to a study carried out by Michael Halliday on the emerging language of his infant son, Nigel.

Halliday (1975) claimed that Nigel's babbling had acquired some elementary functions of speech long before anything resembling words or sentences were used. He reported that from the age of nine months, Nigel was systematically using particular, recognisable vocalisations to accomplish particular functions. Functions are not strictly the same thing as meanings that we might speak of in adult language because they do not yet consist of words, phrases or sentences; and Halliday could not easily translate them into meanings as adults might understand the term. He described them and attempted to explain them in the following manner:

- instrumental (the 'I want' function)
- regulatory (the 'do as I tell you' function)
- interactional (the 'me and you' function
- personal (the 'here I come' function).

What makes Halliday's approach interesting is his view that language is not so much a system of rules, as Chomsky proposed, as it is a means of performing particular socially communicative functions. For Halliday, learning language is a matter of learning the kinds of meanings that can be shared in particular situations. It isn't at all clear that every family would provide the environment for these particular functions. On Heath's and Wells' evidence it seems unlikely, but it does seem plausible that each particular social context in which an infant was developing would provide its own means of interpreting, and thus shaping, what the child's first attempts at communication could mean.

Halliday's description has been misunderstood by some writers who have recommended that teachers should plan to develop each of these functions. These writers have missed the point that, by the time the child starts school, these separate single functional language forms have been replaced by a much more complex way of speaking in which multiple functions are used. Furthermore, different contexts and interactions may well produce different kinds of language use altogether.

Bearing in mind the reservations about observations of development being true for all children, the research on the meaning and function of beginning sentences is still interesting. As far as making references to objects, it has been noted that children seem to be quite selective in what they choose to mark by naming or comments. Not everything in their world seems to get the kind of attention that warrants being named and its name becoming part of the child's language. Lindfors (1987) cites the work of Katherine Nelson who studied the early vocabularies of a group of eighteen children for one year. Nelson found that of these children, eleven used 'shoe', five used 'hat', four used 'socks', but only one used 'crib' and none used 'diaper' (nappy— Nelson's study was conducted in the USA). Similarly six used 'key' and

Halliday suggested that language is not so much a set of rules as a means of performing particular socially communicative functions.

Each particular social context in which an infant was developing would provide its own means of interpreting, and thus shaping, what the child's first attempts at communication could mean.

none used 'table'. The problem is to explain why some words seem more likely to appear in children's early vocabularies than others that name or label objects at least as likely to be encountered by the child. Lindfors draws an explanation from the work of Swiss psychologist Jean Piaget. For Piaget cognitive (or thinking) development could be described in several stages, each with distinctive characteristics. In the first of these, which he called the sensorimotor stage, the child up to about two years of age understands the world in terms of his or her ability to do things physically to it. Lindfors goes on to point out that certain objects in the child's life are much more likely than others to be acted on by the child in some way. Other objects that are present in the child's world are not so easily differentiated from other aspects of that world because they are not so easily manipulated.

> Until the age of two years, the child understands the world in terms of his or her ability to do things physically to it, and this has implications for language learning.

The kinds of meanings that children choose to realise in their early one-word and two-word sentences have been documented by various researchers. Table 9.1 shows some results of this research. Beyond the two-word sentence, the child's language production makes rapid and complex changes. The early two-word sentence becomes a three-word sentence as the child begins to use more complex grammatical structures to realise more complex semantic possibilities and, shortly after, four-word sentences begin to appear. This early language has been called 'telegraphic speech' because it seems to resemble the kind of

Table 9.1   Meaning relations in early utterance

Kind		Form	Example
1	Naming	that + N	that book
2	Notice	hi + N	see house
3	Recurrence	more + N	more milk
		'nother + N	'nother raisin
4	Non-existence	allgone + N	allgone egg
		no more + N	no more milk
5	Attribute	Adjective + N	big train
6	Possessive	N + N	mummy nose*
7	Locative	N + N	doll bed*
		V + N	put box*
8	Agent-Action	N + V	Eve read
9	Agent-Object	N + N	mummy sock*
10	Action-Object	V + N	throw ball

> Children's early speech is tightly bound to the context in which it occurs.

*These items are really quite ambiguous when set out in a table, but a reader could soon imagine a context in which the utterance would have the meaning given to it here. The point is that children's early speech is tightly bound to the context in which it occurs.

Adapted from R. Brown, *A First Language: The Early Stages*, and J. Lindfors, *Children's Language and Learning*.

language adults use when they send telegrams. However, to regard it as merely a shortened or abbreviated version of adult language would miss several important points. In the first place, there seems to be a considerable difference between what the child can say and what the child can understand, so we must not confuse the child's growing language capacity with the development of speech. In addition to speech, the child is developing a range of social conventions relating to the use of language. Conversational turn-taking and even an understanding of the structure of conversation and exchanges are being learned in every encounter in which the child participates or overhears.

Conversational turn-taking and even an understanding of the structure of conversation and exchanges are being learned in every encounter in which the child participates or overhears.

What do children say in three-word sentences and what do they seem to understand? We can try to answer the question in several ways. We can do it in terms of the grammar (or structure) of their sentences, we can look at the meanings they seem to make, or we can examine the social interactions they seem to be negotiating with others.

Development by stages: some problems

A guide to the sequence of early grammatical development was developed by Roger Brown and some of his students from Harvard University in the early 1970s. Brown suggested that the clearest indication of development in language was the increasing length of sentences used by children. His method of measuring length was to count the individual morphemes (units of meaning) used in utterances produced by the child. Of course the utterances used by any child varied in length each time something was said. However, Brown proposed that an average, or mean, could be calculated which could provide a useful index of the grammatical complexity of children's utterances. Furthermore, it was possible to subdivide their development into stages about which useful generalisations could be made. In all, Brown was able to suggest five stages of development on the evidence of the data he and his colleagues analysed, as shown in Table 9.2. Each stage seemed to reflect further levels of grammatic and semantic complexity. Beyond the fifth stage, however, the system was unhelpful because of increasing structural complexity and combination of sentences, rather than the simple addition of more units.

Table 9.2   Brown's developmental stages as mean length of utterance (MLU)

Stage	MLU
1	1.75
2	2.25
3	2.75
4	3.50
5	4.00

An approach that seems to divide children's development into clear, identifiable stages is attractive to those who want to make comparisons between children and extract general rules about the nature of language development from these comparisons. However, it is also dangerous for those who want to accept some responsibility for the continuing development of children's language at school, such as teachers. The problem is, as Harste et al. (1984) pointed out, that these approaches seem to rest on assumptions that language is a closed system of structures and meanings to be acquired by children, rather than a system by which children interpret their experience. The difference is one of focus. Brown and his colleagues, and other language researchers, regarded the developing language as their primary interest. As educators, Harste et al. argue for a focus on the learners and the strategies they use.

What use can we make of all the data collected, analysed and written about during the years of intensive study of children's language development? Brown and his colleagues' research involved the most intensive analysis of only three children—named Adam, Eve, and Sarah—from which developmental stages were identified. The transition to stage 2 was evidenced by the first appearance of fourteen grammatical morphemes (the smallest meaningful units of a language) or inflections in the children's speech. The evidence provided by Adam, Eve, and Sarah was highly consistent and is shown in Table 9.3.

Although the evidence was drawn from a small sample of children, subsequent studies tended to confirm the general order that indicates grammatical relationships which children used to develop these morphemes. These children did not begin to use the grammatical morphemes shown in Table 9.3 simply because they had now learned a

Language could be considered as a system by which children interpret their experience.

Table 9.3 First appearance of grammatical morphemes

Morpheme	Example
The present progressive	-ing
Prepositions	'in', 'on'
The plural marking of nouns	cat—cats; dog—dogs
The irregular past tense	'went' (from 'go')
Possessives	'Mummy's nose'
Uncontracted *be* as a main verb	'Where is it?'
Articles	'a', 'the'
The regular past tense	'walked' (from 'walk')
Third person singular verbs	'she goes'
Third person irregular verbs	'has he?', 'does she?'
Uncontractible *be* as auxiliary	'is he', 'were they'
Contractible copula (linking verb)	'that's'
Contractible *be* as auxiliary	'they're running away', 'he's sitting down'

part of the grammar of English as used by adults. In the samples of speech recorded by Brown and his associates, his subjects did not cross a line that showed clearly that they had now learned a particular grammatical form. Sometimes months separated the first usage of one of the fourteen morphemes from the times when they seemed to be used consistently. The learning proceeded in such a way that the researchers had to devise careful ways of analysing the distribution of omissions and usage.

Perhaps the most interesting observation made by the study is that the order of acquisition didn't seem to depend on the frequency with which the children were likely to hear each of the morphemes. The most likely explanation was that when the grammatical and meaning complexity of each was combined, the resultant complexity seemed to correspond closely to the order of acquisition (that is, the more complex patterns are acquired later). To this extent there was some evidence that, in searching for pattern and order in language, children were sensitive to basic rules of language that underlay the speech they heard and produced each day.

Even more striking evidence of children's active search for and application of their own rules of pattern and order in language comes from the phenomenon called 'overgeneralisation' or 'over-regularisation'. The grammatical morphemes that have already been mentioned as ways of marking different grammatical functions, such as tense and number, are regular and quite predictable for many English verbs and nouns, as shown in Table 9.4.

You will notice that the spelling rules for English do not reflect the pronunciation rules in that the past tense morpheme for walk and kiss, /t/, is pronounced differently from the morpheme used to mark the past tense for hug and sag, /d/. Similarly, the plural morpheme takes different pronunciations for cat, /s/, and dogs and boxes, /z/. Even so, these forms can be said to be regular with the variations being due to regular phonological rules.

The order of acquisition does not depend on the frequency with which children are likely to hear each morpheme.

Children actively search for and apply their own rules of pattern and order over the language they are learning, as is evidenced by 'overgeneralisation' and 'overregularisation'.

Table 9.4 Regular verb and noun inflections

Verb	Past tense	Noun	Plural
walk	walked	cat	cats
kiss	kissed	sock	socks
hug	hugged	dog	dogs
sag	sagged	box	boxes

In addition to these regular ways of marking past tense and pluralisation, the language includes a number of frequently used irregular verb past tenses and noun pluralisations, as Table 9.5 illustrates.

Table 9.5   Irregular verb and noun inflections

Verb	Past tense	Noun	Plural
sleep	slept	sheep	sheep
come	came	child	children
run	ran	mouse	mice

In the early stages of language development, children do not use inflected forms that would indicate they are sensitive to tense or number distinctions. Even when their speech first begins to include forms that mark these, they may well use them with apparent correctness. However, shortly after this many children begin to use 'incorrect' forms that indicate that they are beginning to recognise and apply regular rules. Children's speech will include expressions such as 'sleeped', 'comed', 'runned', 'sheeps', 'childs' and 'mouses'.

These examples may seem trivial and they certainly are childish, but what they indicate is an active, constructive process being used by children as they impose a pattern and order over their developing language.

Brown's study showed how, when sampled over time, children's language continues to change rapidly but not in discrete steps. Sentences become longer and grammatically more complex as children begin to combine semantic roles into single sentences. What might have been two two-word sentences just a month or so earlier in a child's life becomes a single sentence as additional meanings and grammar are combined. The sentence that expresses 'agent + action' as in 'Adam write' was recorded in Adam's early language as was a sentence that included 'agent + action + instrument + locative + object' as in 'I like pick dirt up firetruck'.

What stands out in this study is not merely the similarity of children's developing speech patterns or the validation that Brown and his co-workers received from other studies. What was striking from studies into children's language was the apparent fact that they were constructing a language that was systematically different from what they heard around them, yet increasingly came to resemble the speech that they heard. There was no doubt that children were applying some sort of systematic processes to the business of gaining control over the language they heard spoken about them. The precise nature of that process, however, was not really clear and many came to believe that learning language was not due to a special capacity of the mind, but a reflection of a general learning capacity that humans possess.

There were further difficulties in understanding children's language development from the perspective of describing rules that children seemed to have acquired. Chomsky had been insistent that the rules of any speaker's language would have to explain more than the actual

In the early stages of language development, children do not use inflected forms that would indicate they are sensitive to tense or number distinctions.

It has been shown that children construct a language that is different in systematic ways from what they hear those around them using, yet which continues over time to resemble more closely the speech that they hear.

Learning language is not due to a special capacity of the mind, but is a reflection of a general learning capacity that humans possess.

Chomsky had insisted that
the rules of any speaker's
language would have to
explain more than the actual
utterances a speaker was
heard to make. The rules
would have to explain the
speaker's competence.

utterances a speaker was heard to make. The rules would have to be able to explain a speaker's competence, that is, the total range of utterances a speaker could produce or understand in an appropriate context. In trying to understand this aspect of adult language knowledge, a researcher can always ask a speaker whether an utterance is acceptable or not. This is not possible with young children, however, because they often have not yet developed the kind of self-awareness that would allow them to reflect on what they may and may not do with their language. A researcher who is seeking to understand aspects of children's language learning is therefore stuck with analyses of what the child utters or appears to understand.

Another problem arises in this approach because elements of adult language appear in young children's speech long before the child could be expected to have the language knowledge or cognitive awareness to use these appropriately. For example, expressions such as 'It's a' and 'I'm a' may appear long before the child shows any other evidence of having learned how to control the verb 'to be' or contract it. The child appears to have learned these expressions, and others, as single expressions rather than grammatical constructions. Finally, there have been objections to the notion that language should be singled out for attention in such a way that its development is separated from the social and cognitive development of the child as a whole.

Later changes in children's language

The development of speech that occurs in the period following the emergence of two- and three-word utterances is complex and rapid. Children's language does not remain fixed in anything that could clearly and unambiguously be called a stage. They continue to develop more complex ways of expressing more complex meanings, and their language increasingly comes to resemble the language of those with whom they interact.

Children continue to
develop more complex
ways of expressing more
complex meanings, and their
language increasingly comes
to resemble the language of
those with whom they
interact.

Children's capacity to
understand others who use
conventional ways of making
sentences seems to be
better established than their
capacity to produce the
conventional forms
themselves.

Children know more about
language than they can
necessarily do with it.

The development of different ways of making negatives, asking questions, and combining sentences within other sentences provides considerable opportunity for speech changes in the first five years of a child's life. Their capacity to understand others who use these conventional ways of making meanings seems to be better established than their capacity to produce the conventional forms themselves. Yet again the difference between children's productive and receptive capacity for language illustrates that when we think about language, we should consider more than speech. Or if you prefer, it illustrates the value of distinctions like Chomsky's concern to separate performance from competence. There is abundant evidence that children know more about language than they can necessarily do with it.

Children at Brown's stage 1 typically make negatives by adding a negative marker to what might otherwise be declarative utterances, for example:

No Teddy
No drink milk
No like custard

Fromkin et al. (1990) illustrate the further development of negatives as it occurred for one child.

Declarative:	I want some food.	
Negative 1:	No want some food.	(*no* attached to beginning of sentence)
Negative 2:	I no/don't want some food.	(negative element inserted; no other change)
Negative 3:	I don't want no food.	(negative element inserted: negation 'spread'—*some* becomes *no*)
Negative 4:	I don't want any food.	(negative element inserted correctly: *some* changed to *any*)

V. Fromkin et al., *An Introduction to Language*, p. 360 emphasis added.

Questions show a similar development with the first being declarative statements delivered with a question intonation, or as a declarative statement preceded by a 'wh' term ('where', 'who', 'why', 'what'). The first set of questions are often termed 'yes/no' questions because they can be answered satisfactorily with a 'yes' or 'no'. The second set are called 'information' questions, because they generally require information to be provided. The following examples are taken from Clark and Clark (1977):

Fraser water?	**Where Ann pencil?**
See hole?	**Where Mama boot?**

As for the development of negatives, children quickly find more complex ways of asking their questions:

See my doggie?	**What book name?**
I have it?	**Why you smiling?**

The next development commented on is the introduction of an auxiliary verb and the inversion of subject and verb:

Does lions walk?	**What I did yesterday?**
Oh, did I caught it?	**What he can ride in?**

In addition to refinements of negation and questions, the most significant change to the structure of children's early language begins at about three years of age when complex sentences first appear. These are sentences in which two or more clauses are combined into one complex sentence.

There are three basic ways of combining sentences in English. The first is by conjoining two sentences of equal 'value' usually with a conjunction as in:

Roula likes Con and Con likes Roula.

The second is by making one sentence relative to the subject, or the object of another sentence as in:

The boy who I play with took the bat.
The boy took the bat that we use for cricket.

The third way to combine sentences is by adding a complement that modifies the main verb rather than the subject or object. These clauses are often referred to as 'adverbial clauses' because they modify the verb as in:

The boy took the bat after the game.
When the game was over the boy took the bat.

Other complements can replace or expand the object of the verb in sentences like:

The boy lives over there.
I played with the boy from next door.

Children seem to combine sentences first by adding complements to the object noun-phrase of sentences, as shown by the following examples from a study by Limber and quoted in Dale (1976):

I think it's the wrong way.
I mean that's a D.
I see you sit down.
Watch me draw circles.
I don't want you read that book.

Using these examples, Dale then commented: 'From these extensions of simple sentences children move into sentences that use relative clauses to modify objects and at about the same time begin to use conjoined sentences'.

Beyond these first complex sentences, the structure of the sentences that children use continues to grow in complexity, as does the complexity of the sentences they seem to understand. Therefore, there is some justification for the claim made by some linguists that by the time children are six years of age they have mastered the major structures of the language they are learning. The claim is true enough when based on an analysis of language as a system of generating and understanding sentence structures. However, as all teachers know, children continue to modify and develop their language in many ways after they commence school.

Generally by the time children are six years of age they have mastered the major structures of the language they are learning, but they continue to modify and develop their language in many ways after they commence school.

In addition to an expanding vocabulary and growing self-confidence in mastery of the rules for generating and interpreting sentences, children show increasing subtlety of understanding in the use of terms indicating time and space relations between themselves and others. Conventional use and understanding of expressions like 'before' and 'after'; 'in front of' and 'behind'; 'to' and 'from' in conversation indicate growing social awareness. The use of terms like 'ask' and 'tell', and 'buy' and 'sell', show increasing awareness of the subtle differences of meaning conveyed by language, as well as an awareness of the social contracts that are maintained between speakers and listeners if language is to be communicative.

Some aspects of speech development that occur after five years of age that have been identified (C. Chomsky 1969) are noted in Table 9.6.

Table 9.6   Course of speech development after five years of age

Approximate age	Major oral language development
5–6 years	Settles the use of pronouns and verbs in present and past tenses, using the inflections of the family. Complex sentences appear more frequently.
6–7 years	Additional progress occurs in using complex sentences, particularly those using adjectival clauses. Conditional dependent clauses, such as those beginning with 'if', appear.
7–8 years	Use of relative pronouns as objects in subordinate adjectival clauses. ('I have a cat which I feed every day.') Subordinate clauses beginning with 'when', 'if', and 'because' appear frequently. Gerund phrases as the object of the verb appear ('I like washing myself').
8–10 years	Connectors ('meanwhile', 'unless', 'even', 'if') are used to relate concepts to general ideas. Use of present participle active begins to appear ('Sitting up in bed I look around'). Use of the perfect participle appears ('Having read Tom Sawyer, I returned it to the library'). The gerund as the object of a preposition begins to be used. ('By seeing the movie, I didn't have to read the book.')
11–13 years	Complex sentences with subordinate clauses of concession introduced by connectives ('provided that', 'nevertheless', 'in spite of', 'unless') are used to frame hypotheses and imagine their consequences. Auxiliary verbs such as 'might', 'could', and 'should' appear more often than at earlier stages. Logical constructions such as 'if ... then' begin to be used. Longer communication units are used.

In addition to a growing capacity to do things with language, children develop an increasing awareness of language itself.

In addition to a growing capacity to do things with language, children develop an increasing awareness of language itself. They become verbally playful and, as they move through the primary school, if all goes well they can explain how and why jokes, stories, and other texts work.

What teachers can expect

By the time they start school some children will be entering sustained contact with English for the first time, while others may find that the English they hear in school is used for different purposes and in different ways from those they have experienced out of school.

Teachers have learned to expect considerable differences between children by the time they start school. Some children will be encountering sustained contact with English for the first time, while others may find that the English they hear in school is used for different purposes and in different ways from their experiences out of school. These children may at first seem to be backward or deficient as far as language development is concerned, but studies in language development provide evidence that this view cannot be sustained. Whatever children's background when they start school, we can be certain that their language development enables them to participate adequately in the roles required of them in their home. The course of language development in school depends to a large extent on how these children understand and choose to accept the roles the school requires of them. Difficulty in school may be the result of *differences* in school practices rather than *deficiencies* in the child.

Difficulty in school may be the result of *differences* in school practices rather than *deficiencies* in the child.

Processes of language learning

What are the processes and strategies used by children as they grow into language from birth? Any answer to this question can be based only on indirect evidence. The behaviourists were right in their assertion that the operation of the mind could never be directly observed. It is sometimes said that a new baby is a mouth surrounded by an appetite, which is one way of putting the view that newborns have little sense of themselves as individuals or as 'things' that are separate from their environment. If this is so, then the newborn has to learn to differentiate itself from its surroundings before any sort of learning can occur.

How the child discovers its separateness from others must be by an internal process that imposes a pattern and predictability on experience. All processes of learning language may be driven by the human need to make sense of what is going on around us, and by the equally pressing need to try things out for ourselves.

We've already seen how infants are sensitive to the sound of human voices and this may well reflect the beginning of the process that leads to an awareness of self and others. At any event this is a necessary, early step in developing language. We know it happens because very young infants come to focus attention on specific objects that they stretch out and reach for. They also quickly learn to fix attention on particular objects that care-givers direct attention to.

The child's discovery of the separateness of itself from others must be by an internal process that imposes a pattern and predictability on experience. Indeed, all of the processes of learning language may well be driven by the human need to make sense of what is going on around us, and then by the equally pressing need to try things out for ourselves. It ought to be quite clear that children play a role in their own language development that goes far beyond imitation of what they hear others saying. The research literature on children's language abounds with examples of children ignoring invitations to repeat or imitate structures they haven't yet developed for themselves. The following example illustrates just how tenaciously children maintain their 'own' language in the face of adult models:

She said, 'My teacher holded the baby rabbits and we patted them'.

I asked, 'Did you say your teacher held the baby rabbits?'

She answered, 'Yes'.

I then asked, 'What did you say she did?'

She answered, again 'She holded the baby rabbits and we patted them'.

'Did you say she held them tightly?' I asked.

'No', she answered, 'she holded them loosely'.

J. B. Gleason, Do Children Imitate?, p. 1.

Even direct invitations to imitate can be refused as in the following example:

Child:	*Nobody don't like me.*
McNeill:	*No, say 'Nobody likes me.'*
Child:	*Nobody don't like me.*
(eight repetitions of this dialogue)	
McNeill:	*No now listen carefully; say 'Nobody likes me.'*
Child:	*Oh! Nobody don't likes me!*

D. McNeil, Developmental Psycholinguistics, p. 69.

Most researchers accept the idea that children actively construct their own language by a process that involves selecting particular aspects of the language they hear and then constructing working theories about what they are, what they mean, and what they can be used for. This view has led many writers on language education to suggest that learners take on a major responsibility for their own language learning.

Indeed, the errors made by adult literacy users can sometimes be traced back to a working theory they constructed as children that has continued uncorrected. For example, one of the authors noticed an adult student in her literacy class occasionally misspelled the word 'they' as 'thay'. He continued to do so despite the error having been brought repeatedly to his attention during the six-week course. Frustrated, the teacher finally discussed the seemingly simple error with the student, asking him why he sometimes spelt 'they' incorrectly. Showing a similar degree of frustration, the student finally blurted out,

> Children actively construct their own language by a process that involves selecting particular aspects of the language they hear and then constructing working theories about what they are, what they mean, and what they can be used for.

'Well, that depends, doesn't it!' The comment prompted the teacher to ask what it depended on. He said, 'Well, it's because "they" refers to males and "thay" is for females'. The teacher was now in a position to explain to the student that 'thay' was not a word in English and could never be used (to which he commented, 'Well, why didn't you tell me that weeks ago?'). Similarly, the same student sometimes misspelled 'full' as 'ful' to indicate that something was half full. In his mid 40s, he had held these misconceptions since childhood. The significance of this anecdote is that it shows the way in which children are active learners of language, seeking to make sense of language and the world around them. As a child, the 'theories' this student had constructed were plausible (as rules related to gender do exist in other languages), yet they were incorrect. In this instance it was only when the teacher understood the reasons for the student's errors that teaching and learning took place.

Language learning as social interaction

Carol Edelsky (1989) has described the process of language development as being 'profoundly social'. By this she means that what children learn is learned as part of the social process of doing things with other human beings. This view has led many writers on language education to insist on the importance of the contexts in which language is learned. It is in the social contexts in which people do things together that children see and hear demonstrations of the language they are learning. Under these conditions they not only learn the language as a system of formal rules, but they learn it as a set of social rules governing the way people relate to each other.

Halliday's views on language and language learning address the relationship between social meaning and language form. Instead of describing language as a self-contained system of rules, he has attempted to describe it in terms of its use as a symbolic system reflecting the meanings generated and shared within social groups. Halliday has written extensively about the way language forms, and how systems are reflections and shapers of the social functions they serve. We have already referred to his research involving the emerging language of his infant son. He identified a number of single-function utterance-types in Nigel's language from the age of about 9 to 16.5 months (Halliday 1975). These utterances, which were not yet verbal, were in order of appearance:

> **instrumental (or the 'I want' function)**
> **regulatory (or the do as 'I say' function)**
> **interactional (or the 'I see you' function)**
> **personal (or the 'here I come' function).**

It is in the social contexts in which people do things together that children see and hear demonstrations of the language they are learning.

Later functions to appear were:

heuristic (or the 'I can find out' function)
imaginative (or the 'let's pretend' function)
informative (or the 'I've got something to tell you' function).

Between 16.5 and 18 months, Nigel's language underwent a transition in which the functions that had previously been separate began to be absorbed into multifunctional utterances (his speech was now doing several things simultaneously within a single utterance). Halliday claimed that much of Nigel's language could now be regarded as falling into either a pragmatic function that involved interaction with others, or what he called a mathetic function that involved language being used to learn about the environment and language itself. This function becomes the base of internalised uses of language in later development. It was only at this point that the first recognisable words began to appear. However, they were firmly located in a functional base in which the child was learning what he could do with this developing way of dealing with the world symbolically.

In taking a functional approach, Halliday can escape some of the concerns faced by purely linguistic or cognitive approaches. Linguistic and cognitive accounts don't offer much by way of explanation of why a child's language changes in the early years. The linguistic or cognitive account has to be supplemented by a social dimension that a functional account includes. Even so, Halliday's approach still leaves unanswered the question of the processes by which children learn how to map their social relationships on to language. Perhaps it is for this reason that Halliday has given a good deal of attention to the theories of Basil Bernstein (see chapter 3), who has tried to explain how different family structures and patterns of interrelation lead to different styles of making meaning.

An Australian educator, Brian Cambourne, has written extensively on the kinds of conditions under which successful language learning occurs. The conditions he identifies are not processes used by learners, but they certainly imply that language learners actively construct their own language (Cambourne 1989). He asserts that language learning proceeds without planned, direct instruction when learners are immersed in an environment in which the language they will ultimately learn is used in purposeful ways. In this environment they are given multiple demonstrations of language in use. While both these conditions are necessary for successful learning, Cambourne argues that they must be accompanied by what he calls engagement, which is the focused attention that learners give to demonstrations when they see themselves as potential 'doers' of what they see being demonstrated. The probability of engagement is enhanced when the learner and others have high expectations that the learners will be successful and are

According to Cambourne, successful language learning occurs under the following conditions: immersion, demonstrations, engagement, expectations, responsibility, approximations, and responses.

permitted to take responsibility for choosing which aspects of language to attend to. The successful language-learning environment, he argues, provides opportunities for the learner to use the language being learned, and early approximations to adult forms are tolerated by more expert language users who provide appropriate responses to the learner.

Cambourne's explanation of the success of first-language learning has been criticised (Luke et al. 1989) because the role of parents and others in the language-learning process varies so much between cultural groups that it is unlikely that generalisations can be made that might fit every cultural group. It is granted that different groups will interact differently with children, but there can be little doubt that the meanings children learn to recognise and share will be those they engage with as they are immersed in the language of others.

Shirley Brice Heath's study of two communities—Trackton and Roadville—in south-eastern USA identified significant differences in the ways each brought its children into accepted ways of making and sharing meaning through language (Heath 1983). In Trackton, her name for a black, working-class, rural community, she noted that babies hardly ever had time to coo and babble by themselves or that they were rarely in quiet situations where their babbling sounds could be heard above the general talk that seemed to go on around them most of the time. Children were 'listeners and observers in a stream of communication which flows about them but is not especially channeled or modified for them'.

When infants begin to utter sounds that could be interpreted as referring to items or events in the environment, these sounds received no special attention. Trackton adults believe a baby 'comes up' as a talker; adults cannot make babies talk: 'When a baby have sumptn to say, he'll say it'. Now this attitude challenged many ideas about the interaction between infants and mothers that had come to be regarded as universal before Heath's study was published. Heath cited instances in which adults ignored the meaning potential of children's early utterances because they believe they should not have to depend on their babies to tell them what they need or when they are uncomfortable. Adults are the knowing participants; children only 'come to know'. The experience of families in Trackton stood in some contrast to the families of Roadville, a white working-class community where parents took pains to act as teachers and conversationalists in baby talk. Heath reported that parents would expand combined items (between 18 to 22 months) into well-formed utterances and would 'seize upon nouns used by the child and build a discourse around it'.

Roadville parents took on a teaching role by asking and answering questions, and made sure that their children 'say things right', which varied from naming things appropriately to using the verbal formulations such as 'I'm sorry' and 'excuse me' in appropriate situations. What is important to note here is that both groups of

Different communities have different adult–child interactions, with the result that children are socialised into rich but different language environments.

children were being socialised into rich but different language environments with marked differences in styles of adult–child interaction. Too often, schools interpret these differences as deficits, and children's learning can be hindered as a result.

A longitudinal study carried out in the English city of Bristol by Gordon Wells (1987) followed the language development of thirty-two children from 15 months to the end of their primary school careers. The study showed that one of the most significant roles for parents or adults was as conversationalists who were sensitive to the communicative needs and proficiency of the children to whom they were talking. In following the progress of these children, Wells noted that class and cultural differences were not significant in the kind of interactions the children enjoyed before school, but that from the beginning of their school careers, differences emerged. These differences were most clearly related to the ease with which the children expanded their language to include the use of reading and writing.

> Wells' study showed that one of the most significant roles for parents or adults was as conversationalists who were sensitive to the communicative needs and proficiency of the children to whom they were talking.

Second-language learning

ACTIVITY AND DISCUSSION

Make a list of the factors that you think might be involved in successfully learning a second language. Discuss your list with fellow students.

In multilingual societies such as ours there are always new learners taking up the challenge of learning another language. There will be very young children simultaneously learning two or more languages within multilingual families. There will be children from non-English-speaking families who begin learning English informally from the media and other children before they start school, and who then start more formal learning when they start school. There will be children from monolingual English-speaking families who begin learning a language other than English as part of a school program, and there will be adults learning English in government-funded programs for new arrivals.

In some respects the processes of learning a second language are similar to first-language learning—similar conditions are necessary, such as immersion in the language, hearing and seeing the language in purposeful contexts, and the opportunity to use the language and to receive feedback.

> The processes necessary for second-language learning are similar to first-language learning, but there are a number of factors that determine how successful the learning will be.

Each learner faces a task unique to his or her circumstances, but there are some factors likely to influence the ease and kind of proficiency the learner will achieve. The learner's age and attitude to the new language and culture, reasons for learning the new language, amount of exposure to the new language, the learner's preparedness to take risks to experiment and use the language, and the type of support and response received in the learning environment all contribute to the likely success in learning a new language. Some of these factors and the implications for teaching will be discussed later.

What does the second-language learner have to learn?

The task of the second-language learner is to figure out how the sound system of the new language's speech code is organised, how meaning is organised into words, sentences and texts, and how the written language works.

The second-language learner has to work out how the sound system of the new language's speech code is organised; how meaning is organised into words, sentences and texts; and, if learning the written language, how the written code works. In addition, the second-language learner has to learn how the language is used in different contexts—the sociocultural aspects, which include verbal and non-verbal variations.

The nature of the task will vary depending on the age, previous experience, and attitudes of the learner. Second-language learners who have already substantially acquired a first language do not have to develop the basic concepts and understandings about the world that are necessary in first-language learning. However, new ways of expressing meanings need to be learned and some reorganisation of meanings need to be made, because different languages do not always label ideas, perceptions, and processes in exactly the same way. Those readers who are bilingual will be well aware that exact translations from one of their languages to the other are often quite difficult. The greater the language–culture differences between the two languages, the greater the reorganisation of thought that will be necessary for a successful language learner.

The second-language learner who has already successfully learned a first language, and has had solid experience in using cognitive processes, is well suited to working out how a language works. These second-language learners know about language and how it works, and, if literate, know about print and its role.

Second-language learning should be easier than first-language learning, but many factors can influence the process.

To this extent second-language learning should therefore be easier than first-language learning, but many factors can influence the process. Many of us can attest to the difficulty of learning a second language.

Factors that influence second-language learning

For discussion purposes the factors that influence the learning of a second language can be categorised as those centred on the learner and those that are centred on the environment.

Factors centring on the learner include neurological, cognitive, affective, and linguistic factors.

Neurological factors

There has been much discussion about a critical period for learning one or more languages. Language-learning research indicates that it is very difficult to learn languages after puberty. It is believed that specialisation of various parts of the brain is involved and parts of the left hemisphere reserved for language get taken over by other functions if they are not used by language learning within the critical period. Steven Pinker (1994, pp. 293–6) argues that there are biological advantages in terms of safety and survival for vulnerable infants to learn language very rapidly, but once having accomplished this, the advantages for such rapid learning ability disappear.

Certainly many adults find learning a second language difficult; however, there is evidence of a tribe in South America where adults learn a number of languages successfully (Brown 1987). This success may be due to the multilingual environment and attitudes towards language learning.

It is difficult as adults to acquire authentic control of the phonology or sound system of a second language. People who learn another language as adults tend to retain much of the sound system of their first language in the form of an accent, but this is only a small aspect of learning a language. Most researchers now agree that older is faster, but younger is better (Larsen-Freeman & Long 1991).

Cognitive factors

It has been suggested that second-language learning is more difficult as an adult because of cognitive differences. The adult, being at a more sophisticated cognitive level, fully appreciates the complexity of the task and may be overwhelmed by it, and discouraged from learning and proceeding a step at a time as a younger learner would. However, research indicates that second-language learning can be achieved at any age, and difficulties may be due to attitudinal and personality factors.

Affective factors

Age and risk-taking

As we grow older we generally become more self-conscious and inhibited and are not prepared to take risks and make mistakes that are essential for language learning.

Attitudes

Attitudes towards the second language will greatly influence the learning process. Negative attitudes towards the speakers of a language, the language itself, and the cultures associated with the language will be detrimental to the learning process. The learner who is positively predisposed towards a second language and culture is more motivated to become like its speakers and likely to experience greater success than a learner with negative attitudes towards the language and its speakers. The learner who feels positive about the language and speakers will

Negative attitudes towards the speakers of a language, the language itself, and the culture associated with the language will be detrimental to the learning process.

actively seek interaction with speakers, which is basic to language learning. In this respect, age might be a factor. Young children will generally not have negative attitudes towards a language or the speakers of a particular language, whereas adults may have learned negative attitudes.

Peer pressure

The need to belong seems very influential with young children who are learning a second language. Hence the playground and interactive classroom are important learning contexts in which children seek to be like everyone else.

Purposes

The purposes for learning the language seem to be significant. If there is a strong desire to learn the language, obviously the learner will put in much more effort, which can only enhance the learning process. This may be one reason why children in parts of the world where there are social or economic advantages in speaking more than one language seem to be more successful in becoming bilingual. If this is so, then school programs in second languages need to be constructed so that learners' purposes can be identified and supported.

Linguistic factors

Children who are learning two languages simultaneously acquire them by similar strategies. Maintaining separate contexts for the two languages helps to avoid any possible confusion in the learning process. Sometimes the development may be slower than if only one language were being learned, but such bilingualism does not retard intelligence. If anything, bilinguals may be slightly superior as 'they have an additional language asset, are more facile at concept formation and have a greater mental flexibility' (Lambert 1990).

Linguistic and cognitive processes similar to those used in first-language learning are used in second-language learning.

Research on non-simultaneous second-language learning in childhood indicates that linguistic and cognitive processes similar to those used in first-language learning are used (Brown 1980). Contrary to popular opinion, there seems to be minimal first-language interference.

It is more difficult to determine what strategies would be naturally used in adult second-language learning, as there are few cases of research of untutored learning of second languages by adults. Teaching methods shape the learning process for so many learners. However, research does indicate that adults approach a second language systematically and attempt to formulate linguistic rules on the basis of whatever linguistic information is available to them—information from both the native language and second language. Adults appear to manifest some of the same types of errors found in children learning their first language.

Adults approach a second language systematically and attempt to formulate linguistic rules on the basis of whatever linguistic information is available to them—information from both the native language and second language.

Where second-language learners may need some special attention in the classroom is in the development of the kind of language required in education. Teachers need to guard against the assumption that because children have developed fluency in playground English they will also be able to deal with the language requirements of the curriculum. Gibbons (1991, pp. 14–25) identifies the major classroom functions of language as:

- classifying
- comparing
- giving and following instructions
- describing
- questioning
- evaluating
- expressing a position
- explaining
- hypothesising
- planning and predicting
- reporting
- sequencing
- social uses such as asking for permission, assistance, directions denying, promising, requesting, suggesting, and expressing wishes and hopes.

Summary

Research and theory building in relation to language and language learning is always carried out within a framework of theoretical assumptions that may not directly relate to teachers' concerns. Teachers need to be aware of the differences between the assumptions and theories that underpin particular research. Behaviourist research into language has been directed to apply general theories of learning to language learning, while cognitive research has attempted to describe the rule-based organisation of learners' language knowledge. Functional theory and research attempts to identify how learners come to use the available resources of the language to meet communicative needs within their families and beyond.

The most valuable research and theory for teachers is likely to be that which takes the learner as its focus and concentrates on interpreting the kinds of interaction and context that children engage in as they learn the kinds of meanings that can be made and shared through language.

Children are remarkably successful in making sense of the linguistic and social rules that apply to their particular language group, and this success is accomplished with varying kinds of support but little direct teaching from their care-givers.

A second language is best learned where the learner can apply the language-cognitive strategies used in learning the first language—

namely by discerning the underlying rules of structure and use in the language being spoken around them, and by continually hypothesising, testing and revising in the light of subsequent interaction. The learner creatively constructs novel text on the basis of the rule system being built. Errors will occur as in first-language learning. Since the learner already has one language, when they lack the means of expression in the second language they will use the resources of the first language. It is critical, therefore, that the learner is immersed in the target language, otherwise the processes will not be able to be used effectively. This makes learning a foreign language difficult.

Second-language learners will, if given the appropriate environment:

- use non-linguistic understandings as a basis for working out the language (this can only occur if the speakers in the environment are using language directly relevant to the situation; teachers and others need to use language in predictable routines and contexts)
- use whatever is salient and interesting to them—we engage in what interests us and this is how we learn
- produce language and see how others respond and/or observe how others express meaning
- ask questions to elicit data
- imitate what others say
- use general language-operating principles to work out the language
- make the most of whatever they know.

Implications for teaching

1   At several places in this chapter we have referred to the fact that, while all children seem to be successful language learners out of school, the same cannot be said about their progress at school. If we accept behaviourist and cognitivist views of language learning, we may be inclined to blame the learner for failing to be as successful at school. This would be a little odd as we would then have to explain why children could learn quite adequately without planned teaching for five years, only to become problem learners when someone sets out to teach them systematically.

2   The interactionist focus on language development shows children as active constructors, in negotiation with others, of their own knowledge of and about language. It would seem to be sensible then to discover how school could support ways of learning that had already been successful. This approach is sensible, but it is unusual, and could be difficult. Many school tasks and rituals require children to use language in ways their out-of-school experiences may not have prepared them.

3   The task of the school is not to give students more language, or even to attempt to change their language; rather it seems to be to extend their experience through new interactions so that the process

of making and sharing meaning can continue with new forms of experience and a wider world of others. It may be that the wisest thing for teachers to do would be to follow Britton's (1976) advice that instead of concentrating on language they should concentrate more on doing things with students and let the language to some extent look after itself.

4   If we want our students to use language to explain, describe, persuade, and report, then we need programs that require them to do these things. So teachers will need to devise activities that require students to take on the demands of these uses of language. It also means that teachers will need to be well informed about how these ends can be accomplished in language. Teachers need to know how to construct coherent explanations, descriptions, persuasive arguments or cases, and clear reports.

5   Obviously some kinds of classroom experiences will invite and support a student's use of effective language-learning strategies more than others. Since second-language learning seems to involve many of the same strategies as first-language learning, supportive classrooms for first-language and second-language learning will share similar characteristics. This means:

   • a classroom where language is whole and meaningful, and used for authentic purposes of interest to the learner which will provide better linguistic data, enable the learner to use non-linguistic cues, and engage the learner in the task. Whole activities such as shared book experience, story-telling, drama, and experiential activities are much more effective than drills, workbook exercises, and use of basic reading texts

   • a classroom where oral and written language are both demonstrated and used purposefully. Literacy learning occurs with oral language learning. There is not a definite sequence from listening, to speaking, to reading, to writing

   • a classroom where the atmosphere is collaborative and non-competitive, and where learners can support each other and where the learner is prepared to take risks, to have a go

   • a classroom where the learner has lots of opportunities to use language for real purposes in order to practise language, and integrate and refine new skills and knowledge

   • a classroom where supportive feedback is provided to assist learning.

References and further reading

Aird E. & Lippmann (eds) *English is Their Right: Strategies for Teachers in the Multilingual Classroom*, AE Press, Melbourne, 1983.

Bloom L. *Language Development: Form and Function in Emerging Grammars*, MIT Press, Cambridge, MA, 1970.

Braine M. D. 'The Ontogeny of English Phrase Structure Rules', in *Language*, 1963, Vol. 39, pp. 1–13.

*Braunger J. & Lewis J. *Building a Knowledge Base in Reading*, Northwest Regional Educational Laboratory's Curriculum and Instruction Services, NCTE, Urbana, IL & IRA, Newark, DE, 1999.

Brown H. Douglas *Principles of Language Learning and Teaching*, 2nd edn, Prentice-Hall, Englewood Cliffs, NJ, 1987.

Brown R. *A First Language: The Early Stages*, Harvard University Press, Cambridge, MA, 1973.

Cazden C. B. *Child Language and Education*, Holt, Rinehart & Winston, New York, 1972.

Chomsky A. N. 'Review of Skinner's verbal behaviour', in *Language*, 1959, Vol. 35.

Chomsky C. *The Acquisition of Syntax in Children From 5 to 10*, Research Monograph 57, MIT Press, Cambridge, MA, 1969.

Clark H. H. & Clark E. V. *Psychology & Language: An Introduction to Psycholinguistics*, Harcourt Brace Jovanich, New York, 1977.

Dale P. S. *Language Development: Structure and Function*, 2nd edn, Holt, Rinehart & Winston, New York, 1976.

De Villiers P. A. & De Villiers J. G. *Early Language*, Harvard University Press, Cambridge, MA, 1979.

*Fromkin V., Rodman R., Collins P. & Blair D. *An Introduction to Language*, 2nd Aust. edn, Holt, Rinehart & Winston, Sydney, 1990.

Garton A. & Pratt C. *Learning to be Literate: Development of Spoken and Written Language*, Blackwell, Oxford, 1998.

Gibbons P. *Learning to Learn in a Second Language*, PETA, Newtown, NSW, 1991.

Gleason J. B. 'Do Children Imitate?', Paper at International Conference on Oral Education of The Deaf, Lexington School for The Deaf, New York, June 1967.

Halliday M. A. K. *Learning How To Mean*, Edward Arnold, London, 1975.

*Hammond, J. (ed) *Scaffolding: Teaching and Learning in Language and Literacy Education*, Primary English Teaching Association, Newtown, NSW, 2001.

*Heath S. B. *Ways With Words: Language, Life And Work in Communities And Classrooms*, Cambridge University Press, Cambridge, 1983.

Lambert R. 'Persistent issues in bi-lingualism', in Harley B., Allen P., Cummins J. & Swain M. (eds) *The Development of Second Language Proficiency*, Cambridge University Press, Cambridge, 1990.

Larsen-Freeman D. & Long M. *An Introduction to Second Language Acquisition Research*, Longman, Essex, 1991.

*Lindfors J. *Children's Language And Learning*, 2nd edn, Prentice-Hall, Englewood Cliffs, NJ, 1987.

McNeill D. 'Developmental Psycholinguistics, in Smith F. & Miller G. (eds) *The Genesis of Language*, MIT Press, Cambridge, MA, 1966.

Nelson K. *Structure And Strategy in Learning To Talk*, Monograph for the Society for Research in Child Development, No. 149, The Chicago University Press, Chicago, 1973.

Skinner B. F. *Verbal Behavior*, Appleton-Century-Crofts, New York, 1957.

*Wales L. 'Literacy for learners of English as a second language', in Christie F. (ed.) *Literacy for a Changing World: A Fresh Look at the Basics*, ACER, Melbourne, 1990, pp. 167–86.

*Wells C. *The Meaning Makers Children Learning Language and Using Language to Learn*, Hodder & Stoughton, London, 1987.

*Wignell P. (ed.) *Double Power: English Literacy and Indigenous Education*, The National Languages and Literacy Institute of Australia, Melbourne, 1999.

*Wing Jan L. *Write Ways: Modelling Writing Forms*, Oxford University Press, Melbourne, 1991.

CHAPTER 10

LEARNING LITERACY

FOCUS

This chapter focuses on the understanding that:

- *literacy is a social and cultural practice that occurs for particular purposes existing within a social context*
- *literacy is inherently tied to issues of power*
- *we now talk in terms of multiple literacies to reflect the different contexts and types of texts literacy users interact with*
- *literacy learning means much more than learning the 'skills' of reading and writing*
- *learning to read and write means learning the conventional nature of a variety of text types*
- *interaction with significant others is the most significant factor in children's literacy development*
- *children learn much about written language before coming to school.*

PRE-READING ACTIVITY

1   Write down what you can remember about learning to become literate.

2   Who was significant in helping you learn to read? What did they do to assist you? Share your responses.

Introduction

When we started out to tell the story of children's language development, we had to spend some time discussing what it was that children learned when they learned language. This was because the view that we took of language determined what we considered to be significant in the process of development. The same is true when we consider the learning of literacy. It is true that learning to use written language involves the use of different senses from those used in learning to speak. However, when we argued that learning language involved more than learning to speak, we had in mind, among other things, that reading and writing refer to special uses of language. From our point of view then, learning to read and write involves learning to use language in new ways for new purposes; that is, different social practices.

The most significant difference between written language and spoken language is that written language persists in time and space. That is to say, it does not evaporate, as does spoken language, which can be recalled only by memory unless recorded in some electronic way. Until about the 1970s, reading and writing was widely considered to be a set of discrete skills such as 'word attack', word recognition, phonic skills, and discrete comprehension skills. Over the past twenty years, there has been a significant shift to what is called a sociocultural perspective of literacy. That is, literacy is seen as 'a matter of social practices – something to do with social, institutional, and cultural relationships' (Gee et al. 1996, p. 1). By considering literacies as social practices, rather than mechanical skills undertaken by individual learners, we become aware of the way in which literacy is context-bound and tied up with the distribution of power (Lankshear 1997). The changing nature of our understanding of literacies has resulted in shifts in classroom approaches, characterised by Lankshear as traditional (skills-based, phonics), progressive (whole language, process writing), and post-progressive approaches (genre-based, critical language awareness, multiliteracies).

The term 'multiliteracies' is widely used to reflect the multiple nature of literacy and the integration of multiple modes of meaning-making (Cope & Kalanztis 2000). Take, for example, the World Wide Web and consider the multiple ways in which meanings are represented through the use of visual images, sound, video, and text. Lankshear and Knobel (in Lankshear 1997, p. 152) describe the way in which reading and writing are transformed by digital or electronic text: 'With digital text we shift from an author-controlled textual environment where words are fixed on the page in a top-down, left-right, beginning-end materiality to a reader-controlled environment, infinitely flexible and open to manipulation'. Hence literacy is now being defined quite broadly. For example Luke, Freebody and Land (2000, p. 20) define literacy as: '... the flexible and sustainable mastery of a repertoire of practices with the texts of traditional and new communications technologies via spoken language, print, and multimedia'.

As literacy teachers, we need to also acknowledge the way in which literacy (and more generally, education) is political. Maria Sweeney (in Edelsky 1999, p. 97) explains the political as it applies to education and literacy teaching:

I strive to create a classroom atmosphere and curriculum that prepares my students to build and participate in a critical democracy. I help my students gain the necessary skills and knowledge to critique their world, unveil injustices and needless

Learning to read and write involves learning to use language in new ways for different purposes.

The most significant difference between written and spoken language is that written language persists in time and space.

Literacy is now seen as a 'matter of social practices'.

The term 'multiliteracies' is used to reflect the multiple nature of literacy.

suffering, and equity, and I urge children to get angry and do something. I don't pretend that my teaching is neutral or objective; education never is. Behind everything taught is a point of view of particular perspective. Value-free education is a myth and, in fact, an impossibility.

Sweeney goes on to cite Ira Shor (1992, p. 12): 'Critical education is not more political than the curriculum which emphasizes taking in and fitting in. Not encouraging students to question knowledge, society, and experience tacitly endorses and supports the status quo …' As Freire said, education that tries to be neutral supports the dominant ideology in society.

Extending this thinking, Luke and Freebody (1999, p. 5) describe literacy education as being: '… ultimately about the kind of society and the kinds of citizens/subjects that could and should be constructed. Teaching and learning just isn't a matter of skill acquisition or knowledge transmission or natural growth. It's about building identities and cultures, communities, and institutions'.

Children begin to learn what reading and writing are used for (the practices) before knowing exactly how the system works. Walter McGinitie, an American researcher, relates a personal anecdote of talking to a child who had spelled the word 'up' correctly, long before his classroom structured spelling/reading program had introduced this particular sound letter combination. When McGinitie asked the child how he knew to spell 'up', the child replied with expansive confidence that it was easy. He learned it from '7up' (an American soft drink trade name). The child told McGinitie that 'u, p' spelled 'up' and then, secure in his mastery of the whole system, added and 'p, u, spells down'. It is an amusing story, but the point is to remind us that written language can make sense in useful ways long before we know exactly how, and children are active language learners, constructing meaning from texts in contexts.

The research literature contains many stories like McGinitie's in which very young children demonstrate that they know reading is different from talking; and writing is used for filling out forms, making notices, lists, and labels, even before the individual letters and words can be written or recognised. How children come to recognise the function of written language may well depend on the examples of written language they see being used around them. Children are immersed in a world in which written language is used to do things. Through their experiences in everyday life, children are provided with examples of ways in which written language is used and valued in their society.

In Heath's 'Trackton' (see chapter 9), where learning to talk involved learning about a variety of social roles, learning to read also had a social dimension. 'Reading was a public group affair for almost all members of Trackton from the youngest to the oldest … but to read alone was frowned upon, and individuals who did so were accused of

---

Children begin to learn what reading and writing are used for before knowing how the system works.

Daily life demonstrates to children both the example of written language that others use and how they use reading and writing.

being anti social' (Heath 1983). In 'Roadville', parents used reading for a variety of purposes that were mostly related to getting something else done, but from an early age they read their children bedtime stories. The bedtime story did not persist beyond the start of school and the interaction seemed to be marked by a concern to 'say it right' and drew appropriate moral lessons; the same approach was evident among 'Roadville' parents when teaching their children to talk. At any event, Heath noted that, 'neither community's ways with the written word prepares it (the child) for the schools' ways'.

In his report on the Bristol study, Wells (1986) commented that: 'If some children made little progress in learning to read and write, the problem as we observed it was not that they had insufficient oral language resources, but that they had not yet discovered the purposes of reading or writing or the enjoyment to be gained from these activities'.

Harste et al. (1984) noted that a two-year-old child who took the comic section from the family Sunday paper and announced that he was going to 'read the funnies' was entering into a social action that demonstrated a number of understandings about the nature of reading. Similarly informed is the two-year-old who takes a blank deposit form from a bank counter and writes what at first sight seems to be scribble in the blank spaces on the form while a parent writes a cheque. Just as we learned to take a broad view of the development of oral language, we need to see that the development of literacy does not begin when children bring home their first reading book from school.

> The development of literacy does not begin when children bring home their first reading book from school.

More recently, children's interaction with electronic or digital texts is an example of learning about different literacies. Unsworth (2001) cites examples by Davidson (2000) and Wilson (2000), respectively, of fifth grade students who make their own 30-minute movies using a computer movie maker, downloading movies from the internet, and using email to swap ideas and communicate internationally; and of a studious year five reader who has a huge collection of Nintendo 64 magazines.

Children's daily lives provide countless demonstrations of the social meanings, purposes, and functions of literacy. Street signs, billboards, television commercials, computer programs, and printed materials are examples they see and interpret. Their parents' and others' interaction with these texts shows them how and why written language is used. How closely they engage with these demonstrations will depend on how important the activity seems to them at the time (Cambourne 1988).

> Children's daily lives provide countless demonstrations of the social meanings or purposes and functions of literacy.

Literacy—what is to be learned?

Given the multiple nature of literacies and the social contexts in which they are embedded, becoming literate is much more than using an alphabetic writing system to map oral language. While decoding skills (knowledge of the relationship between sounds and letters or grapho-phonics) are part of the task, they constitute only one of the resources a literate person brings to texts. Freebody and Luke (1990, 1999) identify four roles or resources: text decoder, text participant or meaning-maker, text user, and text analyst, which are important for the literate person today. In the past, teaching methods tended to focus on only some of these roles; for example, phonics and whole word methods focused on the code-breaker role, whole language emphasised the text meaning-maker and user practices, genre approaches focused on the text user, and critical literacy emphasised the text analyst role.

Figure 10.1   Freebody and Luke (1990, 1999)

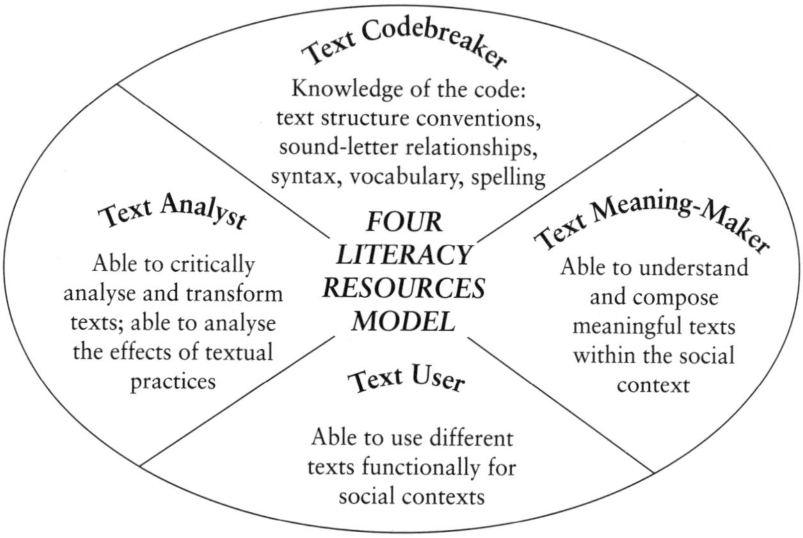

Text codebreaker

Here the emphasis is on learning and using appropriately the code or conventions of language. For written language, the role of the text decoder foregrounds letter/sound relationships, and the understanding of letters/words/sentences, paragraphs, spelling, syntax (grammar), and other conventions of texts.

Text meaning-maker

The emphasis is on understanding and composing meaningful texts using the knowledge as code-breaker, plus knowledge of the topic and context. The role of the text participant draws on background knowledge comparing your own experiences with those described in the text, relating previous experiences with similar texts, seeing your own interests and lifestyles reflected in texts, and constructing meaning from texts based on your own prior knowledge.

Text user

The emphasis here is on using texts appropriately. Hence the learner needs to understand the purposes and uses of different texts, and how the purpose and function of texts shape the way texts are structured. The role of the text user foregrounds using appropriate text types for particular purposes.

Text analyst

The role of the text analyst foregrounds understanding how texts are crafted according to the views and interests of the author/developer; and identifying how the ways in which information or ideas are expressed influence reader, listener, or viewer perceptions. Depending on your purposes for engaging with texts, as text analyst you interrogate the text for the values and assumptions informing the text and consider what action you need to take in reconstructing meaning. The emphasis in literacy education, then, is on developing an understanding that, from children's earliest experiences with literacy, ideas and information in texts are not neutral but represent particular views that can be challenged.

A key concept to understand is that our choice of language and literacies depends on the social context in which they are to be used. This includes the values, behaviours, and language shared by a particular group, which are known as Discourses (Gee 1990, 1995). Familiarity with these are necessary for the effective use of literacy, as they shape and are integrated with the literacy practices. In Gee's view, therefore, literacy means the fluent control of the practices of a Discourse.

Our choice of language and literacies depends on the social context in which they are to be used.

Competence in literacy therefore not only entails how to read and write identifiable text types or genres, but also requires strategic knowledge of how to read social situations and institutional rule systems. Literacy is about cultural knowledge and social power.

Strategic knowledge to read social situations and institutional rule systems is a part of literacy competency.

Shirley Brice Heath (1986) has noted that the community often gives higher value to instrumental uses of literacy over the critical, aesthetic, organisational, and recreational uses that are valued by schools.

What these views lead to is a realisation that if literacy is to be seen as fluent control of a Discourse valued by a community, then schools need to be aware of which texts and Discourses are valued in their communities.

This does not mean that the kind of literacy that has been the usual business of the curriculum is made irrelevant. All the stories, rhymes, and poems that form the traditional content of the curriculum still have a place, but teachers need to recognise that some children will not be familiar with them and that any lack of immediate response is not to be taken as evidence of a 'deprived', 'disadvantaged', or 'illiterate' background. For example, deaf children may not be familiar with traditional nursery rhymes that often rely on rhythm or rhyme, and may include archaic language (think of 'Little Miss Muffet', a nursery rhyme that appeared on a state-wide standardised literacy test for children in Grade 3).

Heath's studies in the United States, Well's studies in the United Kingdom, and McNaughton's studies in New Zealand have pointed to the power of interactions within the family, and between the family and its community, in shaping the child's expectations of literacy and schooling. McNaughton (1995) in particular has shown how in Auckland Pakeha (European), Maori, and Samoan families provide contexts for children's literacy development that reflect and build social and cultural identity. While common purposes for literacy and literacy practices were identified across social groups, there were some distinctive differences. For example, Samoan families set high value on reading for religious purposes and to maintain links with family members in Samoa. Thus for students in these families, early literacy practices emphasised reading and writing of letters, and routines for devotions.

At a time when literacy is increasingly thought of as participation in social practices, rather than a neutral psychological skill, it becomes important to recognise the practices and values students may bring to school. It seems that in some cases we may be presenting literacy as something foreign to the child's culture and experience, despite the fact that the child may have a wealth of experience with particular literacies and literacy practices that we haven't recognised (use of electronic games, surfing the internet, reading a 'form guide' and so on).

Learning how written language works

If children learn the social meanings of written language from the demonstrations of literacy events provided by their daily lives, can they learn in a similar way how written language works? It would seem that they can. The apparent scribble on the bank deposit slip by an English-speaking child runs in a line from left to right and doesn't spread into the printed parts of the form. Older children show an understanding of some of the features of print, even though they haven't yet discovered all of what Yetta Goodman (1983) calls the 'operational and linguistic principles of written language'. Five-year-old Amanda refused a student teacher's invitation to write, saying that she could not write. However, she produced the following sample when she was coaxed to do some 'pretend writing':

She then offered the following example of what she called 'Grandma' writing:

Before she has learned the precise nature of the alphabet letters that she will use later, she shows that she already knows something of the differences between print script and cursive handwriting. By insisting that her writing was 'pretend writing', she demonstrated a clear understanding that while pretend writing may be okay in play, it isn't normally accepted in school. Amanda was aware of a range of social expectations that change the rules in different contexts.

Quite clearly the anecdotes repeated here are of children showing some self-assurance in dealing with written language, but we need to be careful in drawing conclusions from these stories. Not all children will have the self-assurance of Amanda; for some, the experience of school will not maintain and sustain the progress they may have made before entering school.

> Children are aware of a range of social expectations that change the rules of writing in different contexts.

Learning the writing system

School literacy, as distinct from family or community literacy, requires children to recognise and become familiar with the language of books. Marie Clay (1991) points out that children need to acquire the ability to 'talk like a book'. Frank Smith (1978, 1985) suggests that teachers need to issue invitations to join the Literacy Club so that students will want to learn to do what the teacher has made so attractive. Neither of these suggestions implies a new sure-fire, never-fail teaching method as much as they advise careful understanding of what it is the child is to learn, and then the presentation of literacy as attractive (meaningful) as possible to the life and culture of each student.

Making sense of print is not just decoding words and understanding sentences. It also means bringing meaning to the text to make meanings that connect with the life and culture of the learner.

The beginning reader and writer should experience written language in a variety of forms and for achieving a variety of purposes. The perceptive and sensitive teacher will be alert to opportunities that show how written language can be used and how it works. Captions, labels, notes, messages, lunch orders, songs, poems, stories, recounts of daily experience, and reports will all have a place in the program as demonstrations of language in use, which can generate talk and teaching about language and the writing system.

> It seems that our capacity to read would break down if we tried to process every piece of information available from the interaction between print and our knowledge of our language and the writing system.

The learner needs to engage with the organisational principles (Y. Goodman 1983) or underlying rules about how written language is organised. At a basic level, the learner has to discover that it's the print or writing on the page that has to be attended to. The next step is to discover that the message is organised from left to right and generally proceeds down the page. Marie Clay (1979) points out that some learners, having learned to write from left to right, then, as in early writing systems, begin the next line at the right hand end of the page and move to the left. Attending to the print, moving from left to right and scanning down the page are important organisational principles.

It is also important for the beginning reader and writer to discover the linguistic nature of the writing system. For English, the alphabetic writing system, in which alphabetical symbols are arranged in systematic ways to represent words, has to be learned. There are other aspects of the writing system that are not immediately obvious even to very successful oral language learners. Punctuation, as a means to capture something of the intonation of oral language and make the meaning unambiguous and clear, needs to be noticed first then gradually mastered, as does the regularity and stability of the spelling system.

Yetta Goodman (1983) pointed out that the young learner also has to learn a number of relational principles in becoming literate. By this she means that children come to know that there is a relationship between written language and meaning, and oral language. Print does not just serve as an aid to memory; it actually specifies the language and shared cultural meanings of the text.

How children come to these understandings is a fascinating topic for research and debate. How they should be helped by teachers in school to learn them is often fiercely contested in the pages of the popular press. What can be done to separate what is known from what is folk wisdom at best and mythology at worst?

When we read we bring considerable knowledge about language and the world to the marks on the printed page. We use our knowledge of sound-letter relationships (grapho-phonics), the structure or grammar of the language (syntactics), and our knowledge of the meanings of words, sentences, whole texts and how these meanings relate to the world (semantics). Fluent readers rely on semantic and syntactic cues rather than just grapho-phonic cues. They use their knowledge of language, text, and world knowledge to predict what is written on the page. As they become more familiar with the style, content, and topic, their predictions about the text become more accurate.

K. S. Goodman (1976) described the process of reading as requiring reading effectiveness (the ability of a reader to keep a focus on meaning while reading) and reading efficiency (a reflection of the amount of information in the text that has to be processed to get to the meaning). Learning to read effectively and efficiently involves learning to use as little of the visual information as possible in getting to the meaning. There is something of a problem here because the more experience we

When we read for meaning we take short cuts by predicting what we think we see on the page.

Successful readers are always engaged in a trade-off between processing the information provided by the print and in anticipating not just the print but the language and the meaning of a particular text.

Learning to read effectively and efficiently involves learning to use as little of the visual information as possible in getting to the meaning.

have of reading, the fewer pieces of information we are likely to need; and the less experienced we are, the more information we are likely to need before we are prepared to take a risk and jump straight to meaning. This means that reading is likely to be more arduous for younger or less experienced readers than it is for practised readers. This also means that one important way to make reading easier for students is to ensure that they have the content knowledge to bring to the process. Students who already enjoy and have a wide experience of reading are likely to find the task easier and perhaps more rewarding than those who still have to plod a little. The challenge for teachers is that our society values more highly those who read effectively and efficiently than it does those who do neither.

> Children who already enjoy and have a wide experience of reading are likely to find the task easier and perhaps more rewarding than those who still have to plod a little.

Writing

By commenting about learning to write after remarking on reading, we run the risk that the reader will see these as two separate developments in the life of the child, when in fact they are intimately related. We've already seen how children engage in writing-like behaviours long before they write conventionally. It would be easy, but quite mistaken, to dismiss this as unimportant. It seems that just as children learn the purposes of reading long before they learn to read, so they seem to learn the purposes of writing long before they learn the actual conventions of handwriting, spelling, and composition (although Amanda's two attempts at writing show that aspects of the conventions can be recognised from an early age). By the time children begin school they may well have seen a variety of demonstrations of writing in their family culture. Shopping lists, personal letters, reminder notes, birthday and seasonal greeting cards, emails, faxes, and business transactions are just some of the possible uses of written language that will have been seen. What is significant, though, is that each of the uses of writing that children encounter will have been grounded in a strong and often obvious social context. In this way they will have had demonstrations not just of the act of writing but also of its purposes. When children come to school there will be a wide variation in the kind of experiences and understandings they have. However, just as their experiences have led them to understand how oral language is used in their home culture, so they will have understandings of the role of writing in that culture. The task of the school is not simply to teach students to write in a nice hand, to spell conventionally and to compose written texts. Underpinning all of these is the need to demonstrate, in strong and obvious contexts, what writing is used for and how the particular uses shape the writing, and the language.

> Each of the uses of writing that children encounter early in their lives will have been based on a strong and obvious social context.

> Underpinning the task of the school is the need to demonstrate, in strong and obvious contexts, what writing is used for and how the particular uses shape the writing and the language.

Throughout most of the 1980s the 'process writing' approach (Walshe 1981; Graves 1983; Parry & Hornsby 1985) significantly influenced the teaching of writing in Australia. The basis of this approach requires that teachers act as editors or tutors who, in individual and group 'conferences', help learners become aware of their intentions as writers, and at the same time become aware of the needs of their readers, as they begin and revise self-selected and teacher-suggested pieces. The approach depends on teachers being able to provide rich and varied reading and writing environments in which students become aware of different kinds of texts or genres. In addition, the approach requires teachers to become skilled and sensitive at asking questions that enable students to first improve their own writing and then ask appropriate questions about their writing that will lead to improvement. Kamler (1994) has raised questions about the content of children's writing and argues that teachers need to ensure students are aware of the language they use and the values expressed in their texts. As teachers of writing, we cannot ignore racist, sexist, or violent content in texts.

It is misleading to describe 'process writing' as an approach or a method because there is no simple set of steps or procedures to be followed in every circumstance.

In many respects it was misleading to describe 'process writing' as an approach or method as there was no simple set of steps or procedures to be followed in every circumstance. There is published evidence (Graves 1983; Calkins 1986) that approaches to teaching writing in this way, or related ways, can be very successful. However, there have also been claims that where some classrooms purport to take this approach, students are limited to routine kinds of writing that have little relevance to writing outside classrooms, or even to the kinds of writing tasks that they will have to complete as part of their education.

Some critics (Martin 1985) have claimed that, in school, young children typically get to write pieces that have been called 'recounts' of their own personal experience. Christie (1985) has argued that these recounts occur as a result of the way teachers introduce and set limits on what and how students write. In short, they set out what can be meant by a piece of classroom writing. This view has been accompanied by the development of teaching strategies (Callaghan & Rothery 1988; Derewianka 1990) that led to teachers and students jointly constructing pieces of writing in educationally valued forms such as exposition, argument, and informational report. This approach has been controversial (Reid 1988), and it is not clear whether direct teaching and modelling of different genres is likely to be more successful than careful demonstration and immersion in representative samples of already published writing in an environment where there are meaningful purposes for student writing.

It is not clear whether direct teaching and modelling of different written genres is likely to be more successful than careful demonstration and immersion in representative samples of already published writing.

Summary

A strong sociocultural emphasis on literacy raises critical questions about language use. Critical literacy theorists (Freebody 1992; Shor 1992; Kamler 1994; Luke 1994) stress the importance of viewing literacy users as meaning-makers, and texts as constructed. Readers need to be aware of the way in which they are positioned by texts and ask critical questions about what has been foregrounded by the author, what has been included, and what has been excluded. Readers need to learn to deconstruct texts through linguistic analysis, identifying the way in which writers choose particular words (where others could have been chosen). Writers also need to become aware of the way in which they use language to make particular meanings (and not others). Just letting students read and write is insufficient. They need to become, among other things, critical text users, sensitive to the types of meanings and values in texts, aware of stereotypes and discourses operating in texts. We want our students to compose texts that are not sexist or violent.

Writers need to become critical text users, sensitive to the types of meanings and values in text.

In Freebody and Luke's (1990) four resources model (see figure 10.1), the text-analyst role positions the reader or writer as a critical language user. That is, we want our students to question the texts they are reading and producing; to consider who produced the text and why; and to ask: How am I meant to respond to the text? How do I want to respond to it? The emphasis is on understanding the values and power relations evident in the text. Critical literacy is the process of developing 'Habits of thought, reading and writing, and speaking which go beneath surface meanings, first impressions, dominant myths, official pronouncements, traditional clichés, received wisdom, and mere opinions, to understand deep meanings, root causes, social context, ideology and personal consequence of any action, event, object, process, organisation, experience, text, subject matter, policy, mass media or discourse' (Shor 1992, p. 129).

Learning to read and write involves learning to use language to achieve authentic purposes in particular contexts. The first steps towards literacy are taken as children discover some of the things that can be achieved with reading and writing through demonstrations by significant others in their daily world. They use the same process of trying out ideas about the function and nature of the writing system as they did when they were learning to speak.

Learning to read and write involves learning to use language to achieve authentic purposes in particular contexts.

The reading process requires readers to construct meaning by bringing what they know about the world and language to help them predict and make sense of the visual cues on the page. Beginning readers find the process more arduous than experienced readers because they don't know as much about the world or written language. Beginning readers, of any age, are more likely to persist at the task if they find it rewarding and satisfying. Therefore the texts presented to students must make the effort seem worthwhile.

Implications for teaching

1   Learning to read is not simply a case of learning a 'value-free' set of skills that can be applied by an individual in every encounter with print. Students' backgrounds have prepared them with a variety of responses to different kinds of literacy. Different families and

different contexts each generate their own uses of and values for literacy. The intimacy of shared bedtime stories in which whole worlds of adventure and fantasy are opened to children may be valued in some settings while, in others, the values of workshop manuals, knitting patterns or even so-called junk mail catalogues may be seen as useful. Furthermore, digital literacies, such as those required to play electronic games, may be highly valued by children and not by adults at home or at school. Whatever backgrounds children have come from, not all will have learned the range of uses of literacy that success at schooling will depend on. The different uses of literacy need to be acknowledged and a range of materials used. There are many different routes to teaching and achieving literacy.

2   The school's first task, therefore, seems to be to issue as winningly as possible what Frank Smith (1985) calls 'invitations to join the literacy club'. Teachers need to present, as seductively as they can, a wide variety of literacy demonstrations that will show the usefulness of and pleasures to be gained by literacy to students who may or may not have already learned of them.

3   When Cambourne (1989) writes of the 'natural' learning that can occur when what is to be learned is demonstrated so that the learner is immersed in the activity, he doesn't simply mean that classrooms need to be covered in displays where print becomes wallpaper that can be looked at or ignored by children. Children deserve to be in classrooms where print is used to capture their imagination; to send and receive messages, emails, or lunch orders; and for directions, requests, reports, and explanations about whatever is the focus of attention at the time.

4   Beginning readers need texts where their rich and varied experiential knowledge can be used to construct meaning from the texts. Texts with predictable language patterns should be provided in order to support the learners' development of visual processing and integration of different kinds of information necessary for making meaning. Familiar stories, rhymes, chants, and songs should be used frequently.

5   Students should have many opportunities to discover the regularities of the writing system by using it themselves right from the first day at school.

6   There must be many opportunities for teachers and students to share, discuss, and question their reading and writing. Reading circles, writing conferences, and classroom publishing of students' writing are valuable in achieving this.

References and further reading

*Butler A. & Turbill J. *Towards a Reading–Writing Classroom*, Primary English Teaching Association, Rozelle, NSW, 1984.

*Cairney T. *Pathways to Literacy*, Cassell, London, 1995.

*Calkins L. M. *The Art of Teaching Writing*, Heinemann Educational Books, Portsmouth, NH, 1986.

*Callaghan M. & Rothery J. *Teaching Factual Writing: A Genre Based Approach*, Report of the DSP Literacy Project, Metropolitan East Region, Sydney, 1988.

*Cambourne B. *The Whole Story: Natural Learning and The Acquisition of Literacy in The Classroom*, Ashton Scholastic, Gosford, NSW, 1989.

Campbell R. & Green D. (eds) *Literacies and Learners: Current Perspectives*, Prentice Hall/Pearson Education, South Melbourne, 2000.

Christensen L. *Reading, Writing and Rising Up*, Rethinking Schools, Milwaukee, WI, 2000.

Christie F. *Language Education*, Deakin University Press, Waurn Ponds, Vic., 1985.

Clay M. *The Patterning of Complex Behaviour*, 2nd edn, Heinemann, Auckland, 1979.

*Clay M. *Becoming Literate: The Construction of Inner Control*, Heinemann, Auckland, 1991.

Clay M. *By Different Paths to Common Outcomes*, Stenhouse, York, ME, 1998.

Comber B. & Simpson A. (eds) *Negotiating Critical Literacies in the Classroom*, Lawrence Erlbaum, Mahwah, NJ, 2001

Cope B. & Kalantzis M. *Multiliteracies: Literacy learning and the Design of Social Futures*, MacMillan, Australia, 2000.

*Derewianka B. *Exploring How Texts Work*, Primary English Teaching Association, Rozelle, NSW, 1990.

Edelsky C. 'Literacy education: reading and the world', in *English Australia*, 1989, No. 89, pp. 61–71.

Edelsky C. *Making Justice our Project*, National Council of Teachers of English, IL, 1999.

Freebody P. & Luke A. 'Literacies programs: Debates and demands in cultural context', *Prospect: Australian Journal of TESOL*, 1990, Vol. 5, No. 7, pp 7-16.

Freebody P. 'A socio-cultural approach: resourcing four roles as a literacy learner', in Watson A. & Badenhop A. (eds) *Prevention of Reading Failure*, Ashton Scholastic, Sydney, 1992, pp. 48–60.

Goodman Y. 'Beginning Reading Development: Strategies and Principles', in Parker R. & Davies F. (eds) *Developing Literacy: Young Children's Use of Language*, IRA, Newark, DE, 1983.

*Garton A. & Pratt C. *Learning to be Literate: The Development of Spoken and Written Language*, 2nd edn, Basil Blackwell, Oxford, 1998.

Gee J. *Social Linguists and Literacies*, The Falmer Press, London, 1990.

Gee J. P. *Social Linguistics and Literacies: Ideology in Discourses*, 2nd edn, Taylor & Francis, London, 1996.

Gehling K. *A Year in Texts: An Explicit Reading Program*, Primary English Teaching Association, Newtown, NSW, 2000.

Goelman H., Oberg A. & Smith F. (eds) *Awakening to Literacy*, Heinemann Educational Books, Exeter, NH, 1984.

Gollasch F. V. Readers' Perceptions in Detecting and Processing Embedded Errors in Meaningful Text, unpublished doctoral dissertation, University of Arizona, Tucson, AZ, 1980.

Goodman K. S. 'Miscues: windows on the reading process', in Goodman K. S. (ed.) *Miscue Analysis: Applications to Reading Instruction*, ERIC/NCTE, Urbana, IL, 1973.

Goodman K. S. 'What do we know about reading?', in Allen P. D. & Watson D. (eds) *Findings of Research in Miscue Analysis: Classroom Implications*, NCTE, Urbana, IL, 1976.

Goodman Y. M. 'Beginning reading development: strategies and principles', in Parker R. and Davis F. (eds) *Developing Literacy: Young Children's Use of Language*, IRA, Newark, DE, 1983.

Graves D. H. *Writing: Teachers and Children At Work*, Heinemann Educational Books, Exeter, NH, 1983.

*Hammond J. 'Is learning to read and write the same as learning to speak?', in Christie F. (ed.) *Literacy for a Changing World: A Fresh Look at the Basics,* ACER, Melbourne, 1990.

*Hammond J. (ed) *Scaffolding: teaching and learning in language and literacy education*, Primary English Teaching Association, Newtown, NSW, 2001.

*Hancock J. (ed) *The Explicit Teaching of Reading*, International Reading Association, Newark, DE, 1999.

*Harste J. C., Woodward V. & Burke C. *Language Stories and Literacy Lessons*, Heinemann Educational Books, Portsmouth, NH, 1984.

*Harste J., Short K. with Burke C. *Creating Classrooms for Authors: The Reading and Writing Connections*, Heinemann Educational Books, Portsmouth, NH, 1988.

*Healy A. *Teaching Reading and Writing in a Multiliteracies Context: Classroom Practice*, Post Pressed, Flaxton, Qld, 2000.

Heath S. B. *Ways with Words: Language, Life, and Work in Communities and Classrooms*, Cambridge University Press, New York, 1983.

*Hill S. *Guiding Literacy Learners*, Eleanor Curtain, Armadale, Vic., 1999.

*Hill S. *Phonics*, Eleanor Curtain, Armadale, Vic., 1999.

*Hornsby D. *A Closer Look at Guided Reading*, Eleanor Curtain, Armadale, Vic., 2000.

Kamler B. 'Lessons about language and gender', *The Australian Journal of Language and Literacy*, 1994, Vol. 17, No 2, pp. 129–38.

*Knobel M. & Healy A. *Critical Literacies in the Primary Classroom*, Primary English Teaching Association, Newtown, NSW, 1998.

Lankshear C. *Changing Literacies*, Open University Press, Buckingham, 1997.

*Luke A. *The Social Construction of Literacy In The Primary School*, Macmillan, South Melbourne, 1994.

Luke A., Baty A. & Stebhens C. 'Natural conditions for language learning: a critique', in *English in Australia*, 1989, No. 89, pp. 36–49.

*Luke A & Freebody P. 'A Map of Possible Practices: further notes on the four resources model', in *Practically Primary*, 1999, Vol. 4, No. 2, pp. 5–8.

Luke A., Freebody P. & Land R. *Literate Futures*, Education Queensland, Brisbane, 2000, p. 20.

*Martin J. *Factual Writing: Exploring and Challenging Social Reality*, Deakin University, Geelong, Vic., 1985.

*McNaughton S. *Patterns of Emergent Literacy*, Oxford University Press, Auckland, 1995.

*Parry J. & Hornsby D. *Write On: A Conference Approach To Writing*, Martin Education, Sydney, 1985.

*Moustafa M. *Beyond Traditional Phonics: Research Discoveries and Reading Instruction*, Heinemann, Portsmouth, NH, 1997.

Reid I. *The Place of Genres in Learning: Current Debates*, Centre for Studies in Literary Education, Deakin University, Geelong, Vic., 1987.

*Shor I. *Empowering Education: Critical Teaching for Social Change*. University of Chicago Press, Chicago, 1992.

*Smith F. *Essays into Literacy*, Heinemann Educational Books, Exeter, NH, 1983.

*Smith F. *Reading*, 2nd edn, Cambridge University Press, Cambridge, 1985.

*Strickland D. *Teaching Phonics Today*, International Reading Association, Newark, DE, 1998.

*Temple C., Nathan R., Burris N. & Temple F. *The Beginnings of Writing*, 2nd edn, Allyn & Bacon, Boston, 1988.

*Unsworth L. *Teaching Multiliteracies across the Curriculum*, Open University Press, Buckinham, Philadelphia, 2001.

*Walshe R. *Every Child Can Write*, Primary English Teaching Association, Rozelle, NSW, 1981.

* Wignell P. (ed) *Double Power: English Literacy and Indigenous Education*, The National Languages and Literacy Institute of Australia, Melbourne, 1999.

*Wilson L. *Reading to Live: How to Teach Reading for Today's World*, Heinemann, Portsmouth, NH, 2002

Winch G., Johnston R., Holliday M., Ljungdah L. & March P. *Literacy: Reading, Writing, and Children's Literature*, Oxford University Press, Melbourne, 2001.

CHAPTER 11

LEARNING AND LANGUAGE: A SUMMARY

FOCUS

This chapter focuses on the understanding that:

- *learning is about making new meanings and involves making connections between known and new information*
- *language has a vital role in facilitating learning*
- *the way the teacher structures the classroom environment and uses language is significant in facilitating learning.*

PRE-READING ACTIVITY

1 Write down how you think you learn. Share and discuss this.

What is learning?

Language is central to learning. Learning is central to teaching.

What do we mean by learning? We have said that language is central to learning. We have also said that learning is central to teaching.

Learning occurs when we change or elaborate what is already known by us. Learning is a process of making connections, identifying patterns, organising previously unrelated bits of knowledge, behaviour, activities, etc, into new (for the learner) patterned wholes (Cambourne 1990, unpublished). We learn by attempting to relate new experiences to what we already know or believe. Learning is about making new meanings for the learner.

We learn by attempting to relate new experiences to what we already know or believe. Learning is about making new meanings for the learner.

We have an innate need to make sense of the world we inhabit—individuals seek to identify themselves, their environment, and their relationship to their environment.

At least from the time of birth, the human individual is engaged in a lifelong quest for meaning. We have an innate need to make sense of the world we inhabit—individuals seek to identify themselves, their environment, and their relationship to their environment. The first and prime means that we use for this lifelong process of discovery is our language, for it is through thinking, interaction, and co-operation with other people that our capacity and potential for learning increases and develops. In addition, our individual understandings and ways of thinking arise from, and are formed by, our cultural and social interactions. It is both an individual and social process.

In order to discover and explore meaning we have certain physical, perceptual, and cognitive faculties:

- **physical**: the senses of sight, hearing, smell, touch, and taste enable the reception of stimuli from the environment
- **perceptual**: once the stimuli are received, the individual has the capacity to learn to select, integrate, organise, and to reject meaningless stimuli as noise
- **cognitive**: each individual has the capacity to organise selected perceptions, form a hypothesis about them, test the hypothesis against further selected samples, confirm or reject the hypothesis, and thus formulate rules about meaning that enable the individual to predict further meanings about their world. Furthermore, each individual has the capacity to rehearse their findings or organise them through association in order to remember and recall meaning as a means of selecting stimuli (the basis of perception) and prediction (the basis of further construction of meaning).

It must be remembered that no stimuli have inherent meaning. We can recognise significant stimuli only if we already expect or know that they are meaningful. The culture of the individual and the context of the stimuli will therefore strongly influence the meaning and learning process. Language is significant throughout this process—it is important in the processes of prediction, organisation, remembrance, and recollection.

Most of the learning that takes place in our daily lives is social: it arises from our need to solve problems that involve other people or acquire skills we see other people using from our natural exploration and play in the world, the demands and assistance of other people, and pleasure and importance we take from our interactions with significant people in our lives. Through all this we become initiated into the culture of our environment and competent language-users, able to use language to explore the world as individuals.

A major role of language is to structure our 'world' and to make sense of the environment. This concept underpins our concept of the role of language as central to learning. Language is about making meaning, and through language we explore and develop new concepts and new meanings. As teachers we need to be aware of how we can assist our students to use language effectively in all areas of the curriculum.

All humans endeavour to make sense of the world, to comprehend and to learn, in the same fundamental manner from birth to adulthood. Of course, the content of a person's mind varies with age. Humans cannot help but learn. They are programmed to learn from birth: 'The brain of a child is a superbly efficient and instinctive learning device, so much a part of any normal living creature that it functions automatically' (Smith 1975). Hence, as teachers, we do not have to teach our students how to learn, but we need to facilitate rather than

In order to discover and explore meaning we have certain physical, perceptual, and cognitive faculties.

No stimuli have inherent meaning.

Most of the learning that takes place in our daily lives is social.

A major role of language is to structure our 'world' and to make sense of the environment.

All humans endeavour to make sense of the world, to comprehend and to learn, in the same fundamental manner, from birth to adulthood.

The main purpose of schooling is to assist the learning processes, but too often we work against our students' natural learning abilities. Learning occurs when sense can be made of an experience.

Learning is not merely the act of acquiring and retaining information, and teaching is not merely the dispensing of facts.

Learning is natural and easy if learners are in control of what is to be learned and how it is to be learned, if they are interested in the task, and if they can understand its relevance for them.

One way of making learning more effective in the classroom is to allow greater involvement by the students in the curriculum.

hinder the process. The main purpose of schooling is to assist the learning processes, but too often we work against our students' natural learning abilities. Learning occurs when sense can be made of an experience. It is the teacher's responsibility therefore to be interesting and comprehensive. We need to give the student the whole story so that patterns can be determined. Rather than demystifying the process, too often we confuse the learners by breaking skills down into subskills, teaching skills out of context, and oversimplifying information, thereby distorting it.

Learning is not merely the act of acquiring and retaining information, and teaching is not merely the dispensing of facts. The learner is not just a walking data bank. Rather, learning is being able to see the relationships between pieces of information, in composing meaning, in making sense. The learner has to gather and use facts and information, but must also make judgments about them and develop concepts.

Learning is natural and easy if the learners are in control of what is to be learned and how it is to be learned, if they are actively engaged and are interested in the task, and can see the purposes of the task and understand its relevance for them. Learning will be difficult if the process is forced, if the information is broken into meaningless bits and pieces, and if someone else is in control, especially when feelings are involved. Most of us have a problem of remembering too much and not forgetting some things we wish we would. We can all remember alternative spellings for some words, and some of us can't forget being a poor reader or writer.

One way of making learning more effective in the classroom is to allow greater involvement by the students in the curriculum. Teachers may set a topic on the basis of their knowledge of students' interests and needs and the curriculum requirements, but students can be involved in determining:

- what they already know, assume, and believe
- what they want or need to find out
- how they will go about answering their questions or finding solutions to their problems
- how they will assess what they have accomplished
- how they will know what they have found
- with whom and how they will share their findings.

This is an investigatory or enquiry-based model of learning–teaching that can be used across the curriculum.

The type of environment the teacher creates, the learning experiences that are provided, the type of student control that is allowed, the type of responses the learner receives, and the way language is used will all be critical in facilitating learning at school.

How does language facilitate learning?

As has been stated many times in this book, language is about making meaning, about making sense of experiences. Hence, language is very much a part of learning. We cannot divorce language from thinking and learning or from living. We need language to collect data, investigate, hypothesise, test, analyse, evaluate, and share findings.

It is through language—non-verbal and verbal—that we receive information about the world. At school much of this information is received through listening and reading. Through reading, particularly, we can create new worlds and find out more about ourselves and our relationships with others. We can encourage students to be critical readers of text, to recognise the way in which texts are constructed and readers positioned. Reading critically allows us great independence and power as learners. Hence it is important that students learn how to use reading for learning purposes.

It is through speech and writing that our thinking and development of concepts is most enhanced. In the process of finding words for our thoughts we develop and extend our thinking. In justifying our ideas for others we have to develop and crystallise our thinking further. Hearing others' responses to our thoughts forces us to modify, change, and extend our thinking, as we take on board the ideas of others. It is therefore important that time is allowed for discussion to occur. In particular, it is important that students are encouraged to articulate their ideas and listen to others. Through the discussion process the richness of many ideas can be shared and the learning of many students can be enhanced.

Similarly, writing enables us to extend our thinking and learning, and, due to the permanent nature of writing, to do this more effectively. The process of finding words to express our thoughts enables our thoughts to grow. Most people would have experienced the feeling that, having finished writing an essay, they now know what the topic is about and would like to start all over again. In the process of writing we review our knowledge, actively apply our understanding, analyse and synthesise what we mean, and constantly evaluate the text we are composing as we move back and forth to create meaning for ourselves and others.

Through writing, because we can read and reread our ideas, we can easily evaluate them, reorder them, and change them. Furthermore, writing allows others to evaluate our ideas easily and their responses further enable us to change and develop our thinking. It is important that we allow and encourage learners to express their ideas through writing, and that we allow them time to explore a topic through writing before we expect a final product. However, in order to enable students

> We cannot divorce language from thinking and learning or from living.

> In the process of finding words for our thoughts, we develop and extend our thinking.

to use writing to its best effect, we need to ensure that they have been shown how to use their thinking capacities to reflect, infer, hypothesise, generalise, and conclude.

The use of language needs to be a conscious part of learning sessions in all areas of the curriculum. Students need to be able to use listening and reading to obtain new data, to create new meanings, and for learning purposes. Hence they need to know how to take notes, and use these notes to hypothesise, infer, and draw conclusions. Students need to be encouraged to explore ideas through talk and then through writing. In addition, students need to learn how to read and write appropriately for different purposes and different discipline areas.

Language is involved in every part of the learning process:

- **acquiring/generating knowledge** — listening, reading, note-taking, graphing, keeping diaries and journals

- **processing/making connections** — collating notes, identifying cause and effect relationships, sharing ideas, grouping similar ideas together, constructing flow charts

- **drawing conclusions/hypothesising** — writing reports, giving oral reports, putting on plays, producing charts, answering questions

- **consolidating and applying knowledge/evaluating one's learning** — writing in different forms, asking new questions, creating new productions.

The way in which the teacher uses language can be significant for learning. Too often teachers ask 'test' questions, where students have to guess the answer that is in the teacher's mind, rather than asking 'real' questions. This certainly does not facilitate the development of thinking processes. Consider the following examples:

T: What time is it Sean?　　　T: What time is it Sean?
S: Twelve o'clock.　　　　　　S: Twelve o'clock.
T: Thanks.　　　　　　　　　 T: Very good.

ACTIVITIES AND DISCUSSION

Think of something that you have learned recently. List the conditions and factors that facilitated the learning. Share your responses with a friend.

Q How many factors were similar?

Think of an occasion when your learning was not successful, and try to determine the conditions and factors that make learning difficult.

The way in which the teacher uses language can be significant for learning.

Language and learning in the classroom

Smith (1983) and Cambourne (1984, 1988) have written in some detail about the implications of language learning for the classroom. Smith has discussed the importance of demonstrations of what is to be learned, of the learner engaging with the demonstrations and the task, and the learner's sensitivity to the learning. He believes that many of us are desensitised to learning certain things because of experiences with them. Many of our teaching strategies can actually discourage the student from learning to read and write!

As discussed in chapter 10, Cambourne (1988) examined the conditions that operate when a child successfully learns spoken language. He then hypothesised that these conditions would be important for learning literacy. Figure 11.1 summarises his views. These conditions are invaluable as a checklist to evaluate how conducive our classrooms are for learning. Smith, Cambourne, and Holdaway (1979), as well as others, believe that the conditions necessary for language learning are important for all types of developmental learning.

Goodman (1986) has summarised what makes language easy or hard to learn:

It's easy when:	*It's hard when:*
It's real and natural.	*It's artificial.*
It's whole.	*It's broken into bits and pieces.*
It's sensible.	*It's nonsense.*
It's interesting.	*It's dull and uninteresting.*
It's relevant.	*It's irrelevant to the learner.*
It belongs to the learner.	*It belongs to somebody else.*
It's part of a real event.	*It's out of context.*
It has social utility.	*It has no social value.*
It has purpose for the learner.	*It has no discernible purpose.*
The learner chooses to use it.	*It's imposed by someone else.*
It's accessible to the learner.	*It's inaccessible.*
The learner has power to use it.	*The learner is powerless.*

K. Goodman, *What's Whole in Whole Language?* p. 8.

Our programs aim to expand the student's communication and meaning making potential. Hence we believe that activities that involve ways of knowing, other than linguistic, should be an integral and natural part of the language curriculum. As an alternative to answering questions verbally students can be asked to draw and share a sketch of what they think a story means. Acting out stories that they have read, pantomiming the actions of their favourite character, putting their stories to music, and other such activities heighten awareness and story appreciation. Similar activities can be used in reading in other areas of the curriculum.

Our programs aim to expand the student's communication and meaning potential. Activities that involve ways of knowing other than linguistic should be an integral and natural part of the language curriculum.

Figure 11.1   The conditions of learning. A schematic representation of Cambourne's model of learning as it applies to literacy learning

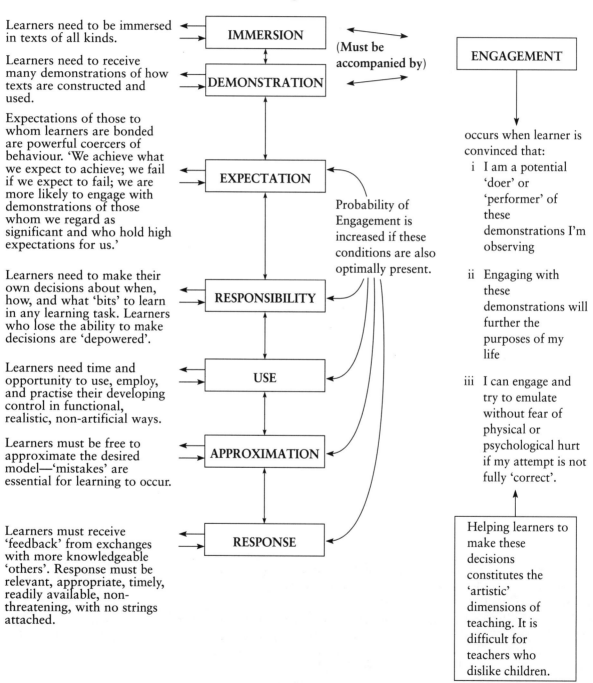

Learners need to be immersed in texts of all kinds.

Learners need to receive many demonstrations of how texts are constructed and used.

Expectations of those to whom learners are bonded are powerful coercers of behaviour. 'We achieve what we expect to achieve; we fail if we expect to fail; we are more likely to engage with demonstrations of those whom we regard as significant and who hold high expectations for us.'

Learners need to make their own decisions about when, how, and what 'bits' to learn in any learning task. Learners who lose the ability to make decisions are 'depowered'.

Learners need time and opportunity to use, employ, and practise their developing control in functional, realistic, non-artificial ways.

Learners must be free to approximate the desired model—'mistakes' are essential for learning to occur.

Learners must receive 'feedback' from exchanges with more knowledgeable 'others'. Response must be relevant, appropriate, timely, readily available, non-threatening, with no strings attached.

IMMERSION

DEMONSTRATION

(Must be accompanied by)

EXPECTATION

Probability of Engagement is increased if these conditions are also optimally present.

RESPONSIBILITY

USE

APPROXIMATION

RESPONSE

ENGAGEMENT

occurs when learner is convinced that:

i   I am a potential 'doer' or 'performer' of these demonstrations I'm observing

ii Engaging with these demonstrations will further the purposes of my life

iii I can engage and try to emulate without fear of physical or psychological hurt if my attempt is not fully 'correct'.

Helping learners to make these decisions constitutes the 'artistic' dimensions of teaching. It is difficult for teachers who dislike children.

B. Cambourne, *The Whole Story*, p. 33.

Art can be used as a vehicle to help students organise their thinking prior to writing, or as a 'keep-going' strategy when they experience writer's block. Drama can help students get in touch with their feelings and facilitate quality writing. Music can be used to set a mood for reading or writing. Students can be encouraged to select music to go with their oral readings of the stories they write. Students should be encouraged to create their own props, put on their own plays, create story murals, etc., in response to literature.

Reading and writing are aesthetic experiences in their own right. Living through a story read aloud, sensing the rhythm of a poem, a well-written novel, a joke, a jingle, are real, written-language experiences in their own right. Written-language experiences need not be formally dissected and analysed for them to be good learning experiences.

Research insights, many of which have been discussed in this book—particularly about the nature of language, language use, and language learning—highlight that many teaching practices seem to rest on inadequate or inappropriate assumptions. We need to examine our beliefs about language, and about reading/writing and learning in order to match current practice to recent research, and consider ways of creating a curriculum built on coherent, theoretical foundations. We need to provide an environment in which students will want to read and write, and in which they can learn to read and write. They need to be responsible for their learning, that is, to select their reading material, to 'own' their writing. We need to provide resources, time, and settings that encourage a wide range of reading and writing experiences. We need to read and write with them; to show them, not to tell them.

From their earliest encounters with both written and spoken language, children expect language to be meaningful. They use what they know about the world to make sense of their interactions with print. They take risks in their intent to create meaning and use what they know about one form of language to refine another. These strategies must be allowed to operate in the classroom. Students must feel comfortable exploring written language in whatever way interests them. Learning to become a writer involves a constant sharing with others, talking and writing about ideas, and getting feedback on whether their ideas have worked or not. A silent, orderly classroom with students working in their own workbooks is not such an environment. Learning to read and write is a process of experiencing language for getting something done.

Competency is not a state that is finally attained; rather, one is continually arriving at it. We need to understand how we either limit or enhance development by the experiences we set for our students. Activities that involve fragments of language, discourage students from taking chances or do not permit the exchanging of ideas, can only make learning to read and write more difficult.

Reading and writing are aesthetic experiences in their own right.

Many teaching practices seem to rest on inadequate or inappropriate assumptions. It is necessary for us to examine continually our beliefs about language, and about reading/writing and learning in order to match current practice to recent research, and to consider ways of creating a curriculum built on coherent theoretical foundations.

From their earliest encounters with both written and spoken language, children expect language to be meaningful.

Students must feel comfortable exploring written language in whatever way that interests them.

Learning to read and write is a process of experiencing language for getting something done.

Competency is not a state that is finally achieved: rather, one is continually arriving at it.

Language develops in many directions at once, it develops continually, sometimes inconspicuously, sometimes in dramatic spurts.

To understand what our students are doing, we need to discover or rediscover language for ourselves.

It is only by observing language in use, by watching language-users, that our understandings can grow.

Language develops in many directions at once; it develops continually, sometimes inconspicuously, sometimes in dramatic spurts. It needs a real environment where there is action and reaction. Learners need to be able to discover strategies that work for them and solve problems that occur when they are using language and literacy in the real world. Frank Smith (1983) has described one way to make learning to read (and by implication learning to write) easy. He believes that, as teachers, we need to understand what our students are trying to do and then help them to do it. To understand what our students are doing, we need to discover or rediscover language for ourselves.

It is only by observing language in use, by watching language users, that our understandings can grow. And it is only from such understandings that we will be able to make curricular decisions that better match our students' intuitions about how language works.

Conclusions

All that has been discussed should assist you to understand how we can best help students learn and use language effectively to serve their own purposes.

Different sections of this book have emphasised the following:

- the global nature of language—the language arts, often defined as listening, speaking, reading and writing (and more recently, including viewing and performing) are arbitrary categories, not separate entities in the learner's mind, and hence should not be taught separately
- there are ways other than verbal ways of making meaning and these should be integrated with the verbal ways in the classroom
- language, including reading and writing, is concerned with constructing/composing meaning, and language should be used and fostered as such in the classroom
- the ways of making and expressing meaning are culturally determined; they are social practices and thus need to be developed within a social context
- the purposeful use of language is important for language development to occur
- facilitation of learning, and the relationship between language and learning
- developing language across the curriculum through real learning activities catering for the students' purposes
- the complex nature of language—the use of language involves a complex interplay of many systems, and in order to develop it whole language activities must be used rather than isolated bits of language
- the nature of the processes of literacy as part of language and culture

- the purposes and values of acquiring literacy and the role of literacy in the community.

The understandings derived from these points are significant in determining the type of learning environment you create and your role in fostering language, in particular literacy. The teacher's role in promoting literacy can be broadly divided into two parts:

- creating a facilitative environment that will invite and encourage learners to use language for a variety of purposes. In such an environment, learners are able to:
  - — see demonstrations of purposeful use of language in its different forms
  - — experiment and take risks in using literacy for their purposes
  - — have their approximations accepted
  - — receive appropriate responses
  - — have time for purposeful use and practice of different forms of language.
- directly assisting to provide specific help when needed for any aspect of language development. This may involve, for example, two minutes of direct instruction, a small group session, or a class session. The intervention occurs, however, at the learner's time of need and not as prescribed by an external program. The intervention will generally mean focusing on some part of language within the context of whole language.

We believe that, if the appropriate environment is created, many learners will succeed in achieving their purposes in literacy with the minimum of additional help, allowing the teacher to concentrate on those learners who require more assistance. The emphasis in the program needs to be on student learning, on using language to achieve a purpose, not on the language as an end in itself. The student needs to have some control over the learning where the curriculum can be negotiated. Learning needs to centre on problem-solving, answering student questions, and investigating issues.

Learners will learn best if they are in an environment where they can engage actively with the task, where their explorations are supported through collaboration with peers and teachers, and where they have the opportunity to reflect upon their learning, to stand back from it, and assess what and how they have learned. In this type of environment they will learn effectively and will be developing and refining their learning strategies.

Smith (1983) says of learning to read: 'Children learn to read by reading, and the sensible teacher makes reading easy and interesting, not difficult and boring'. The same could be said about learning to write. He goes on to say:

All the evidence indicates that it is not so much inadequacy on the part of children that makes learning to read (and to write) such a hassle as the way we expect them to learn—through instructional

> *procedures that systematically deprive them of relevant practice and necessary information. The more difficulty children experience in learning to read, the less reading and the more nonsense drills we typically arrange for them to do.*
>
> F. Smith, *Essays into Literacy*, p. 5.

Students need to see literacy being used for authentic purposes and have real purposes for their own use of literacy. We need to provide an environment that encourages risk-taking that uses open-entry and open-ended activities that allow all the learners to benefit. Too often our activities suit only a few students. We may have better success in teaching literacy if we concentrated on developing the desire to become literate—essentially an inner attitude to reading and writing—rather than focusing on teaching the skills. Currently, too many adults are able to read but see little purpose in reading beyond providing some specific information they may need or as a way of passing time. Many students gain the impression that reading is all about decoding. Commonly used texts that are written for teaching tend to emphasise decoding and word recognition and are often empty of meaning.

The facilitative environment should provide a range of uses for literacy, as well as a variety of materials—children's literature, information books, magazines, etc. However, as teachers, we must be aware that every piece of printed material we offer our students influences their values and attitudes to reading and knowledge of their environment and life. Reading can be used to shape the minds of readers to make them conform to the dominant culture, or it can be used to enhance their capacity to be free through developing their ability to think for themselves, form their own values, test their own attitudes, and change or expand previously learned behaviours. In one sense we cannot teach students to read and write, but we can facilitate their development and provide them with strategies that expand their capacity to think through reading and writing. It is neither an insignificant nor an easy task, but it is crucial for the future of our society.

It is imperative that, as teachers, we value the multiple literacies used in students' lives and emphasise the development of critical literacy—the use of literacy, and not merely the teaching of skills.

Sidenote: Students need to see literacy being used for authentic purposes and have real purposes for their own use of literacy.

Sidenote: It is imperative that we value the multiple literacies used in students' lives and emphasise the uses of literacy, and not merely the teaching of skills.

Postscript

Bissex (1980) gives us this message, written by Paul, aged 5.5 years:

DO NAT DSTB
GYNS AT WRK

The GYNS AT WRK (genius at work) is our human capacity for language. DO NAT DSTB (do not disturb) is a caution to observe how this capacity works, for the logic by which we teach is not always the logic by which students learn.

References and further reading

Bissex G. *Gyns at Work: A Child learns to Read and Write*, Harvard University Press, Cambridge, MA, 1980.

*Brown H. & Mathie V. *Inside Whole Language: A Classroom View*, Primary English Teaching Association, Rozelle, NSW, 1990.

*Cambourne B. 'Language, learning and literacy', in Butler A. & Turbill J. (eds) *Towards a Reading and Writing Classroom*, Primary English Teaching Association, Rozelle, NSW, 1984.

*Cambourne B. *The Whole Story: Natural Learning and the Acquisition of Literacy in the Classroom*, Ashton Scholastic, Gosford, NSW, 1988.

Cazden C. *Classroom Discourse: The Language of Teaching and Learning*, Heinemann, Portsmouth, NH, 1988.

Cook J. 'Negotiating the curriculum: programming for learning', in Boomer G. (ed.) *Negotiating the Curriculum*, Ashton Scholastic, Gosford, NSW, 1982, pp. 133–49.

*Dwyer J. (ed.) *A Sea of Talk*, Primary English Teaching Association, Rozelle, NSW, 1989.

*Gilles C., Bixby M., Crowley P., Crenshaw S., Henrichs M., Reynolds F. & Pyle D., with Watson D. *Whole Language Strategies for Secondary Students*, Richard C. Owen, New York, 1988.

*Goodman K. *What's Whole in Whole Language?* Scholastic-TAB Publications, Ontario, 1986.

*Harste J. & Short K., with Burke C. *Creating Classrooms for Authors*, Heinemann Educational Books, Portsmouth, NH, 1988.

*Harste J., Woodward Y. & Burke C. *Language Stories and Literacy Lessons*, Heinemann Educational Books, Portsmouth, NH, 1984.

*Holdaway D. *Foundations of Literacy*, Ashton Scholastic, Gosford, NSW, 1979.

*Hynds S. & Rubin D. *Perspectives on Talk and Learning*, National Council of Teachers of English, Urbana, IL, 1990.

*Jones P. (ed.) *Talking to Learn*, Primary English Teaching Association, Newtown, NSW, 1996.

McVitty W. (ed.) *Children and Learning*, Primary English Teaching Association, Rozelle, NSW, 1984.

*Murray J. & Smith F. (eds) *Language Arts and the Learner*, Macmillan & Co., South Melbourne, 1988.

*Reid J. with Green B. & English R. *Managing small-group Learning*, Primary English Teaching Association, Newtown, NSW, 2002.

Smith F. *Comprehension and Learning*, Holt, Rinehart & Winston, New York, 1975.

Smith F. *Essays into Literacy*, Heinemann Educational Books, Exeter, NH, 1983.

*Stewart-Dore N. *Writing and Reading to Learn*, Primary English Teaching Association, Rozelle, NSW, 1986.

*Watson D. (ed.) *Ideas and Insights: Language Arts in the Elementary School*, National Council of Teachers of English, Urbana, IL, 1987.

*Watson D., Burke C. & Harste J. *Whole Language: Inquiring Voices*, Scholastic, Richmond Hill, Ontario, 1989.

*Wing Jan L. *Write Ways: Modelling Writing Forms*, Oxford University Press, Melbourne, 1991.

APPENDIX 1

Australian English phonemes

The following International Phonetics Alphabet (IPA) symbols are used to represent Australian English phonemes:

Consonants

p	pill	t	till	k	kill
b	bill	d	dill	g	gill
m	mill	n	nill	ŋ	ring
f	feel	v	veal	tʃ	choke
h	high	θ	thigh	ð	thy
s	seal	z	zeal	j	you
l	leaf	r	reef	w	witch
ʃ	shrill	ʤ	Jill	ʒ	azure
ʍ	which				

Vowels

i	beet	ɪ	bit
ɛ	bet	æ	bat
a	part	ʌ	but
ɒ	pot	ɔ	port
ʊ	put	u	boot
з	bird	ə	about
aɪ	buy	ɪə	beer
eɪ	bay	ɛə	bear
ɔɪ	boy	ʊə	tour
aʊ	how	oʊ	hoe

APPENDIX 2

Glossary of language terms

abstract	Used to refer to the semantic features of nouns that denote quality or state, ideal or theoretical concepts, e.g. happiness, sadness, democracy. Compare with **Concrete**.
acronyms	Words made from combining the initials of a number of words, e.g. radar.
affricative	A class of consonant sounds with the characteristics of stops (plosives) and fricatives, as in the initial sounds in 'church' and 'jump'.
allomorph	A positional variant of a morpheme. The endings of 'cats', 'dogs' and 'churches' all have the meaning 'plural', but differ in phonemic representation, and are therefore allomorphs of the 'plural' morpheme.
allophone	A positional variant of phoneme. The initial sound in 'pin' [pʰ] and the second sound in 'spin' [p] are phonetically different, but this difference is quite predictable in English and never results in a difference in meaning; it is therefore an allophonic difference, not a phonemic difference.
alveolar	Refers to the hard ridge behind the top teeth. The sounds at the beginning of 'Ted', 'dead' and 'Ned' are alveolar consonants.
anaphora	Reference to something that has already been mentioned through a process of substitution. For example, 'did too' in 'I said it and he did too' avoids the repetition of 'said it'.
anaphoric pronoun	A pronoun that makes reference to a noun phrase in a sentence or series of sentences; for example, 'he' in 'I spoke to the man and expected he would answer'.
animate	Having life and movement; however, plants are excluded. 'Boy', 'dog' and 'caterpillar' are animate nouns and are assigned the semantic feature (+ animate) as opposed to 'tree' and 'rock' which are (– animate or inanimate).
antecedent	The word or group of words to which a pronoun refers. In 'He gave it to the people who came', 'the people' is the antecedent of 'who'.

aspiration	A puff of air accompanying the release of a stop (plosive), as with the initial stops in 'pam', 'tan', 'can'.
babbling stage	The early months of a child's linguistic development, during which the sounds the infant makes have no particular meanings but signify contentment; the infant begins to make imitative sounds as well.
base	A morpheme to which affixes (other morphemes) can be added, as 'wise' in 'unwisely'. Also called root or stem.
bilabial	A speech sound produced by putting the upper and lower lips together, like [b] and [m].
bound morpheme	A morpheme which does not/cannot stand alone; it must occur with at least one other morpheme, such as 'un' in 'unfair'.
code	The term is used in a variety of ways: language codes—speech, writing, body language; elaborated and restricted codes—types of speech possessed by an individual.
competence	Language competence—the ability to understand and produce grammatical sentences in one's native language, even if one has never heard the sentences before; communicative competence—the ability to communicate effectively in a range of situations. Compare with **Performance**.
complex sentences	A sentence containing one independent clause and one or more dependent clauses or embedded verbals.
compound sentence	A sentence containing two or more independent clauses and no dependent clauses.
concrete	Having discernible features. 'Man', 'rock' and 'plant' are concrete nouns and are marked with the semantic feature (+ concrete). Compare with **Abstract**.
connotative	Referring to the suggested or inferred associations that, along with the literal meaning, go with a word, e.g. 'fire' suggests warmth, pain, cooking, terror. Compare with **Denotative**.
consonant	A speech-sound produced by partial obstruction or complete stoppage of the airstream somewhere in the speech organs, e.g. [b], [g], [s]. Also refers to the letter that symbolises the sound.
constituent	One of the parts of a construction—often used to refer to parts of a sentence.
content words	Words such as 'man', 'go', 'slow' and 'red', which are often inflected and have considerable semantic content. Compare with **Function words**.

deep structure	The basic form of a sentence, containing the meaning, which underlies the sentence as it is actually spoken or written (the surface structure).
denotative	Referring to the literal meaning of a word, as opposed to the connotative, or suggested meanings.
dental	A speech-sound formed with the tip of the tongue touching the upper teeth, e.g. the initial sound in the word 'this'.
descriptive grammar	The systematic listing of the elements of a particular language at a particular time, based on observed characteristics of the language, with no attempt made to evaluate correctness.
descriptive linguistics	Also called 'synchronic linguistics'; the study of a language at a particular time.
determiner	A word such as 'the', 'a', 'my', 'his', 'this', 'that', usually followed, though not always immediately, by a noun.
dialect	A variety of language spoken in a particular area (regional dialect) or by a particular social group (social dialect or sociolect).
discourse	A group of sentences related in some sequential manner.
discourse analysis	The study or analysis of the structure of discourse.
distinctive feature	A member or feature of one of the basic oppositions in sounds or letters, e.g. front–back, high–low, voiced–voiceless, straight–curve, out of which the phonemic and alphabetic systems are formed.
ellipsis	A deleted part of a construction that can be recovered from knowledge of the part that remains.
embedded sentence	A sentence that is included in another sentence, e.g. '(when) I arrived' is included in 'He left when I arrived'.
eponyms	Words derived from people's names.
free morpheme	A morpheme that can stand alone, such as 'fair'. Compare with **Bound morpheme**.
fricative	A speech-sound formed by partial closure of the air passages, resulting in friction, e.g. [s], [v], [f], [z].
function words	Also called 'structure words'. Words such as 'the', 'not', 'in', 'to', 'quite', 'very', which do not take inflections and often have little lexical meaning, but which perform important syntactic functions. Compare with **Content words**.

generative-transformational grammar	A grammar that attempts to explain how an infinite number of simple and complex sentences can be generated and transformed from a limited number of basic structures.
genre	A term used by linguists to refer to a particular form of language used for particular purposes and context.
gerund	A participle, e.g. 'playing', used as a noun in a sentence.
grammar	A system or description of rules inherent in a language by which sounds (phonemes) and forms (morphemes) are arranged to produce sentences; also, the study of these rules.
icon	A sign that resembles the object, e.g. photographs, some road signs.
ideolect	The unique speech pattern of an individual.
immediate constituent	A linguistic analysis based on the principle that a sentence is a two-part construction at several levels. The first two-part breakdown is into subject and predicate; next the subject is divided into immediate constituents, etc.
index	A sign that is causally connected to the object it signifies, such as smoke to represent fire.
inflection	The addition of affixes to the base word to indicate grammatical changes, e.g. plural, verb tenses.
International Phonetic Alphabet (IPA)	A uniform, standardised, notational system, based primarily on the Latin alphabet, to represent all the speech-sounds of all the world's languages.
intonation pattern	The combination of pitch, stress and juncture with which an utterance is spoken. See also **Suprasegmental phoneme**.
juncture	The breaks or transitions between syllables, words, phrases, and sentences.
kernel sentence	A simple, active, declarative sentence used in generative-transformational grammar. Other sentences can be derived from a core of these sentences.
labial	Referring to the use of lips in the articulation of sounds as in 'pat', 'bat'.
labiodental	A speech sound formed with the lower lip and the upper teeth touching, e.g. [f], [v].
language acquisition device	The inherent abilities necessary for language acquisition.
language competence	See **Competence**.

language performance	See **Performance**.
language universals	Characteristics that all languages share.
lateral	A speech-sound formed by passing breath along the sides of the tongue, e.g. [l].
lexeme	Word.
lexicology	The study of words of a language.
lexicon	The vocabulary of a particular language.
metalanguage	A language for describing language, a second-order language.
metalinguistic knowledge	The ability to perceive language as a system.
minimal pair	Two utterances distinguished by a single contrast, as are 'pat' and 'bat'. Minimal pairs are used to determine the phonemes of a language.
morpheme	The smallest unit of meaning or grammatical structure, e.g. the word 'cats' contains two such units, 'cat' and 'plural'.
morphology	The study of morphemes and their combination in words.
neutral vowel	The schwa, the lax mid-central vowel symbolised by [ə], e.g. the first syllable in 'alone'; an unstressed vowel.
palatal	A speech-sound formed by placing the front of the tongue near or against the hard palate, e.g. 'y' and 'you', 'sh' and 'she'.
paralanguage	A system of phonetic characteristics overlaid on the phonological system and conveying certain meanings.
performance	A person's actual speech production.
phone	A separate speech-sound as it is actually produced by a speaker, e.g. [b], [g].
phoneme	A class of phones that is a minimal significant contrastive unit in the phonological system of a language, a speech-sound as it is interpreted by the hearer, e.g. /b/, /g/.
phoneme–grapheme correspondence	The relationship between a sound unit (phoneme) and a contrastive alphabetic unit (grapheme or letter), e.g. /æ/ and 'a'.
phonemics	The study of the use of speech-sounds in language.
phonetics	The systematic study of the sounds of language and their production.

phonics	Sound–letter knowledge (a teaching term).
phonology	A term covering both phonemics and phonetics, that is, the study of the sounds of language—their use and production.
phrase-structure grammar	A grammar that describes the grammatical structures.
phrase-structure rule	A rule in the phrase-structure grammar.
pivot grammar	A type of grammar used to describe young children's two-word utterances where there appeared to be a number of key words (pivot words) to which a number of other words were attached to form the utterances.
portmanteau words	Two words blended together to make a new word, e.g. 'brunch' from 'breakfast' and 'lunch'.
pragmatics	A study of how contextual variables are relevant to meanings of utterances.
prescriptive grammar	A grammar that sets forth rules of 'correct' usage, often without logical basis, such as the 'shall'/'will' rule.
psycholinguistics	The study of the relationship between language and human thought, perception, and behaviour.
register	Refers to a variety of language used by an individual in particular contexts.
Whorf hypothesis	The hypothesis that a person's perception of the world and their way of thinking about it are deeply influenced by the structure of the language they are raised in and speak. Also called linguistic relativity.
schwa	See **Neutral vowel.**
semantics	The study of meaning in language.
semiotics	The study of signs to convey meaning.
semi-vowel	A vowel-like sound functioning as a consonant, e.g. /j/, /w/.
social dialect	The dialect spoken by a particular social group; a sociolect.
sociolect	A social dialect that is determined by socio-economic factors, for example, working-class English.
sociolinguistics	The study of language in social contexts.
stop (plosive)	A consonantal sound made by completely blocking the airstream, e.g. /p/, /b/.

stress	The intensity with which a sound is produced relative to that of other sounds. Varying the stress in some instances alters the word altogether, e.g. 'present' and 'present'.
structural grammar	A grammar that attempts to describe a language from strictly observable data, concentrating first on the form and function of the elements of utterances; meaning is considered secondary. See also **Descriptive grammar**.
structure words	See **Function words**.
suprasegmental phoneme	One of the phonemes of stress, pitch or juncture. See also **Intonation pattern**.
surface structure	The grammatical relationships among the words of an actually observed sentence as opposed to deep structure.
syllable	A unit in the phonological system of a language with a vowel as its nucleus, e.g. pen/cil.
symbol	A sign that is arbitrarily and conventionally related to its referent or object.
syntax	The arrangements and interrelationships of words, phrases, clauses, and sentences.
top-level structure	The overarching structure of a text such as comparisons and contrasts; lists and descriptions; problems and solutions.
transformation	A rule of changing one grammatical structure into another by adding, deleting, or rearranging constituents.
transformational grammar	See **Generative-transformational grammar**.
tree diagram	A schematic representation of a sentence according to generative-transformational rules.
universals	Linguistic features common to all languages, such as the fact that all languages have sentences as their fundamental units.
vowel	A speech-sound produced by tongue and lips, with practically no obstruction to the airstream.

INDEX